The

HARVEST BAKER

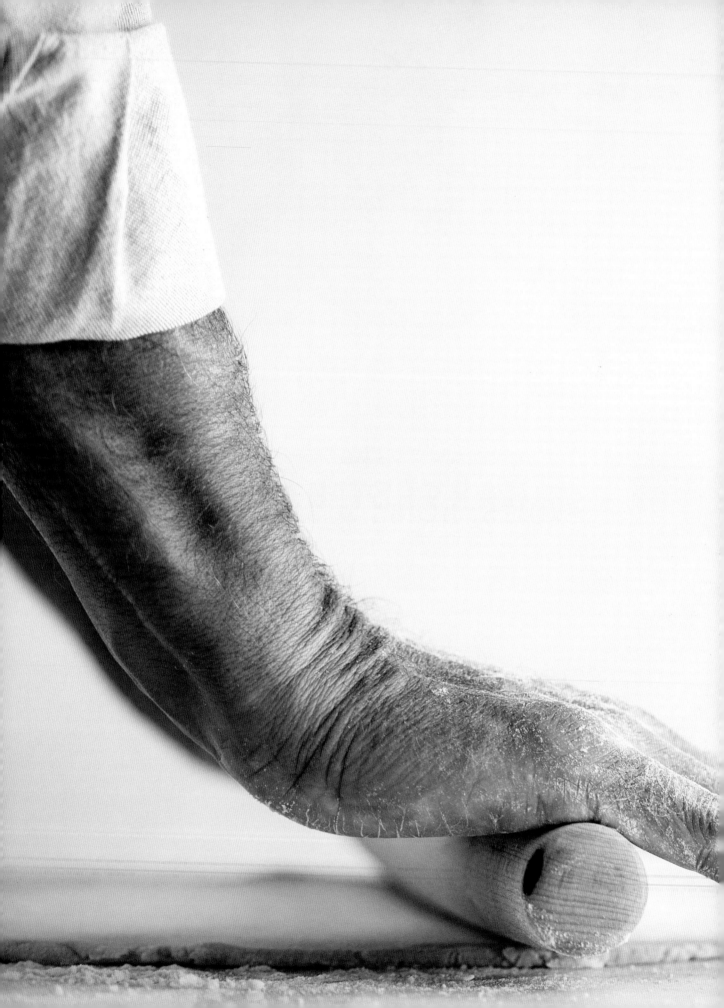

KEN HAEDRICH

THE
HARVEST BAKER

150 SWEET & SAVORY RECIPES

— Celebrating —

THE FRESH-PICKED FLAVORS OF FRUITS, HERBS & VEGETABLES

Photography by Johnny Autry

Storey Publishing

The mission of Storey Publishing is to serve our customers by publishing practical information that encourages personal independence in harmony with the environment.

Edited by Hannah Fries
Art direction and book design by Jeff Stiefel
Text production by Erin Dawson
Indexed by Samantha Miller

Cover photography by © Johnny Autry
Interior photography by © Johnny Autry

Additional photography by © 1MoreCreative/Getty Images, 165, 229; © Aberration Films Ltd./Science Photo Library/Getty Images, 209; © alfonso90/iStockphoto.com, 178; © Barcin/Getty Images, 255; © Bill Brady Photography/Getty Images, 93; © Brent Hofacker/Alamy Stock Photo, 35; © BruceBlock/iStockphoto.com, 173; © budgetstock-photo/iStockphoto.com, 177; © chang/Getty Images, 231 (background only); © DNY59/iStockphoto.com, 175; © Getty Images, 143; © Hans Geel/Alamy Stock Photo, 246; Jeff Stiefel, 261; © Kemter/iStockphoto.com, 214 (background only); © Lauri Patterson/iStockphoto.com, 190; © Magone/iStockphoto.com, 169, 205; Mars Vilaubi, 41, 95, 122, 226; © mashuk/iStockphoto.com, 75; © merc67/iStockphoto.com, 133; © meteo021/iStockphoto.com, 131; © OJO Images Ltd./Alamy Stock Photo, 89; © Pachai-Leknettip/iStockphoto.com, 159; © Patrick Swan/Getty Images, 161; © double_p/Getty Images, 101; © The Picture Pantry/Lisovskaya Natalia/Getty Images, 91; Roberta Sorge/Unsplash, 225; © Taras_Bulba/iStockphoto.com, 135; © Todd Bertrand/EyeEm/Getty Images, 64; © trait2lumiere/iStockphoto.com, 24 (background only)

Storey Publishing
210 MASS MoCA Way
North Adams, MA 01247
storey.com

Printed in China by R.R. Donnelley
10 9 8 7 6 5 4 3 2 1

LIBRARY OF CONGRESS CATALOGING-IN-PUBLICATION DATA

Names: Haedrich, Ken, 1954– author.
Title: The harvest baker / Ken Haedrich.
Description: North Adams, MA : Storey Publishing, [2017] | Includes index.
Identifiers: LCCN 2016059746 (print) | LCCN 2017006312 (ebook) |
ISBN 9781612127675 (pbk. : alk. paper) | ISBN 9781612127682 (ebook)
Subjects: LCSH: Bread. | Pastry. | Baking. | LCGFT: Cookbooks.
Classification: LCC TX769 .H226 2017 (print) | LCC TX769 (ebook) |
DDC 641.81/5—dc23
LC record available at https://lccn.loc.gov/2016059746

THE HARVEST BAKER

is dedicated to the pleasures of home cooking,
to the foot soldiers of scratch baking, and
to the farmers, gardeners, and other producers
who keep us in provisions.

CONTENTS

PREFACE

Hello, and welcome to my harvest baker's kitchen. Please, pull up a chair, have a slice of warm Tomato Slab Pie (page 195), and let's talk. You might have a few questions, after all — such as, What does it mean to be a harvest baker, and how is it different from "regular" home baking? Do I have to grow my own food? Will my kids/spouse/partner eat it? And will I have to spend a lot of money on kitchen equipment I don't already own?

First of all, relax. There's nothing mysterious or complicated about harvest baking. You don't have to grow a garden, though many harvest bakers do (even if it's just a few herbs on the kitchen windowsill). Nor will you need to shell out a lot of money for kitchen tools.

Indeed, you may not realize it, but chances are you're a harvest baker already, at least some of the time. Ever made zucchini bread? Or piled fresh veggies on your homemade pizza? That's harvest baking right there, the kind everyone relishes and wants more of. This book will simply take you farther down that path and help you discover fresh new ways to bake with the harvest, with delicious recipes you'll return to time and time again.

Harvest baking is part of a larger movement that's gained tremendous momentum over the past few years. It's a movement toward wholesome foods, locally sourced as much as possible, and prepared in ways that nourish body and soul and look great on your plate. Just look around; there are signs of this movement everywhere. Farmers' markets are more popular than ever, and the farm-to-table phenomenon is exploding. Supermarkets carry a wider selection of produce than ever before, much of it local and organic. Finding inventive ways to use fresh produce is the driver behind numerous food blogs. And the number of home gardens continues to soar.

Is it any wonder, then, that we're experiencing a corresponding surge of interest in baking with the harvest? Harvest baking is right in step with the way people are cooking today — an incredibly gratifying development for someone who's been at it for more than 30 years. If you have a minute, I'd love to tell you how I got started.

A BIT OF PERSONAL HISTORY

I can scarcely remember a time when I didn't like to bake. My mom and dad were avid fruit pie makers, and when I left home in my teens it didn't take long to realize that I'd inherited some of their baking DNA. No matter where I was living, and even in the tiniest and most challenged of kitchens, I'd spend hours combing through cookbooks and baking everything that caught my eye.

It wasn't until the early '80s that fresh produce became a dominant theme in my baking. A few years out of the navy and looking for a new adventure, I packed a few belongings and moved from New Jersey to rural New Hampshire to take a position as the chief cook and bottle washer at a group home for kids who'd been dealt a lousy hand and gotten off to a rough start in life. Frankly, my qualifications for the job were pretty slim — about as slim as the salary they were offering — so we bit our respective tongues and quietly agreed to ignore these shortcomings.

Besides, I was not overly concerned about the money. All this young cook saw was a golden opportunity: my meager pay would be offset by the fact that I could design my own culinary education and cook virtually anything I wanted, provided I didn't kill anyone or act off a hunger strike. Everything I prepared had to be vegetarian, and pretty healthy, but I was fine with that, too, because it more or less reflected my own diet at the time.

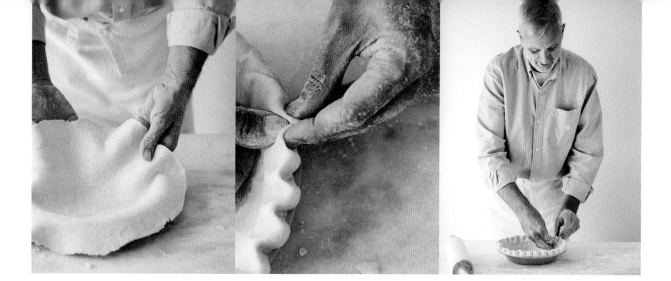

There was another perk that came with the job, and his name was Michael, our groundskeeper and gardener. Michael was born with dirt under his fingernails. He was a vegetable whisperer, someone who could miraculously turn patches of dense New Hampshire clay dirt into rich, organic soil capable of producing fat tomatoes, the most vivid greens, and the tastiest onions you have ever eaten. All of which, sooner or later, landed in my kitchen with a hefty thud.

"What's that?" I would ask when he dropped off several bushel baskets of something unfamiliar.

"Kale. It's sorta like spinach on steroids."

"What am I supposed to do with it?"

"You're the cook. You figure it out."

And that's how it began. Michael would grow it, I'd cook it, and sooner or later I'd find a way to work it into yeast breads, rolls, pizzas, calzones, biscuits, cakes, cookies, and the like. The critics could be merciless: since diplomacy wasn't their strong suit, the kids I cooked for left no doubt as to whether I'd struck out or hit a home run.

I've seen a lot of kitchens in the 30-some years since. And I've been incredibly fortunate to have had a career figuring out how to make the best of the harvest and showcase it on our plates — especially in our baked goods.

SEE YOU IN THE KITCHEN

I hope you'll spend a few moments flipping through these pages and taking a look at what's in store for you as a harvest baker. If you're not halfway to the kitchen within 5 minutes, some freshly dog-eared recipes flapping in the breeze as you sprint, I'll be very surprised.

Whether you're new to baking or an old hand at it, there's a lot to discover here. If you're an experienced baker, these recipes are going to expand your horizons. There's at least a little of the artist in every home baker, and in that respect I think you'll gain a deeper appreciation for the ways in which produce can be our palette. The harvest provides the colors, flavors, and textures we depend on to turn our baking into edible works of art.

If you're a relatively new baker, you're incredibly fortunate to be starting out at a time that's so rich with possibility. You have a wonderful world of fresh ingredients at your fingertips and — more likely than not — family, friends, and associates who are food savvy, curious, and anxious to sample your baking and offer words of encouragement. If you haven't discovered this already, you will soon: good bakers are never at a loss for good friends.

— *Ken Haedrich*

TOOL TALK

OUTFITTING THE HARVEST BAKER'S KITCHEN

My wife and I have a friend who, it seems, can't go more than a few days without purchasing the latest and greatest shiny new object for his kitchen. Outsize boxes arrive on his doorstep like clockwork, holding rice cookers, slow cookers, omelet and quesadilla makers, knife sets, high-tech pans, pasta extruders, casseroles, and one contraption that I swear, when it was fully operational, bore an uncanny resemblance to a tanning bed for a whole chicken. It's as if he feels he won't be complete as a cook without this paraphernalia. His kitchen counter is so crammed with stuff it looks like the Washington Beltway on the day before Thanksgiving.

I'm pretty much the polar opposite. I am not a kitchen tool gadgeteer, and if the economy ever depended on me for any sort of stimulus spending, our country would be in deep trouble. For one thing, I don't like clutter: it takes up space and makes other stuff hard to find. For another, I'm something of a tightwad, and if one tool can serve multiple purposes, I'll find a way to make it happen. This probably explains why one of my food processors and several of my baking sheets and other bakeware, not to mention a lot of my enameled cast-iron cookware and knives, are more than 35 years old. I have a skillet that's nonstick in name only; the nonstick stuff has long since retired and moved to Florida.

What I'm getting at is this: if someone like me can indulge his passion for harvest baking with a modest assortment of cookware and tools, so can you. Indeed, you probably already own much of the equipment you need. And if you do have to acquire some new gear, you can do it organically, buying items that reflect your interests and passions in the kitchen as they evolve.

That being said, I think it's a mistake — when you do buy kitchen gear — to go cheap when a few more bucks can make a world of difference. For instance, you can spend $8 at a superstore for a flimsy baking sheet that'll buckle every time you put it in a hot oven. Or you can spend $25 somewhere else and get one that you can pass on to your kids.

The following is not meant to be an exhaustive buying guide. But perhaps my observations will prove useful when you want to add to or upgrade the collection of baking gear you already own.

BAKEWARE BASICS

When I talk about bakeware, I'm referring to the assorted cake pans, bread pans, baking sheets, pie pans, and the like that you bake things in or on. My first rule of thumb when it comes to these items is this: weight matters. Good bakeware almost always has an unmistakable heft that's missing from cheaper versions. Weightiness means the bottom and sides of the item will be thicker, and thickness translates into better distribution of heat with fewer "hot spots" that can cause scorching. It also means the pan will cost more because it requires more raw material.

The second rule of thumb is that unless you like scrolling through endless online product reviews, make it easy on yourself and buy from a source that's already vetted these items and carries the best brands. Don't shop for them in a supermarket. I have no vested interest in promoting any particular brand, but I find that Williams-Sonoma has excellent bakeware. Anything they sell with the USA Pan label is reliably good, especially their nonstick Goldtouch line of products. The surface of many nonstick pans is too dark, causing your baked good to cook too hot and resulting in excessive browning or burning. The surface of the Goldtouch bakeware has, literally, a specially treated, gold-colored surface and bakes things to an even, light-amber finish.

Cake Pans

Many of the cakes and bars in this collection are baked in a 9- by 9-inch pan, an 8- by 8-inch pan, or a 13- by 9-inch pan. These pans measure 2 to 2¼ inches from your counter to the top of the pan. My favorite pans in this category have squared edges where the corners meet, not rounded edges, so your bars and cakes have a more professional look. These are workhorse pans, so buy good ones. Again, steer clear of nonstick pans with very dark or black surfaces.

I should note that while I like and own both glass and ceramic pans in the above sizes, I seldom use them

for bars and cakes. They don't heat as quickly or bake as evenly as heavy metal, so they're generally more suited to casseroles than baked goods.

For whatever reason, I don't make many round or layered cakes, but I make just enough of them that a pair of 8- and 9-inch round pans are good to own. I like a heavyweight aluminum cake pan with a rolled upper edge, which is generally an indication that the pan is durable and otherwise well made.

Rounding out a basic cake pan collection is a 9-inch springform pan or cheesecake pan. Springform pans have relatively high sides, about 3 inches, to accommodate a thick cake. This is perhaps the most idiosyncratic baking pan you'll ever have to buy, for the simple reason that it's made up of two parts — a base and a buckled removable collar for the sides. They don't always fit perfectly, or they become less snug over time, and as a result butter can leak out and into your oven, creating a smoky mess. So no matter how new your pan is, it's always a good idea to wrap the base in aluminum foil when baking a cheesecake (see page 257) or anything else with a buttery crust — a tart, for instance. Some of the newer models have a base that's a little wider than the pan, with a continuous shallow trench to trap butter leaks.

Tube Pans

A handful of cakes here are baked in one-piece tube pans (not the two-piece ones with removable bottoms). I own both a fluted Bundt pan, which has a 14-cup capacity, and — my favorite — a really big 18-cup nonstick cast-aluminum pan made by Nordic Ware. The latter has straight sides, which I actually prefer to the fluted pan. The cakes here will work in most any of the larger tube pans, but don't panic if you have too much batter for your pan: if it fills the pan by more than about two-thirds, just bake the extra batter in small loaf pans or large ramekins. These will, of course, bake more quickly than the large cakes.

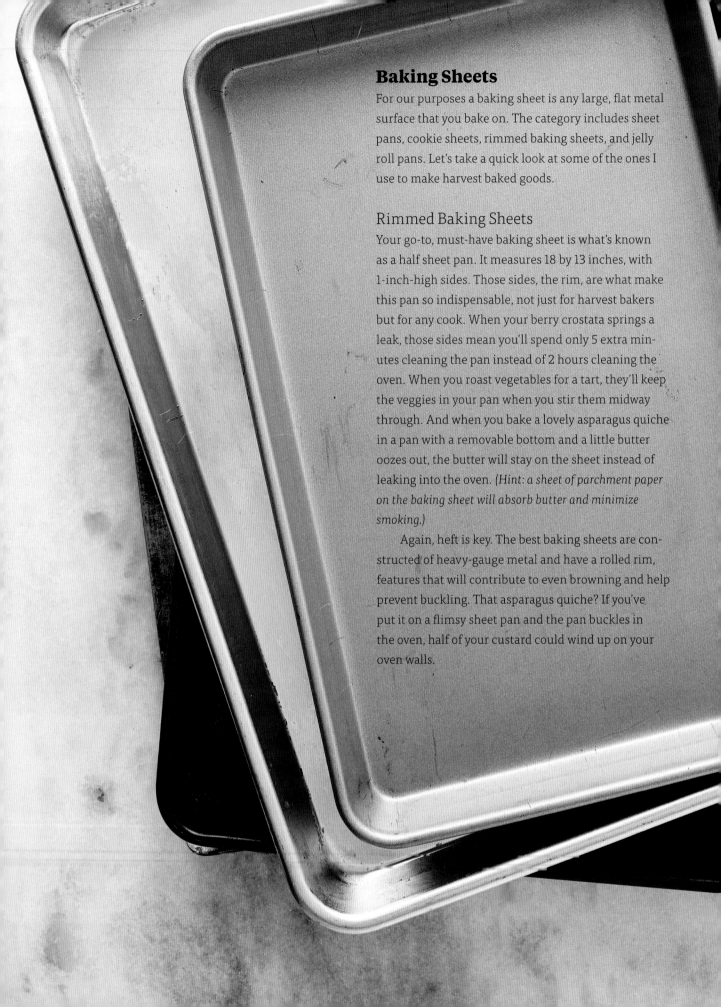

Baking Sheets

For our purposes a baking sheet is any large, flat metal surface that you bake on. The category includes sheet pans, cookie sheets, rimmed baking sheets, and jelly roll pans. Let's take a quick look at some of the ones I use to make harvest baked goods.

Rimmed Baking Sheets

Your go-to, must-have baking sheet is what's known as a half sheet pan. It measures 18 by 13 inches, with 1-inch-high sides. Those sides, the rim, are what make this pan so indispensable, not just for harvest bakers but for any cook. When your berry crostata springs a leak, those sides mean you'll spend only 5 extra minutes cleaning the pan instead of 2 hours cleaning the oven. When you roast vegetables for a tart, they'll keep the veggies in your pan when you stir them midway through. And when you bake a lovely asparagus quiche in a pan with a removable bottom and a little butter oozes out, the butter will stay on the sheet instead of leaking into the oven. (*Hint: a sheet of parchment paper on the baking sheet will absorb butter and minimize smoking.*)

Again, heft is key. The best baking sheets are constructed of heavy-gauge metal and have a rolled rim, features that will contribute to even browning and help prevent buckling. That asparagus quiche? If you've put it on a flimsy sheet pan and the pan buckles in the oven, half of your custard could wind up on your oven walls.

Jelly Roll Pans

A scaled-down version of the half sheet pan, this one measures 15 by 10 inches and 1 inch high. It's good for little tasks, such as reheating slices of quiche — nothing you can't do on a larger sheet — and since I almost never make an actual jelly roll, I could probably live without it except for one important consideration: this is the pan I use for slab pies, those rectangular pies, sweet and savory, that I just adore. You will, too, once you've started making them.

I hate to sound like a one-string fiddle, but again, sturdy heavyweight construction is key; you really don't want your slab pies buckling in the oven. The fully 1-inch-high sides are crucial for accommodating a respectable quantity of filling.

Cookie Sheets

Baking sheets with open sides and one or two raised edges for gripping are called cookie sheets. But they're not just for cookies: they're a good choice for free-form breads, too. And because they have open sides, large galettes and crostatas easily slide off them and onto a cooling rack. With cookies, not only do the open sides make it easy to maneuver a spatula underneath them without bumping into a wall, they also allow oven heat to flow more evenly over the surface so that your cookies brown more uniformly.

There's no shortage of cookie sheet designs out there, including "sandwich" sheets that have a layer of air in the middle. This provides a buffer against oven heat and minimizes browning. Problem is, other than for certain cookies, you want some browning on the bottom of your baked goods, so these sandwich sheets aren't exactly multifunctional. The one I have seldom sees use. Better to choose a more multipurpose sheet, and if you do need to temper the heat underneath, you can always line your sheet with parchment paper. I rarely bake without it.

I love my 17- by 14-inch thick aluminum Vollrath cookie sheet; it's more than 30 years old and will probably outlast me.

Bread Pans

My bread pan collection is not as extensive as my collection of 30-plus pie pans, but it's considerable. I have stoneware ones, glazed and unglazed, lots of everyday metal pans, and an antique cast-iron pan from the 1800s. (In case the sheer volume of this pan collection seems hypocritical for someone who professes to dislike clutter — a point my wife likes to make — be assured that it's all in the name of "professional research.")

Nearly all loaf bread recipes, whether quick breads or yeasted ones, require either 9- by 5-inch loaf pans or 8½- by 4½-inch ones. The difference might sound insignificant, but keep in mind that the last ½ inch can make quite a difference, volumewise. There are cosmetic consequences: a recipe meant for the smaller pan but baked in the larger one will come out squattier, and the baking time may need to be adjusted. But it's doable. On the other hand, a recipe meant for the larger pan but baked in the smaller one might overflow. If bread baking is going to be your thing, you should have both sizes.

Which is better, metal or stoneware? I like metal for yeast breads and, usually, stoneware for quick breads. Because metal heats up faster, your yeast breads will get a nice bit of "oven spring" — a quick, noticeable rise — in metal pans. Heavy, dark pans are acceptable for yeast bread, since a good amount of browning is desirable.

You're better off baking quick breads in glazed stoneware pans or weighty and reflective (shiny) metal pans. Quick breads generally contain much more sugar than yeast breads. Sugar promotes browning, so it's best to bake quick breads in a heavy material, like stoneware, that reduces browning. Another way to add a layer of protection against overbrowning is by lining your loaf pans with parchment paper when you bake quick breads. I almost always do, cutting a piece as wide as my pan and long enough to line the bottom and both sides, with a little extra to help loosen and remove the loaf later.

Glass bread pans do a serviceable job, but they're not my first choice for either quick or yeast breads. Glass is slow to heat up, conducts heat somewhat unevenly, and often overbrowns your crust. Some bakers like the fact that glass allows you to see what's happening to the crust, but in the end that's more or less irrelevant because the color of the crust is not a reliable indicator that your bread is done.

Muffin and Popover Pans

Everyone needs a pan with 12 standard-size muffin cups. Each cup holds approximately ½ cup of batter, and it's safe to say that the overwhelming majority of muffin recipes are written with these in mind.

The usual arrangement is a single pan with 12 cups, but if I were starting over I'd probably get two 6-cup pans; they're smaller, easier to store, and easier to move around in the oven. A lot of bakers like to line their cups with muffin liners, but — maybe because they seem a little too dainty — I've never been into them. Instead, I butter my pans well with soft butter and sometimes dust them with flour. I'm in the habit of filling the cups with hot water as soon as the muffins come out of the pan and letting it soak for a few minutes. Makes cleanup easy.

I don't make popovers (page 37) all that frequently, maybe five or six times a year — just enough to have a dedicated popover pan. Mine is glazed terra-cotta. It may have been a gift years ago; I don't recall, nor can I even find one like it online today. Most of the ones you see now are dark metal or heavy-duty cast aluminum with the traditional deep, narrow, steep-sided cups that create tall popovers with dramatically domed tops. If you're not sure whether a popover pan is an investment you want to make, you can bake popovers in muffin cups or ramekins to get acquainted, but the result will be squattier and not quite the same.

Pie Pans

Pie pans are one of my favorite subjects (predictable for someone who has written several books about pie). I have far more to say about them than anyone of sound mind would want to hear, so I will have mercy on you and stick with the basics.

My go-to pie pans are 9 to 9½ inches in diameter and typically 1½ to 2 inches deep, what we call a deep-dish pie pan. By "we" I mean those of us who actually bake pies because, to my knowledge, there is no governing body setting the standards and little agreement as to whether these measurements mean the entire diameter, the diameter from inside to inside or inside to outside, or something else. Or whether a pan 2¼ inches deep is a deep-dish pan or extra-deep-dish pan. Bottom line: if you are — or, more precisely, if your pan is — in the ballpark, you're good.

Unlike a lot of baked goods, pies, by necessity, often come to the table still in the pan, so looks are a consideration. Manufacturers are happy to oblige with all manner of attractive pans. Many are colorful stoneware pans whose brand names — Le Creuset, Haeger, Emile Henry, Staub — are synonymous with quality bakeware. A less expensive but quite serviceable option is tempered glass, such as Pyrex or Anchor Hocking, but glass doesn't have quite the same wow. Ceramic, stoneware, and glass are all a bit slow to heat up but in the end will yield a nicely browned crust.

When oven-to-table looks aren't required, I also like my metal Goldtouch pie pan and several other heavy, not-too-dark metal pans, including some vintage ones like my Table Talk pie pans. I like to pick up inexpensive metal pie pans from secondhand stores because I can bake in them and give the pie away and not be overly concerned about getting the pan back. If I give you a pie in one of my $40 stoneware pans, however, I'll pitch a tent on your front porch till I get it back.

A discussion of pie pans wouldn't be complete without mentioning pot pie pans and mini pie pans, scaled-down versions that are perfect for individual-size servings. These include a wide choice of pans in assorted materials, with a typical capacity in the 1- to 1½-cup range. Some of the same manufacturers make these pans, but they can be as expensive as full-size ones. For everyday pot pie pans, I often use disposable aluminum.

Tart Pans

The most common tart pan, the one that so many recipes require, is a 9- or 9½-inch-diameter pan with scalloped sides about 1 inch high. Every harvest baker needs a pan like this for her vegetable quiches and other types of veggie tarts. Some pans, usually metal ones, have sides that are 2 inches high. They produce beautiful tarts, but they're much less common, and because of the height of the sides, they can be challenging to line with pastry.

Metal tart pans often have a detachable bottom. This allows for easy removal of the tart when it's time to serve. But like other two-piece pans, it also creates a little issue: butter can leak out of your crust, seep through the pan, and drip into your oven. Not good, but there's a simple fix: whenever you bake with a two-piece tart pan, put it on a rimmed baking sheet, preferably one lined with parchment. The butter will stay on the sheet, and the parchment will absorb the butter and minimize any smoking that might occur.

A common complaint with metal tart pans is that the top edge of the pan is sharp. It sure can be. Cuts to the hands are not uncommon; even more common are cuts to one's pastry as you're attempting to get it into the pan. So take care with these metal pans: watch your hands, and don't put any downward pressure on your pastry until you've tucked it safely into the pan.

Given these (admittedly workable) concerns, it's no wonder that some cooks prefer using a one-piece ceramic or stoneware tart pan. You can't remove the entire tart, like you can with the metal pans, for a dramatic presentation. But these pans are pretty enough to bring to the table and come in a variety of colors. If you can only have one, make it basic white so it will go with anything else you put on the table.

THE ZEN OF PARCHMENT PAPER

If you could purchase just one item to make your baking life easier, it would be large sheets of parchment paper. Buy the more economical full sheets (24 by 16 inches) and cut them in half, or purchase half sheets (16 by 12 inches). Once you start using parchment on your baking sheets for tarts, scones, free-form loaves, and the like, you'll save hours a year on cleanup and wonder how you ever did without it. You'll roll your pie dough on it, too. (Waxed paper is great for rolling also.) I always keep a large sheet under my work area when I'm cooking to catch the mess I make during meal prep.

OTHER USEFUL BAKING TOOLS

Pans aren't the only tools you'll reach for when you're baking with the harvest (or just baking, period). There's a variety of task-specific tools you'll find indispensable as your baking repertoire expands. Here are the ones I rely on most.

Rolling Pins

You could get by with either a tapered French-style pin or a much heavier American-style rolling pin with a fat barrel, but it's nice to have both. I like the French pin for small work, such as rolling out mini pie dough circles or starting to roll a cold disk of pie dough; it allows for more pressure and control. But as the circle of dough gets larger, I'll switch over because the straight, 12-inch-wide barrel of my American-made maple rolling pin keeps the dough nice and even.

Rulers

I can't seem to go more than 10 minutes in the kitchen without measuring something: the size of a pan, the diameter of pizza dough, or the thickness of the scones I just patted out. Measurements matter in baking. They're one of the ways we get on the same page, so to speak, so you need to have a ruler nearby. My favorite is a 16-inch ruler I made from a sawed-off yardstick. Because you need a 13-inch-diameter circle of dough to make a 9½-inch deep-dish pie shell, those extra inches come in real handy. Ditto when you're rolling a dough for a slab pie (page 148).

Pastry Brushes

You often need more than one at a time, for wet and dry work, so keep a couple around. A pastry brush is useful for brushing excess flour off doughs, applying a glaze to a top crust, or brushing your calzone with olive oil. Wash and dry them right away; long soakings will lead to their demise. For most baking jobs I like a small, 1- or 1½-inch-wide boar's hair bristle brush, though the thin silicone bristle brushes have become more and more popular. I use an entirely different, much larger brush for basting meats with heavy glazes. Your pastry brushes will last longer if you don't use them for messy work like this.

Pastry Wheel

You use a fluted pastry wheel to trim pie dough, cut lattice strips for your lattice-top pies, and make smaller circles of dough for hand pies. You can pick one up for a few bucks. Be aware that this isn't the same thing as a pizza cutter, which has a very sharp, nonfluted edge that can easily damage a nice wooden table or cut through an expensive silicone mat on your work counter. The blunt flutes on a pastry wheel won't do that.

Pastry Blender and Pastry Fork

Little more than a series of curved wires held in place by a handle, the pastry blender is the tool you use for cutting the fat into the flour for your pie doughs: press repeatedly through your mixture and you soon have little split pea–size clods of fat and flour. Old-timers were fond of using two butter knives, scissor fashion, to achieve the same result. I never quite got the hang of it. I do, however, like using my big pastry fork for cutting in, especially when I'm using softer fats such as Crisco and lard.

Cake Tester

Is your cake baked all the way through? Sometimes the low-tech way is the most reliable: just poke your tester into the middle of the cake and find out. If it emerges with raw batter stuck to it, your cake needs more time. If it's clean, the cake's done. Toothpicks are fine for the job, but they're not long enough to go deep into a big pound cake; you need a long, thin cake tester for that. It's just a length of rigid wire with a handle attached. The thin wooden skewers you find at the supermarket also work great.

Cooling Racks

I love my cooling racks. They have folding legs, so they're easy to store, and they help protect surfaces by keeping hot pans a good 4 inches off your tabletops and counters. They should be as large as your most frequently used baking sheets so the sheets don't hang over the edge and get knocked off.

Food Processor

I could live without my food processor, but I wouldn't want to. I use it nearly every day for making pie dough or pizza dough, grinding nuts, smoothing out rough tomato sauce, making pesto, and more. It's a time saver when you need it most. A caveat: don't go too small. For pizza and pie dough I recommend a machine with a 12-cup capacity or larger. I also own a newer 16-cup processor that I bought a couple of years ago. We had a brief exclusive honeymoon together, but today I use the two more or less equally.

Electric Mixers

Baking involves a lot of taking out and putting away of ingredients, measuring, creaming, waiting, cracking, rinsing, and other activities. It's a good idea to have a machine that can keep working and mixing while you're otherwise occupied. That's the beauty of a heavy-duty stand mixer, and every baker can use one. My own KitchenAid mixer is more than 30 years old. It's gotten noisier over the years, but the only thing I've had to replace is the flat beater when the nylon coating wore off. For many smaller beating jobs, an inexpensive hand mixer works just as well. A hand mixer can beat egg whites and handle a gingerbread batter and the like, but a large quantity of heavy batter is best mixed in a stand mixer. If you're on a budget, consider scouring thrift shops for these items; the last time I went hunting for a mixing bowl, I couldn't believe the selection of mixers being sold for a fraction of the original prices.

Scale

A small digital scale has a place in the harvest baker's kitchen. Perhaps surprisingly, I don't use it for weighing flour; dry measuring cups work just fine. But I often need to know how much those two carrots weigh, or some odd bits of butter and Crisco, or whether I've divided a dough into equal quarters. It comes in handy for weighing parcels and calculating postage, too.

PART 1
FOR THE LOVE OF BREAD

1

MORNING BREADS
Muffins, Biscuits, and Scones

It's virtually impossible to have a bad day when you start with a homemade quick bread. Plump muffins, tender-crusty biscuits, rich scones — these simple pleasures get your day off on the right foot and remind you just how good breakfast can be. These morning breads are even more special when they capture a moment in time by featuring the seasonal harvest, the way they do in the following recipes.

STRAWBERRY RHUBARB MUFFINS

These are so good that they'll have you counting the days until spring, when you can get your hands on fresh berries and rhubarb again. They're certainly worth the wait. (I will use frozen strawberries when good local ones aren't available, but I find it very difficult to find frozen rhubarb.) Light and cake-like, rich and moist, these muffins are laced with cinnamon, cardamom, and lemon zest, just enough to notice but not enough to interfere with the delicate fruit flavor. A sprinkle of sugar on top gives them a crunchy lid that contrasts nicely with the soft interior. Serve them out on the patio or screened porch, on one of those warm spring weekends that melt away the memory of winter.

1 Preheat the oven to 400°F (200°C). Butter a standard-size 12-cup muffin pan and dust each of the cups with a little sugar. Set aside. Combine the rhubarb and 1½ tablespoons sugar in a small bowl. Mix well and set aside.

2 Combine ⅔ cup sugar in a mixing bowl with the flour, baking powder, baking soda, salt, cardamom, and cinnamon. Whisk well to mix.

3 In a separate bowl whisk the eggs until frothy, then whisk in the sour cream, melted butter, milk, vanilla, and lemon zest. Make a well in the dry mixture and add the liquid mixture. Stir gently, until just a few streaks of the dry mixture remain, then add the rhubarb and strawberries and fold them in with as few strokes as possible to minimize staining the batter.

4 Divide the batter evenly among the cups. Sprinkle 2 or 3 big pinches of sugar over each muffin. Bake for 20 to 22 minutes, until the muffins are well risen and golden brown on top. Transfer the muffins to a cooling rack and cool in the pan for 5 minutes. Remove the muffins and continue to cool on the rack, bottoms facing up. These are best served warm. Refrigerate leftovers. Reheat leftovers, loosely wrapped in foil, in a 300°F (150°C) oven for 7 to 10 minutes.

MAKES 12 MUFFINS

Butter and sugar for the cups

1 cup finely chopped fresh rhubarb

⅔ cup plus 1½ tablespoons sugar

2 cups all-purpose flour

2 teaspoons baking powder

½ teaspoon baking soda

½ teaspoon salt

¼ teaspoon ground cardamom or nutmeg

¼ teaspoon ground cinnamon

2 large eggs

1 cup sour cream

6 tablespoons unsalted butter, melted and partially cooled

3 tablespoons milk

½ teaspoon vanilla extract

1 teaspoon finely grated lemon zest

½ cup diced fresh strawberries

Fresh Berries: The Jewels of Summer

Nothing kicks off summer like a roadside sign announcing FRESH BERRIES FOR SALE. For those of us who love to bake, fresh berries are the plump jewels that sweeten our scones and brighten our muffins, the currency that adds immeasurable value to so much of our summer baking.

The first immutable law of berries is this: not all berries are created equal. If they're picked too soon, they won't be sweet and juicy. And if they're flown in from distant lands, they'll be homesick and taste like jet lag. Which leads us to our second immutable law of berries: get 'em fresh and local, straight from the farm if possible. Pick-your-own farms are everywhere these days, and I can't think of a more enjoyable family activity. Better still is a free supply of wild fruit. Years ago, when I lived in New Hampshire, my kids and I knew all the best picking spots. Wild blackberries grew in abundance along old logging roads. We'd thread recycled yogurt containers through our belts, head into the brambles, and in no time flat have enough fruit for a couple of pies.

No matter where you procure your berries, you'll want to keep them in tip-top condition until you use them, which should be as soon as possible — within a couple of days at most.

Handling and Rinsing

As soon as you get your berries home, spread the fruit out on a paper towel–lined baking sheet and remove any debris or mushy fruit. With large strawberries — which typically mark the beginning of berry season — you can cut out soft areas and salvage what's left. Then layer the berries in a colander with an occasional paper towel between them to absorb excess moisture; the colander allows for air circulation and help keeps them fresh. Don't rinse the berries yet. Put another paper towel on top, put the colander on a plate or pie dish, and refrigerate until you're ready to use them.

Contrary to common practice, berries shouldn't be rinsed until just before you use them. Leave the berries in the colander, but remove the paper towels. Give the berries a quick rinse under cold running water, then turn them out onto a rimmed baking sheet lined with paper towels. Gently shake the sheet back and forth so the towels wick away as much water as possible.

Adding Berries to Your Baked Goods

Unless I'm in a real hurry, I like to partially freeze my berries before adding them to my baked goods. It won't diminish the flavors of the berries, and a quick hardening up in the freezer will keep them from squishing or falling apart when you mix them into batter or dough. After you rinse the berries and dry them as well as possible (you don't want any extra moisture added to your recipe), spread the berries out, cut or whole, on a baking sheet and place directly in the freezer. If you're using the berries right away, a 30- to 60-minute freeze should be long enough. For long-term storage, freeze the berries for an hour or two, until they're good and firm, then transfer them to plastic freezer bags, seal, and store in the freezer for up to 1 year.

WHOLE-WHEAT BLUEBERRY BEET MUFFINS

One of the challenges when you're baking with beets, especially puréed beets, is this: The item in question can turn a pretty shocking shade of red. Or blue-red. Or some similarly off-putting shade — really off-putting if you happen to be a kid. One of the best ways to temper this effect is by using whole-wheat flour, as we do here. You still see a bit of red, but the whole grains give it an earthy, appealing hue. The irony is, when all is said and done, you don't really taste the beets anyway, at least not much; they take a backseat to whole-grain goodness, sweet maple syrup, plump blueberries, and warm ginger. Make these for your favorite blueberry muffin lover; you'll be a hero.

1 Preheat the oven to 400°F (200°C). If the beet stems and leaves are still attached, trim them off where they meet the root. Trim off most of the skinny tail also. Tear off a 12- to 14-inch piece of aluminum foil and drizzle the middle with a little cooking oil. Place the beets in the center and sprinkle with 2 tablespoons of water. Close up the foil, place the foil packet on a baking sheet, and bake the beets until they're tender all the way through when pierced with a cake tester or paring knife. This could take anywhere from 50 to 75 minutes, depending on the size of the beets. When they are done, open the foil so the beets can cool.

2 When the beets have cooled, remove the skins by rubbing them off with dry paper towels. Cut the beets into chunks and transfer to a food processor. Process to a smoothish purée. Measure out ¾ cup. (Refrigerate or freeze any leftovers for another use. Blend with fresh herbs and cream cheese to make a nice spread for appetizer toasts.)

3 Preheat the oven to 400°F (200°C). Butter a standard-size 12-cup muffin pan. (You can use muffin cup liners if you like, but you may have to use an additional ramekin or two for excess batter.)

4 Combine the flour, baking powder, baking soda, salt, and ginger in a large bowl. Mix well by hand.

5 Whisk the eggs in a separate bowl until frothy. Add the sour cream, brown sugar, maple syrup, oil, vanilla, and beet purée. Whisk until evenly blended. Make a well in the dry ingredients and add the liquid mixture. Stir until everything is dampened and only a few dry streaks remain. Add the blueberries and ginger and fold them in until the batter is evenly mixed.

6 Divide the batter among the cups. Bake for 20 to 22 minutes, until the muffins feel springy to the touch. Transfer the muffins to a cooling rack and cool in the pan for 5 minutes. Remove the muffins, and continue to cool on the rack, bottoms facing up. Transfer to a cloth-lined basket, and serve warm. If desired, you can glaze them with the Maple Syrup Glaze, but the muffins should cool to lukewarm first. (If they're hot, too much of the glaze will run off.)

MAKES 12 MUFFINS

Oil for the foil sheet

Butter for the muffin pan

3 medium-size fresh beets

2¼ cups whole-wheat pastry flour

1½ teaspoons baking powder

1 teaspoon baking soda

½ teaspoon salt

½ teaspoon ground ginger

2 large eggs

1 cup sour cream, plain yogurt, or vanilla yogurt

½ cup packed light brown sugar

½ cup pure maple syrup

¼ cup vegetable oil or light olive oil

½ teaspoon vanilla extract

1 cup fresh or frozen blueberries

3 tablespoons finely chopped crystallized ginger

Maple Syrup Glaze (page 289; optional)

BACON, CHEDDAR, AND FRESH CORN MUFFINS

Fresh corn, bacon, cheese — how could these muffins be anything short of fabulous? The bacon's salty bite is really important here, so it's worth taking a few minutes to fry it up. (No cheating with packaged bacon bits. In my lazier moments I've used diced pepperoni. It's okay, but it's not bacon.) These are nice as an accompaniment to scrambled or poached eggs, and they can turn any hearty chili, soup, or stew into a feast. If you want to layer another harvest flavor on top of the corn, sauté ¼ cup finely diced onion or sliced scallions in a little of the bacon fat and add it to the batter when you add the corn.

1 Fry the bacon in a large skillet until crisp. Transfer to a paper towel–lined plate and cool thoroughly.

2 Put the corn in a small saucepan with enough water to cover. Bring to a boil and cook at a low boil for 5 minutes. Drain the corn, and set it aside to cool.

3 Preheat the oven to 400°F (200°C). Butter a standard-size 12-cup muffin pan.

4 Combine the flour, cornmeal, sugar, baking powder, baking soda, and salt in a large bowl. Whisk well.

5 Whisk the eggs in a separate bowl until frothy. Whisk in the milk, sour cream, and oil. Make a well in the dry ingredients, add the liquid mixture, and stir with a wooden spoon just until the batter is dampened. Crumble the bacon into the batter, then add the corn and cheese. Stir just until the batter is evenly mixed.

6 Divide the batter evenly among the muffin cups. Sprinkle the tops with a little extra cheese, if desired. Bake for 20 to 22 minutes, until the muffins are slightly domed and the tops are golden brown.

7 Transfer the muffins to a cooling rack and cool in the pan for 5 minutes. Remove the muffins and continue to cool on the rack, bottoms facing up. Serve as soon as possible. Refrigerate leftovers. Reheat leftovers, wrapped in foil, in a 300°F (150°C) oven for about 10 minutes.

MAKES 12 MUFFINS

Butter for the muffin pan

6–8 bacon strips

1 cup corn kernels, preferably freshly cut

1¼ cups all-purpose flour

1¼ cups yellow cornmeal

3 tablespoons sugar

2½ teaspoons baking powder

¼ teaspoon baking soda

¾ teaspoon salt

2 large eggs

1 cup milk

⅓ cup sour cream

¼ cup vegetable oil, light olive oil, or melted butter

1 cup grated sharp cheddar cheese or pepper jack cheese, plus a little extra for sprinkling

RICOTTA, LEMON, AND BLACKBERRY MUFFINS

Crispy on the outside, with a moist, tender, off-white interior, these muffins are a showcase for your fat summer blackberries. They love lemon, so we include lots of zest; lemon thyme, too, if you have it on hand. Some of the blackberries I get from my brother-in-law's garden are real monsters, and I have to cut them in half before adding them to the batter — feel free to do likewise. Oftentimes I'll end up with leftover ricotta cheese when I make a big Italian meal, and this is a clever way to use it up.

1 Preheat the oven to 400°F (200°C). Butter a standard-size 12-cup muffin pan.

2 Combine the flour, baking powder, baking soda, salt, and nutmeg in a large bowl. Mix well by hand or with a whisk.

3 Purée the ricotta, sugar, sour cream, milk, melted butter, egg, lemon zest, and vanilla in a blender. Make a well in the dry mixture and add the liquid mixture. Stir until everything is dampened and only a few dry streaks remain. Add the blackberries and lemon thyme, if using, and fold them in with as few strokes as possible.

4 Divide the batter evenly among the cups. Bake for 20 to 22 minutes, until the muffins are well risen and the tops feel springy to the touch and are light golden brown. Transfer the muffins to a cooling rack and cool in the pan for 5 minutes. Remove the muffins and continue to cool on the rack, bottoms facing up. Serve as is, or drizzle a little Citrus Glaze on the muffins before serving.

MAKES 12 MUFFINS

Butter for the muffin pan

2 cups all-purpose flour

2 teaspoons baking powder

½ teaspoon baking soda

¾ teaspoon salt

¼ teaspoon ground nutmeg

1 cup ricotta cheese

1 cup sugar

½ cup sour cream

½ cup milk

5 tablespoons unsalted butter, melted

1 large egg

2–3 teaspoons freshly grated lemon zest

½ teaspoon vanilla extract

1–1¼ cups blackberries, halved if very large

1 teaspoon fresh lemon thyme (optional)

Citrus Glaze (page 289; optional)

PEANUT BUTTER AND APPLE CRUMB MUFFINS

Muffins are wonderful, but like so many quick breads, they have a limited shelf life before they start drying out. That's one of the reasons I like adding grated fruits and vegetables: their moisture is released gradually into the bread, so the muffins are not as quick to dry out. That's certainly the case with these peanut butter muffins made with grated apple. They're great for breakfast and after-school snacks, and they freeze beautifully. No need to thaw. Just wrap in foil and place in a 350°F (180°C) oven for about 15 minutes. Serve warm, with a slather of butter and drizzle of honey, and applesauce on the side.

1 Preheat the oven to 400°F (200°C). Butter a standard-size 12-cup muffin pan.

2 Combine the all-purpose flour, whole-wheat flour, baking powder, baking soda, salt, and cinnamon in a large bowl. Whisk well to combine.

3 Combine the buttermilk, brown sugar, peanut butter, oil, egg, and vanilla in a separate bowl. Using an electric mixer — a hand-held mixer is fine — beat on medium speed until evenly blended.

4 Make a well in the dry mixture and add the liquid mixture. Using a wooden spoon, mix briefly, until only a few dry streaks remain visible in the batter. Add the apple and raisins, if using, and stir until the batter is well mixed.

5 Divide the batter evenly among the muffin cups. Top each one with about 1 tablespoon of the streusel, gently pressing it into the batter to partially embed it. Bake 20 to 22 minutes, until the muffins are well risen and a tester inserted into the center of the middle muffins comes out dry. Transfer the muffins to a cooling rack and cool in the pan for 5 minutes. Remove the muffins and continue to cool on the rack. Transfer to a cloth-lined basket and serve warm. If you like, drizzle the tops sparingly with Confectioners' Sugar Glaze before serving.

MAKES 12 MUFFINS

Butter for the muffin pan

1 cup all-purpose flour

1 cup whole-wheat pastry flour

2 teaspoons baking powder

½ teaspoon baking soda

½ teaspoon salt

½ teaspoon ground cinnamon

1 cup buttermilk

⅔ cup packed light brown sugar

⅓ cup creamy peanut butter

⅓ cup vegetable oil

1 large egg, at room temperature

½ teaspoon vanilla extract

1 cup peeled and grated apple (about 1½ large apples)

½ cup raisins (optional)

¾–1 cup Brown Sugar Streusel (page 287)

Confectioners' Sugar Glaze (page 289; optional)

GLORIOUS MORNING MUFFINS

This is my take on the popular "morning glory" muffin, countless variations of which you've probably encountered over the years. In case you haven't, the basic idea is a wholesome carrot cake–like muffin with a laundry list of add-ins, from crushed pineapple to nuts and everything in between. It's a delicious way to start the day, and because they're substantial, one of these with your coffee will hold you over till lunch. They freeze beautifully, so I seal mine two at a time in quart-size freezer bags and take them out the night before I serve them for breakfast. Warm them up, split them, and top with yogurt. This makes a big batch because you'll want extras. Use a second pan or ramekins for the extra batter.

1 Preheat the oven to 375°F (190°C). Butter a standard-size 12-cup muffin pan plus 2 or 3 additional cups of roughly the same size. I usually use ramekins. (See tip regarding the optional seeding of the cups.)

2 Combine the all-purpose flour, whole-wheat flour, granulated sugar, brown sugar, baking powder, baking soda, cinnamon, and salt in a large bowl. Whisk well to combine.

3 In a separate bowl, whisk the eggs until lightly beaten. Whisk in the oil, buttermilk, and vanilla. Stir in the can of pineapple. Make a well in the dry ingredients and add the liquid mixture. Mix until everything is just dampened and only a few dry streaks remain; then fold in the apple, raisins, walnuts, coconut (if using), and ginger. Fold in the carrots and stir just until the batter is evenly mixed.

4 Divide the batter evenly among the cups. Bake for 10 minutes, then turn the heat down to 350°F (180°C) and bake about 20 minutes more, until the muffins are golden on top and a toothpick inserted into the center of the muffins comes out clean. Transfer the muffins to a cooling rack and cool in the pan for 5 minutes. Remove the muffins, and continue to cool on the rack, bottoms facing up. Serve warm if possible. Store leftovers in plastic freezer bags. Refrigerate what you'll eat within a couple of days, and freeze the rest. Reheat muffins, wrapped in foil, in a 300°F (150°C) oven for 15 minutes if they're frozen, 7 to 10 minutes if they've been refrigerated.

TIP: To give these Glorious Morning Muffins a handsome, wholesome profile, I often coat the cups of the muffin pan with sunflower seeds or rolled oats. Use plenty of soft butter so they will stick to the sides, and drop a little pile into each cup. Rotate the pan to distribute the seeds or oats, and you're good to go.

MAKES ABOUT 15 MUFFINS

Butter for the muffin pan

1¼ cups all-purpose flour

1 cup whole-wheat pastry flour

½ cup granulated sugar

½ cup packed light brown sugar

2 teaspoons baking powder

1 teaspoon baking soda

1 teaspoon ground cinnamon

1 teaspoon salt

3 large eggs

½ cup vegetable oil

½ cup buttermilk or plain yogurt

1 teaspoon vanilla extract

1 (8-ounce) can crushed pineapple, including the juice

½ cup finely diced peeled apple

½ cup dark or golden raisins

½ cup chopped walnuts or pecans

¼ cup flaked sweetened coconut (optional)

2 tablespoons finely chopped crystallized ginger

1½ cups grated carrots

BUTTERNUT SQUASH CRUMB MUFFINS

Serve these amber-colored muffins throughout the fall, when you're looking for new ways to use up your stash of winter squashes. They've got cinnamon, spice, and everything nice, including the crumb topping I never get tired of. If you happen to grow butternut squash, a nice gift would be a little tray of these muffins along with the recipe and a squash so your recipient can make them herself (and perhaps even reciprocate with a muffin gesture of her own).

1 Preheat the oven to 400°F (200°C). Butter a standard-size 12-cup muffin pan.

2 Combine the flour, baking powder, salt, cinnamon, ginger, and nutmeg in a large bowl. Whisk well to mix.

3 Combine the squash purée, brown sugar, milk, oil, egg, and vanilla in a separate bowl. Whisk well, until evenly blended. Make a well in the dry mixture and add the liquid mixture. Mix the batter until just a few streaks of the dry mixture remain. Stir in the pecans.

4 Divide the batter evenly among the muffin cups. Top each one with about 2 tablespoons of streusel, gently pressing it into the batter to partially embed it. Bake for 20 to 22 minutes, until the muffins are well risen and the streusel is golden brown. Cool the muffins in the pan on a rack for about 5 minutes, then loosen with a butter knife. Transfer the muffins to the rack and continue to cool. Serve warm or at room temperature, with a drizzle of Confectioners' Sugar Glaze, if desired. To reheat, wrap the muffins in foil — leaving the tops partially exposed — and place in a 300°F (150°C) oven for 8 to 10 minutes.

MAKES 12 MUFFINS

Butter for the muffin pan

2¼ cups all-purpose flour

1 tablespoon baking powder

¾ teaspoon salt

½ teaspoon ground cinnamon

½ teaspoon ground ginger

½ teaspoon ground nutmeg

1 cup butternut squash purée (see box at right)

¾ cup packed light brown sugar

¾ cup milk

⅓ cup vegetable oil or light olive oil

1 large egg, lightly beaten

1 teaspoon vanilla extract

1 cup finely chopped pecans

1½ cups Brown Sugar Streusel (page 287)

Confectioners' Sugar Glaze (page 289; optional)

HOW TO MAKE BUTTERNUT SQUASH PURÉE

Puréed butternut squash has many uses in the kitchen. It can add flavor and body to soups, stews, and curries. And it makes a great side dish mixed with butter, a bit of brown sugar or maple syrup, and salt and pepper. Try it in your baked goods, too, as an occasional substitute for pumpkin or sweet potato purée.

Here's how you make it: Preheat the oven to 375°F (190°C).

Line a large rimmed baking sheet or roasting pan with parchment paper or oiled aluminum foil. Rinse and dry one large butternut squash. Halve it lengthwise and scoop out the seeds. Rub the cut surfaces with cooking oil; salt lightly. Place the halves, cut sides down, on the sheet. Pour ½ cup of water on the sheet and bake the squash for 40 to 60 minutes, until the skin is shriveled and

the squash is soft and tender when pierced with a paring knife. Place the baking sheet on a cooling rack, turn the squash over, and allow to cool. Spoon out the flesh and transfer it to a food processor. Process to a smooth purée. Transfer the purée to a sealed container and refrigerate for 2 to 3 days or freeze for up to several months.

HERBED PARMESAN POPOVERS

In the pantheon of dramatic breads, nothing quite compares to popovers. Tall, bulging, and gorgeously golden, these impressive breads start out in the most unlikely of guises — a thin, pancake-like batter. This batter inflates like a balloon, leaving behind a crusty shell. Fresh herbs have a special affinity for popovers, which serve as a sort of blank canvas for other flavors. In the summer I'll snip off a handful of several herbs from my garden, chop them fine, and sprinkle them over the batter with a little Parmesan. (Other cheeses work well, too, but Parmesan is my favorite.) I like chives and dill in these, but it's hard to go wrong with most any herb combination. Serve the popovers shortly after they come out of the oven. I love them with scrambled or poached eggs for breakfast, served with honey butter. For dinner I'll serve them with soups or stews, or split them and pour on a big ladle of creamy beef stew or chicken-and-vegetable stew to make free-form pot pies.

1 Drizzle a little of the melted butter into each cup of a popover pan, reserving most of the butter. If you have a standard 6-cup popover pan, you'll probably need to butter two additional cups of some sort; I use 1-cup capacity custard cups. A muffin pan will also work, but because the cups are wider than popover cups, your popovers won't rise as high. Either way, you'll need to butter about 8 cups. Adjust the oven rack so it is one setting below the middle. Preheat the oven to 450°F (230°C).

2 Whisk the eggs in a large bowl; use a spouted bowl if you have one, because it makes pouring the batter nice and easy. Whisk in the milk. Add the flour and salt and whisk well, until smooth. You should see lots of little air bubbles. Whisk in the remaining melted butter.

3 Divide the batter evenly among the buttered cups, filling them about three-quarters full, but no more than that. Sprinkle a generous teaspoon of the chopped herbs over each one, followed by about 1 tablespoon of cheese. Do not stir it in.

4 Bake for 20 minutes without opening the oven door, or the popovers may fall. Reduce the heat to 375°F (190°C) and bake an additional 15 minutes, again without opening the door. When the popovers are done, they'll be tall, crusty, and well browned. Transfer the pan to a cooling rack, let the popovers rest for a minute or two, then remove them from their cups. Serve as soon as possible, but be aware that there may still be hot steam inside when you serve them. Let folks know to poke them with a knife to release the steam. Popovers will lose their structure and stature within minutes, but they'll still taste good. Refrigerate leftovers. You can reheat them, wrapped in foil, in a 300°F (150°C) oven for a few minutes, if desired.

NOTE: If your eggs are cold, take off the chill by placing them in a bowl and covering them with lukewarm water for 5 minutes.

MAKES 8 POPOVERS

- 3 tablespoons unsalted butter, melted
- 3 large eggs, at room temperature
- 1½ cups milk, at room temperature
- 1½ cups all-purpose flour
- 1 teaspoon salt
- 3 tablespoons minced fresh herbs
- ½ cup finely grated Parmesan cheese or about ¾ cup melting cheese, such as cheddar, Gruyère, or Gouda

FRESH INGREDIENTS

Windowsill Herbs

If you have a sunny, draft-free windowsill in or near the kitchen, you've got prime real estate for growing an indoor herb garden during the cooler months. Windowsill herb plants won't be as lush and abundant as your outside plants, but a snip here and there will brighten your winter salads and add a summery accent to your soups, breads, and other recipes.

The ideal window should get at least 6 hours of sunlight each day; less than that and you'll probably need a supplemental grow light. Whether you're starting plants from seed or transplanting a clump from an outdoor plant, use a soilless potting mix for good drainage.

Give each herb its own container so that faster-growing ones (such as mint) don't crowd out the others. Chives are easy to grow indoors, and giving them the occasional haircut stimulates new growth. Parsley grows slowly indoors, but it's low maintenance and has countless uses. Thyme likes a lot of sun (consider growing more than one kind: I use lots of lemon thyme in my baking). Rosemary is relatively unfussy, but allow the soil to dry out between waterings.

As is often the case, trial and error is the best way to learn which herbs grow best where you live, so pick a few of your favorites and go for it.

SWEET POTATO BUTTERMILK BISCUITS

I may be a Yankee by birth and upbringing, but I've always been a Southerner by virtue of my love for tender, mouthwatering biscuits of various persuasions. Those persuasions would include these sweet potato biscuits, crusty on the outside, pillow soft within, and just begging to be split, drizzled with honey, and stuffed with a slice of salty ham. If there's an art to making good biscuits — and there is (see page 41) — adding mashed sweet potato just enhances it. The dough is stickier than that of other biscuits and should be handled with a light touch. It helps to keep your hands and counter well floured. Note that this recipe uses both cold butter for flavor and vegetable shortening for softness. The cake flour helps give the biscuits that melt-in-your-mouth tenderness Southern biscuits are famous for.

1 Preheat the oven to 425°F (220°C). Lightly grease or butter a large baking sheet.

2 Combine the all-purpose flour, cake flour, sugar, baking powder, salt, and baking soda in a sifter or large sieve and sift everything onto a large sheet of waxed paper. Transfer these dry ingredients back into the sifter and sift again into a large bowl.

3 Add the butter and shortening to the dry ingredients. Briefly break up the pieces of fat with your fingers, rubbing them into the dry ingredients; then switch to a pastry blender and cut the fat into the flour until you have mostly split pea–size pieces of fat.

4 Combine the sweet potato and ¾ cup buttermilk in a small bowl; whisk well to blend. Make a well in the dry ingredients and add the liquid mixture all at once. Stir with a wooden spoon just until the batter comes together in a shaggy mass; a dry pocket or two may remain. Wait a minute or two, then stir again, adding another tablespoon or two of buttermilk if the dough seems to need it. The dough will be dampish and a little sticky.

5 Flour your hands and your work counter well. Turn the dough out onto your counter and flour the dough lightly. Gently knead the dough, flattening it out slightly and gently folding it over onto itself. Repeat several times, flattening and folding, dusting the dough with flour as needed. Pat the dough out to a thickness of 1 inch.

6 Using a 1½- to 2-inch biscuit cutter, cut the dough into rounds and place them on the baking sheet, leaving 1½ to 2 inches between them. They'll get crusty all over if you don't place them too close to one another. Brush each one sparingly with any remaining buttermilk. Bake on the middle oven rack for 17 to 20 minutes. When done, the tops will be light golden brown and the bottoms much darker brown. Transfer the baking sheet to a cooling rack. Cool briefly on the pan, then transfer the biscuits to the rack. Serve warm, from a cloth-lined basket. Store leftovers in a plastic freezer bag. Reheat leftovers, loosely wrapped in foil, in a 300°F (150°C) oven for 8 to 10 minutes.

MAKES 12 OR MORE BISCUITS

Grease or butter for the baking sheet

2	cups all-purpose flour
¼	cup cake flour
2	tablespoons sugar
2½	teaspoons baking powder
1	teaspoon salt
½	teaspoon baking soda
4	tablespoons cold unsalted butter, cut into ¼-inch pieces
2	tablespoons cold solid vegetable shortening, in smallish chunks
¾	cup finely mashed sweet potato or sweet potato purée (page 246)
¾	cup buttermilk, plus 2 to 3 additional tablespoons, as needed

SWEET POTATO BUTTERMILK BISCUITS WITH BACON

Cook 4 to 8 slices of bacon until crisp. When they are cool enough to handle, crumble them up. Stir the bacon into the dough when you add the buttermilk and sweet potato.

MASHED POTATO BISCUITS

There was a time when I believed that lots of people used biscuits to recycle their mashed potatoes, but even when I moved down south I was met with surprise and skepticism when I brought up the idea. Why did no one think of this? I considered the possibility that leftover mashed potatoes were a rarity. But now I think it's a simple lack of understanding just how good potato biscuits are — crispy on the outside and feather soft in. If you love working with different doughs, like I do, you'll appreciate just how soft and supple this one feels. Smother these biscuits with your favorite preserves, or serve them with gravy, stews, and hearty winter soups. They go with just about anything.

1 Preheat the oven to 425°F (220°C). Very lightly butter a large baking sheet.

2 Sift the flour, baking powder, and salt into a large bowl. Sift again, if desired. Mix in the pepper. Add the cold butter and shortening and toss with your hands to coat the fat with the flour. Using a pastry blender, cut the fat into the dry ingredients until it is broken into split pea–size pieces.

3 Add the mashed potatoes to the bowl, breaking them up and incorporating them into the dry mixture with a large fork. When the potatoes are well distributed, make a well in the mixture and add all but a tablespoon or two of the milk, plus the chives, if using. Mix well with your fork to dampen everything, then decide if you need to add the remaining milk. If the dough has already cohered nicely, you don't need it. But if a number of dry pockets remain, stir it in.

4 Turn the dough out onto a well-floured work surface. Using floured hands, knead the dough 8 to 10 times and pat it out to a thickness of ¾ inch. Using a 2-inch biscuit cutter, cut the dough into rounds and arrange them, about 2 inches apart, on the baking sheet. Brush the biscuits with the melted butter.

5 Bake on the middle oven rack for 16 to 18 minutes, until the biscuits are golden brown and crusty. Transfer them to a cloth-lined basket, and serve as soon as possible. Store leftovers in a plastic freezer bag. Reheat leftovers, loosley wrapped in foil, in a 300°F (150°C) oven for about 10 minutes.

NOTE: If you prefer, you can use a total of 6 tablespoons cold butter in the biscuits, instead of 4 tablespoons butter plus 2 tablespoons vegetable shortening.

MAKES 14 TO 16 BISCUITS

Butter for the baking sheet

2 cups all-purpose flour

1 tablespoon baking powder

¾ teaspoon salt

¼ teaspoon freshly ground black pepper

4 tablespoons cold unsalted butter, in ½-inch cubes, plus 2 tablespoons melted butter

2 tablespoons vegetable shortening, in small chunks (see note)

1 cup leftover mashed potatoes, at room temperature

½ cup milk

2 tablespoons chopped chives (optional)

THE ART OF BEAUTIFUL BISCUITS

Yes, it is an art, and yes, you can master it. Here are some tips to help get you there:

• For the lightest biscuits, sift your dry ingredients twice.

• Be sure your oven is thoroughly preheated. Your biscuits will get added "spring," or rise, in a really hot oven.

• Don't overhandle the dough or you'll get tough biscuits. (Buttermilk biscuits need a little extra handling. See the box on page 43.)

• If your biscuits touch one another on your baking sheet, they'll rise a little higher because they won't spread out. But they won't be as crusty on the sides. Your choice.

• Have soft butter ready for serving with warm biscuits. You don't want to hack up your pretty little biscuits trying to spread them with cold butter.

CORNMEAL BUTTERMILK BISCUITS

This is not a harvest biscuit per se, but it is the basis for several other harvest baked goods — including Everything Biscuits (page 45) and the Biscuit-Crusted Chicken Pot Pie (page 196) — so this is as logical a place as any to file the recipe. If you're not accustomed to adding cornmeal to your biscuits, I think you'll find it quite agreeable. It alters the texture of your biscuits, adding a barely perceptible crunchiness, as well as the appearance, resulting in a less refined, more rustic look. It's an easy and wholesome way to do a biscuit makeover. I've incorporated a bit of cornstarch and some vegetable shortening, two little tricks for achieving extra-tender biscuits. (If you'd prefer, use another tablespoon of butter instead of the shortening.) For some advice on handling soft buttermilk biscuit doughs, see the box at right.

1 Preheat the oven to 425°F (220°C). Lightly oil a large baking sheet.

2 Sift the flour, cornmeal, cornstarch, sugar, baking powder, baking soda, and salt into a large bowl. (If some of the cornmeal particles get caught in the sifter, add them back to the dry mixture in the bowl.) Sift again, if desired. Add the butter and vegetable shortening. Start by rubbing the fat into the flour, to break up the fat, then switch to a pastry blender and cut the fat into the dry ingredients until the mixture resembles coarse crumbs, with split pea–size pieces of fat.

3 Make a well in the dry mixture and add the buttermilk all at once. Stir thoroughly, until the dough coheres. Let the dough rest for 3 or 4 minutes.

4 Flour your hands and work counter and turn the dough out onto your counter. Gently pat out the dough, keeping it on the thick side, then fold it over onto itself. Repeat a couple more times, patting and folding. You're not trying to knead the dough, but just work it a bit so it has enough strength and structure to rise a little (see page 43). Pat the dough out to a thickness of almost 1 inch.

5 Using a 2-inch biscuit cutter, cut the dough into rounds and place them on the baking sheet, leaving about 2 inches between them. Bake for about 15 minutes, until golden brown and crusty. Transfer the biscuits to a cloth-lined basket and serve as soon as possible. If you're not serving right away, transfer them to a cooling rack. Store leftovers in a plastic freezer bag. Reheat leftovers, loosely wrapped in foil, in a 300°F (150°C) oven for about 10 minutes.

MAKES ABOUT 12 MUFFINS

Oil for the baking sheet

1½ cups all-purpose flour

½ cup fine yellow cornmeal

1 tablespoon cornstarch

1 tablespoon sugar

2 teaspoons baking powder

½ teaspoon baking soda

½ teaspoon salt

4 tablespoons cold unsalted butter, cut into ½-inch cubes

1 tablespoon solid vegetable shortening (Crisco)

¾ cup plus 2 tablespoons buttermilk

How to Build a Better Buttermilk Biscuit

You may have noticed that recipes will often admonish the cook to not "overhandle" biscuit dough, lest ye end up with tough biscuits. That's true up to a point, but it's not so much the case with buttermilk biscuits. Buttermilk is a natural dough tenderizer, so much so that without a little handling, the dough won't develop the muscle to rise at all. A little handling is good. It will activate the gluten in the dough, which creates the structural support — think of tiny 2×4s — that holds the biscuit up. The resulting rise makes for a more attractive and lighter biscuit.

(The method I use for handling buttermilk doughs is outlined in the recipes.) Please note that I'm not advocating a muscular, yeast-bread-type kneading, just some gentle patting and folding.

EVERYTHING BISCUITS

You're familiar with the everything bagel, right? Here's its first cousin, the everything biscuit, chock-full, if not of everything, then certainly of enough to put on a good show. The base of these biscuits is the Cornmeal Buttermilk Biscuits on the page 42, and the theme is savory, not sweet, so you'll want to serve these up with the right partner. I love them with soups, especially tomato-based soups and creamy chowders. They're also excellent with eggs, and because they're full of spinach, I'll occasionally split a couple of them and top with a poached egg for a quick biscuit-and-egg-Florentine sort of thing. Try them; they're harvest biscuit heaven.

1 Sift the flour, cornmeal, cornstarch, sugar, baking powder, baking soda, and salt into a large bowl. (If some of the cornmeal particles get caught in the sifter, add them back to the dry mixture in the bowl.) Sift again, if desired. Add the butter and vegetable shortening. Start by rubbing the fat into the flour, to break up the fat, then switch to a pastry blender and cut the fat into the dry ingredients until the mixture resembles coarse crumbs, with split pea–size pieces of fat. Set aside in the refrigerator.

2 Heat the oil in a large skillet over medium heat. Add the onion and sauté for 4 to 5 minutes, then stir in the spinach and carrot. Add a bit of salt and pepper, to taste. Cook, stirring often, until the vegetables are completely wilted and any moisture in the pan has cooked off. Stir in the garlic, cook for 30 seconds, and remove the pan from the heat. Transfer the vegetables to a plate and cool thoroughly.

3 Line a large baking sheet with parchment paper or foil and butter it lightly; the butter will help keep the cheese from sticking. Preheat the oven to 425°F (220°C).

4 When the vegetables have cooled, make a well in the biscuit mixture. Add the buttermilk and stir just until everything is dampened. Add the vegetables and 1 cup of the grated cheese. Stir well, until the dough coheres. Allow the dough to rest for 2 or 3 minutes.

5 Turn the dough out onto a floured work surface. With floured hands, knead it gently once or twice — it will feel much denser than your typical biscuit dough. Pat it out to a thickness of 1 inch. Using a 2-inch biscuit cutter, cut the dough into rounds and place them about an inch apart on the baking sheet. Lightly brush the tops with some of the glaze. Sprinkle with seeds and then the remaining 1 cup of cheese.

6 Bake the biscuits for 18 to 22 minutes; because they're so dense, and given the moisture in the veggies, they need to bake longer than biscuits typically do. They'll be a rich golden brown and crusty when done. Either tuck the biscuits into a cloth-lined basket and serve at once or transfer them to a rack and allow to cool. Store leftovers in the fridge. Reheat, wrapped in foil, in a 300°F (150°C) oven for about 10 minutes.

MAKES ABOUT 16 BISCUITS

Butter for the parchment paper

1½ cups all-purpose flour

½ cup fine yellow cornmeal

1 tablespoon cornstarch

1 tablespoon sugar

2 teaspoons baking powder

½ teaspoon baking soda

½ teaspoon salt

4 tablespoons cold unsalted butter, cut into ½-inch cubes

1 tablespoon solid vegetable shortening (Crisco)

2 tablespoons light olive oil

⅓ cup finely chopped onion

7–8 cups (about 6 ounces) loosely packed baby spinach, coarsely chopped

1 medium carrot, grated

Salt and freshly ground black pepper

2 garlic cloves, minced

¾ cup plus 2 tablespoons buttermilk

2 cups grated extra-sharp cheddar cheese

1 egg beaten with 1 teaspoon water, for glaze

Sesame or poppy seeds, for sprinkling

BLUEBERRY CREAM SCONES WITH MINT SUGAR

Scones fall all over the place on the richness scale. There are scones made with skim milk and oil, buttermilk, or sour cream; there are buttery ones and, best of all, butter-and-cream ones like these. Calories aside, if you're going to make blueberry scones just a few times a year, they can't taste underwhelming. These are anything but. They've got a creamy texture, almost like a dense coffee cake, with plenty of blueberries in each wedge. Scones usually dry out pretty quickly. But these are rich enough that they'll reheat nicely the next day. I like to top them off with a sprinkling of mint sugar.

1 If your blueberries are fresh, an hour before you plan to bake these — or even the night before — put your blueberries on a plate and place them in the freezer to firm up a bit. (Firm berries won't burst and leave blue streaks in your scones.)

2 Preheat the oven to 425°F (220°C). Line a large baking sheet with parchment if you have it, or butter the sheet very lightly.

3 Combine the flour, sugar, baking powder, salt, and nutmeg in a large bowl. Mix well with your hands or a whisk. Add the butter and gently toss it with the dry mixture to coat the fat. Using a pastry blender, cut the butter into the dry mixture until it is broken into split pea–size pieces.

4 Combine the cream, egg, lemon extract, and vanilla in a measuring cup; stir to blend. Set aside 2 teaspoons of this liquid to brush on the scones. Make a well in the dry mixture and add the rest of the liquid mixture. Mix gently with a few strokes, then add the blueberries. Stir, using as few strokes as possible, until the dough forms a shaggy, cohesive ball.

5 Scrape the dough onto a well-floured work surface. Place a sheet of plastic wrap on top of the dough and press it into a ¾-inch-thick disk. Use a rolling pin if you like to even it out. Either way, press gently to do as little damage as possible to the blueberries.

6 Remove the plastic and cut the disk into six to eight wedges with a knife or dough scraper. Transfer the wedges to the baking sheet, re-creating the circle but leaving about ⅛ inch between the pieces (see note). Brush the scones lightly with the cream glaze.

7 Bake for about 25 minutes, until they're swollen and a rich golden brown. Transfer the baking sheet to a cooling rack and cool for 5 minutes. Cut the scones apart and set them directly on the rack.

8 When the scones are still slightly warm, drizzle with the Confectioners' Sugar Glaze. If you're using the mint sugar, sprinkle it on soon, before the glaze starts to form a skin. Refrigerate leftovers. To reheat the scones, place them on a baking sheet, cover loosely with foil, and place them in a 300°F (150°C) oven for 10 to 12 minutes.

MAKES 8 SERVINGS

- 1¼ cups fresh or frozen blueberries
- 2 cups all-purpose flour
- ⅓ cup sugar
- 2½ tablespoons baking powder
- ½ teaspoon salt
- ⅛ teaspoon ground nutmeg
- 6 tablespoons cold unsalted butter, cut into ¼-inch pieces
- ¾ cup heavy cream
- 1 large egg, lightly beaten
- ½ teaspoon lemon extract or 2 teaspoons grated lemon zest
- ½ teaspoon vanilla extract

   Confectioners' Sugar Glaze (page 289)

   Mint Sugar (page 286; optional)

NOTE: If you want the scones to be as crusty as possible all over, leave more room between them on the baking sheet — about 1 inch.

STUFFED SPINACH AND FETA CHEESE SCONES

This recipe will reshape the way you think about scones, literally. For one, they're savory, not sweet, and instead of cutting them into the usual triangle shapes, we form the scones into round bowls — reminiscent of your first clay project as a kid — then apply a glaze and seeds and fill the cavity high with a blend of sautéed onions, spinach, and cheeses. The result is something like a little filled spinach pizza but with a rich, biscuity crust that will have everyone clamoring for seconds. This is a wonderful brunch bread; you can save time in the morning by making and shaping the dough the day before. The filling can be prepared ahead as well, but don't glaze or assemble the scones until you're ready to bake.

1 Combine the flour, cornmeal, confectioners' sugar, rosemary, baking powder, and salt in a food processor. Pulse several times to mix. Remove the lid and scatter the butter over the dry ingredients. Pulse again, six or seven times, until the largest pieces of butter are about the size of peas.

2 Remove the lid and pour the cup of cream over the flour mixture. Pulse again, four to six times, just until the dough coheres. Stop the machine before the dough balls up around the blade. Turn the dough out onto a very lightly floured surface and knead three or four times.

3 Divide the dough into eight equal pieces and shape into balls. Pinch and mold each one into a bowl about ¾ inch high and 2¾ inches in diameter. Make the depression in the bowl wide and deep so it can hold plenty of filling. As you shape each one, transfer it to a large parchment-lined (or buttered) baking sheet. Refrigerate while you make the filling.

4 Melt the butter for the filling in a large skillet over medium heat. Add the onion and sauté for 5 minutes. Add the spinach and a pinch of salt. Sauté until wilted, 2 to 3 minutes. Stir in the garlic and sauté for 1 minute, then remove from the heat. Transfer the spinach mixture to a bowl. Cool completely, then stir in the feta and Havarti cheeses.

5 Preheat the oven to 400°F (200°C).

6 Work with one scone bowl at a time. Carefully pick it up — it should be firm enough to handle gently — and brush the outside "walls" of the bowl with the yolk. Sprinkle the glazed area with seeds and place the bowl back on the sheet. Repeat for the other scones. Divide the filling among them, mounding it high in each bowl. Drizzle about 1½ teaspoons of cream on top of each scone's filling and press it down gently.

7 Bake the scones for 20 to 22 minutes, until they're light golden around the edge and browned underneath. Transfer the scones to a cooling rack. Serve warm. Refrigerate leftovers. Rewarm, wrapped in foil, in a 300°F (150°C) oven for 10 to 12 minutes.

MAKES 8 SERVINGS

DOUGH

- 1¾ cups all-purpose flour
- ¼ cup fine yellow cornmeal
- 1½ tablespoons confectioners' sugar
- 1 tablespoon finely chopped fresh rosemary or 1½ teaspoons dried
- 2½ teaspoons baking powder
- ½ teaspoon salt
- 4 tablespoons cold unsalted butter, cut into ½-inch cubes
- 1 cup heavy cream

FILLING AND GLAZE

- 2 tablespoons unsalted butter
- ¾ cup finely chopped onion
- 4–6 ounces (several large handfuls) baby spinach, coarsely chopped
- 1–2 garlic cloves, minced
- 1 cup crumbled feta cheese
- 1 cup grated Havarti, Muenster, or cheddar cheese
- 1 egg yolk, lightly beaten
- 2–3 tablespoons sesame seeds or poppy seeds
- 1 tablespoons heavy cream

2

SWEET AND SAVORY
Quick Breads and Tea Loaves

Quick breads and tea loaves, be they sweet or savory, are a staple in the harvest baker's kitchen, and for good reasons: They're relatively simple to toss together, which is why they're called "quick." Also, there's no yeast involved with these breads, making them less intimidating. And perhaps best of all, this next collection is so charmingly versatile and delicious that you can enjoy these breads for breakfast, lunch, snacks — you name it. Add a smear of cream cheese and a slice of cold cuts and you can even make a meal.

WHOLE-WHEAT AND OATMEAL ZUCCHINI BREAD

Zucchini bread is a harvest-baking classic that almost everyone loves. Indeed, the amount of zucchini in American gardens come midsummer is only surpassed by the number of zucchini bread recipes for using it up. Even so, it's not always easy to find a recipe that's not too sweet or too healthy and heavy for its own good. I think this version is the best of both worlds, a zucchini bread that's just sweet enough, perfectly moist, and whole-grain wholesome, a great repository for the yearly zucchini glut. Go ahead and slice some up while it's still warm; nobody can resist. But the beauty of this bread is how good it is on the second and third day, thanks to the moisture in the zucchini. Incidentally, I like to use smaller zucchini here. The oversized fat ones sometimes have too much water in them.

1 Preheat the oven to 350°F (180°C). Butter two 8½- by 4½-inch loaf pans. If you have parchment paper, line the bottom and two long sides with a single sheet, allowing it to extend a little above each rim (this will give you something to hold on to when you remove the loaf later).

2 Combine the all-purpose flour, whole-wheat flour, oats, baking powder, baking soda, salt, cinnamon, and nutmeg in a mixing bowl. Whisk to mix.

3 Combine the eggs, oil, granulated sugar, brown sugar, milk, vanilla, and grated zest in a large bowl. Using an electric mixer (handheld is fine), beat the mixture on medium speed for about 30 seconds, just until evenly blended.

4 Make a well in the dry mixture and add the liquid mixture all at once. Stir well with a wooden spoon, until just a few dry streaks remain. Add the zucchini and walnuts and fold them in until the batter is evenly mixed. Divide the batter between the loaf pans.

5 Bake for 45 to 50 minutes, until a tester inserted in the middle of the bread comes out clean. Transfer the loaves to a cooling rack and cool in the pan for 15 to 20 minutes. Slide out the loaves and continue to cool. Slice and serve warm or at room temperature. Refrigerate leftovers in plastic bags, but serve at room temperature.

MAKES TWO 8½- BY 4½-INCH LOAVES

Butter for the loaf pans

1½ cups all-purpose flour

1 cup whole-wheat pastry flour

½ cup old-fashioned rolled oats or quick oats

2½ teaspoons baking powder

½ teaspoon baking soda

1 teaspoon salt

1 teaspoon ground cinnamon

¼ teaspoon ground nutmeg

3 large eggs

1 cup vegetable oil or light olive oil

1 cup granulated sugar

⅔ cup packed light brown sugar

¼ cup milk

2 teaspoons vanilla extract

Grated zest of 1 orange or lemon

2 cups grated zucchini

1 cup chopped walnuts

ROASTED CARROT TEA LOAF

This is how I feel about carrots: if somebody wants to cut and fuss with them and work a little magic, I'll eat them. But it takes some doing. So the bar was already set quite high when I decided to come up with a carrot bread that I would not just eat but relish. Roasting some of the carrots was a good place to start; roasting concentrates flavor and sweetness, whereas boiling tends to leach it away. Since carrots have a special fondness for orange flavor, I included both the zest and juice of an orange. Then I added some chopped crystallized ginger for warmth and spice. The result is a carrot loaf of such exceptional flavor and moistness that even the most ambivalent carrot eater will devour it.

1 Preheat the oven to 400°F (200°C). Tear off a sheet of aluminum foil about 16 inches long. Cut two-thirds of the carrots — four of them, probably — into 3-inch sections and lay them in the foil. Drizzle them with a teaspoon or two of oil and a pinch of the salt. Wrap them up tightly in the foil and place on a baking sheet. Roast for 50 to 60 minutes, until the carrots are tender. Open up the foil and set aside to cool thoroughly.

2 Meanwhile, butter an 8½- by 4½-inch loaf pan well. If you have parchment paper, line the bottom and two long sides with a single sheet, allowing it to extend a little above each rim (this will give you something to hold on to when you remove the loaf later). Set the oven to 350°F (180°C).

3 Sift the flour, baking powder, baking soda, and remaining salt into a mixing bowl. Stir the milk, orange juice, orange zest, and vanilla together in a separate small bowl or measuring cup.

4 When the carrots are thoroughly cooled, put them in a food processor with about ⅓ cup of the sugar. Process to a finely textured but not totally liquefied consistency. Grate the remaining raw carrots using the large holes of a box grater.

5 Using an electric mixer (handheld is fine), cream the butter. Gradually add the remaining ⅔ cup sugar and beat for 2 minutes on medium-high speed. Beat in the eggs, one at a time, beating well after each addition. Beat in the processed carrots on low speed.

6 With the mixer on low speed, beat half of the flour mixture into the creamed mixture. Beat in the milk-and-orange liquid, then the remaining dry ingredients; switch to a wooden spoon if the batter is too thick for your mixer. Add the grated carrots and ginger and fold them in until the batter is evenly mixed. Transfer the batter to the prepared pan.

7 Bake the bread for 55 to 65 minutes, until the loaf is nicely risen and a tester inserted deep into the center of the bread comes out clean. Transfer the bread to a rack and cool in the pan for at least an hour. Then run a thin knife or spatula around the outside of the loaf and remove the bread from the pan. Slice and serve when you're ready. Refrigerate leftovers.

MAKES ONE 8½- BY 4½-INCH LOAF

Butter for the loaf pan

¾ pound (about 6 medium) carrots, trimmed and peeled

Drizzle of light olive oil or cooking oil, for roasting the carrots

¾ teaspoon salt

1½ cups all-purpose flour

1 teaspoon baking powder

1 teaspoon baking soda

¼ cup milk or half-and-half

2 tablespoons fresh orange juice

Finely grated zest of half an orange

½ teaspoon vanilla extract

1 cup sugar

½ cup (1 stick) unsalted butter, softened

2 large eggs, at room temperature

¼ cup finely chopped crystallized ginger

NOTE: I wouldn't make it up special for this, but if you happen to have a little baggie of streusel (page 287) in the freezer, you can scatter a bit — no more than about ½ cup — on top before baking. Don't pile it on heavily, however; you don't want to impede the rising.

PUMPKIN SODA BREAD

One of the first breads I learned to make was Irish soda bread, a crusty, free-form loaf studded with currants or raisins. If you're not familiar with Irish soda bread, I urge you to try it; this pumpkin variation is as good a soda bread as you'll find. Like most, it has no yeast. And since there's no rising involved, it's quick to prepare. The pumpkin does a couple of things: it helps keep the bread moist (premature dryness is a common issue with soda breads), and with the help of the egg yolk, it makes for a gorgeous soft-orange interior. Slightly sweet and full of flavor, this makes an excellent toast and tastes great with cream cheese and honey.

1 Preheat the oven to 400°F (200°C). Line a large baking sheet with parchment paper, or oil it very lightly and dust with cornmeal.

2 Combine the flour, cornmeal, ½ cup sugar, salt, baking powder, and baking soda in a large bowl. Mix well by hand. Add the butter and toss it with the dry ingredients. Rub the butter and dry ingredients together thoroughly, until the fat essentially disappears into the mix. Add the raisins and nuts and mix in by hand.

3 Whisk the buttermilk, pumpkin, and egg yolk in a small bowl. Make a well in the dry mixture and add the liquid mixture. Mix thoroughly with a wooden spoon until the ingredients form a cohesive dough that, for the most part, pulls away from the sides of the bowl. Scrape the dough out onto a floured work surface and divide it in half. Using floured hands, gently knead each half into a ball. Place the dough balls on the baking sheet, leaving 5 to 6 inches between them. Brush each loaf sparingly with milk and sprinkle the tops with sugar. Using a sharp serrated knife, cut a ½-inch-deep cross in the top of each loaf (this is where the loaves will split and spread).

4 Bake for about 40 minutes, until good and crusty. When done, the bottoms of the loaves will sound hollow when tapped with a fingertip. Transfer them to a cooling rack and cool well before slicing. These loaves keep best in the refrigerator, wrapped tightly in foil and slipped into a plastic food bag. Freeze the second loaf if you won't be eating it within 2 or 3 days.

MAKES 2 GOOD-SIZE LOAVES

Oil and cornmeal for the baking sheet (optional)

4½ cups all-purpose flour

½ cup yellow cornmeal

½ cup sugar, plus a little for sprinkling

2 teaspoons salt

2 teaspoons baking powder

1 teaspoon baking soda

4 tablespoons unsalted butter, at room temperature, cut into ½-inch pieces

1 cup raisins

½ cup chopped walnuts

1⅔ cups buttermilk

¾ cup pumpkin purée, canned or fresh (page 226)

1 egg yolk

Milk, for glaze

HONEYED PARSNIP TEA BREAD

Let's face it: parsnips aren't the first veggie we reach for at dinnertime, and they might be one of the last that come to mind when we think about harvest baking. That's too bad, because with a little imagination and the right company, their sweetness and earthy flavor can be a real asset. There may be no better example than this moist whole-wheat tea loaf, sweetened with honey and full of plumped raisins (or cranberries). As is often the case with grated vegetables, you don't really see the parsnips, but you do pick up on the flavor. I love having a loaf of this in the fridge, where it will last for at least a week. I'll slice it cold, smear it with cream cheese, drizzle it with honey, then let it come to room temperature while the coffee brews. The walnuts are optional but highly recommended.

1 About an hour ahead, put the raisins in a small bowl. Add the hot cider. Set aside for 50 to 60 minutes so the fruit can plump.

2 Butter an 8½- by 4½-inch loaf pan. If you have parchment paper on hand, line the bottom and two long sides with a single sheet, leaving a little overhang on each side (this will give you something to hold on to when you remove the bread later). Preheat the oven to 350°F (180°C).

3 Combine the whole-wheat flour, all-purpose flour, baking powder, salt, cinnamon, and ginger in a large bowl. Whisk well to mix. Stir in the oats.

4 In a separate bowl, whisk the eggs until frothy. Whisk in the oil, honey, brown sugar, milk, vanilla, and lemon zest.

5 Using the large or small holes of a box grater (see note below), grate the parsnips; you should have 1¾ to 2 cups. Drain the raisins; you can discard the liquid or save it for something else.

6 Make a well in the dry ingredients and add the liquid mixture. Stir well, until the batter is dampened and only a few dry streaks remain. Add the grated parsnips, raisins, and walnuts, if using, folding them into the batter until it is evenly mixed. Pour the batter into the prepared pan and smooth with a spoon. Bake on the middle oven rack for 60 to 70 minutes, until the loaf is well risen and doesn't feel "squishy" when pressed gently on top. A tester inserted deep into the center of the loaf should come out clean.

7 Transfer to a rack and cool the loaf in the pan until barely lukewarm. Remove the loaf from the pan and continue to cool on the rack. When the bread is thoroughly cool, transfer to a plastic freezer bag and refrigerate until needed. This loaf slices best when it's cool but tastes best at room temperature.

NOTE: I've used both the small and large holes of a box grater to grate the parsnips, and it doesn't seem to make much difference. Either way, the gratings are practically invisible. However, if your small holes are really small and your grating yields nothing but coarse parsnip sludge, use the larger holes.

MAKES ONE 8½- BY 4½-INCH LOAF

Butter for the loaf pan

1 cup raisins or dried cranberries (sweetened or unsweetened)

1 cup hot apple cider or hot water

1¼ cups whole-wheat pastry flour

½ cup all-purpose flour

2 teaspoons baking powder

¾ teaspoon salt

1 teaspoon ground cinnamon

½ teaspoon ground ginger

¼ cup old-fashioned rolled oats or quick oats

3 large eggs

¾ cup vegetable oil or light olive oil

½ cup honey

½ cup packed light brown sugar

¼ cup milk

½ teaspoon vanilla extract

Finely grated zest of 1 lemon

2 medium parsnips, peeled

½ cup chopped walnuts (optional)

SPICED SWEET POTATO AND CHOCOLATE CHIP BREAD

This is one of the prettiest quick breads going, the orange of the sweet potato crumb serving as a striking backdrop for the dark chocolate chips. What's more, it's as delicious as it is pretty and great for brown-bag lunches, hikes, and road trips. I've said it before, but I'll say it again: bake your sweet potatoes ahead of time, when the oven's already going, just so you'll have the flesh on hand (for breads like this) when you need it. It's a pain to turn the oven on just to bake two spuds. Even if you don't use it right away, the flesh will freeze beautifully.

1 Butter a 9- by 5-inch loaf pan. If you have parchment paper on hand, line the bottom and two long sides with a single sheet, letting it extend slightly above the top on each side (this will give you something to hold on to when you remove the bread later). Otherwise, dust the pan with flour and knock out the excess. Preheat the oven to 350°F (180°C).

2 Combine the all-purpose flour, whole-wheat flour, baking powder, baking soda, salt, allspice, cinnamon, and ginger in a large bowl. Whisk well to mix.

3 In a separate large bowl, combine the eggs, granulated sugar, brown sugar, oil, and buttermilk. Using an electric mixer (handheld works fine), beat the ingredients on medium-high speed for 1 minute. Add the sweet potato, lemon juice, and vanilla and beat them in also.

4 Make a well in the dry ingredients and add the liquid mixture. Stir the batter until just a few dry streaks remain. Add the pecans and chocolate chips and fold them in until the batter is evenly mixed. Scrape the batter into the prepared pan and smooth the top with a spoon.

5 Bake on the middle oven rack for 60 to 70 minutes. When done, the bread will have risen nicely and, like most quick breads, developed one or more lengthwise cracks along the top. A tester inserted deep into the cake should come out clean. Transfer the bread to a rack and cool in the pan for about an hour. Run a thin-bladed knife or spatula around the bread, between the paper and pan, and slide the bread out. Continue to cool. Slice and serve when you're ready. Slip leftovers into a plastic freezer bag and refrigerate, but serve the bread at room temperature.

MAKES ONE 9- BY 5-INCH LOAF

Butter for the loaf pan

1 cup all-purpose flour

1 cup whole-wheat pastry flour

1½ teaspoons baking powder

½ teaspoon baking soda

1 teaspoon salt

½ teaspoon ground allspice

½ teaspoon ground cinnamon

½ teaspoon ground ginger

2 large eggs

1 cup granulated sugar

⅓ cup packed light brown sugar

½ cup vegetable oil or light olive oil

⅓ cup buttermilk or plain yogurt

1½ cups finely mashed sweet potatoes (page 246)

1 tablespoon lemon juice

1 teaspoon vanilla extract

¾ cup chopped pecans (preferably toasted)

¾ cup semisweet chocolate chips

Fall's Calling:
Homemade Applesauce

It would be almost criminal to let fall slip by without making at least one batch of homemade applesauce. Applesauce is one of our go-to accompaniments with sweet quick breads, not to mention a great side dish with roasts. And the best news of all is that it's almost embarrassingly easy to prepare.

To make about 3 cups of applesauce, peel, core, and coarsely chop 5 large apples. Put them in a large nonreactive pot with 1 cup water or apple cider, ⅓ cup sugar, and a pinch of salt. Bring to a boil, then cover and reduce the heat to a low boil. Cook, covered, until the apples are very tender, about 15 minutes, checking several times to make sure there's still plenty of liquid in the pot. Remove from the heat and transfer the contents to a bowl. Cool thoroughly. Transfer the apple mixture to a food processor, add ¼ teaspoon cinnamon, and process to your preferred consistency. Transfer to jars and refrigerate until serving.

APPLE APPLESAUCE OATMEAL BREAD

I love keeping fruit breads like this one around because it gives me something quick, easy, and delicious to have with my morning coffee, and it eliminates the need to think about what to make for breakfast. And because this loaf has both fruit and oats, eating a slice is almost like having a bowl of oatmeal, only in a more convenient package. The applesauce adds moisture, so the bread will keep all week in the fridge, and the streusel topping only sweetens the deal, though you can do without it if you like.

1 Butter a 9- by 5-inch loaf pan. If you have parchment paper on hand, line the bottom and two long sides with a single sheet, letting it extend a little above the top on each side (this will give you something to hold on to when you remove the bread later). Otherwise, dust the pan with flour and knock out the excess. Preheat the oven to 350°F (180°C).

2 Combine the flour, oats, baking powder, baking soda, salt, and cinnamon in a large bowl. Mix well by hand or with a whisk.

3 Combine the eggs, brown sugar, applesauce, oil, sour cream, and vanilla in a separate bowl. Using an electric mixer (handheld is fine), beat on medium speed for 1 minute. Make a well in the dry mixture and add the liquid mixture. Stir well by hand until everything is dampened, then let the batter rest for 3 or 4 minutes. Add the diced apple and raisins, folding them into the batter until it's evenly mixed.

4 Scrape the batter into the pan and smooth the top with a spoon. If you're using the streusel, sprinkle it evenly over the batter. Bake for about 1 hour, until a tester inserted deep into the middle of the loaf comes out clean.

5 Transfer the bread to a rack and cool in the pan for about 30 minutes. Run a thin-bladed knife or spatula around the bread, between the paper and pan, and slide the bread out. Continue to cool on the rack. Slice and serve when you're ready. Slip leftovers into a plastic freezer bag and refrigerate, but serve the bread at room temperature.

MAKES ONE 9- BY 5-INCH LOAF

Butter for the loaf pan

1½ cups all-purpose flour

½ cup old-fashioned rolled oats or quick oats

2 teaspoons baking powder

½ teaspoon baking soda

½ teaspoon salt

1 teaspoon ground cinnamon

2 large eggs

1 cup packed light brown sugar

¾ cup smooth applesauce

½ cup vegetable oil

¼ cup sour cream, buttermilk, or plain yogurt

1 teaspoon vanilla extract

1¼ cups peeled and finely diced apple

1 cup dark raisins

½ cup Brown Sugar Streusel (page 287; optional)

SAVORY VEGETABLE SKILLET BREAD

This recipe goes way, way back to my earliest New Hampshire days, when my kids would devour this bread practically before I could get it out of the skillet. It's difficult to describe, because it doesn't fit neatly into a particular genre, but imagine leftover Thanksgiving stuffing baked up as a big skillet pancake and you'd be getting warm. There's no flour here, just old-fashioned oatmeal, so it's got a pleasantly chewy texture. And the quartet of vegetables — potatoes, onion, celery, and carrots — along with the traditional Thanksgiving seasonings give the bread its familiar flavor. I like to serve it on the side with soups, but it's also good rewarmed for breakfast and served with scrambled eggs or under a poached egg.

1 Preheat the oven to 400°F (200°C). Set the slice of bread on your kitchen counter to dry out for a few minutes while you work.

2 Put the diced potato in a small saucepan and add just enough water to cover. Bring to a boil and cook at a low boil, uncovered, until tender, about 10 minutes. Drain the potato, pouring the water into a liquid measuring cup and leaving the potato in the pan. If you have more than ½ cup of potato water, pour some off until you have just ½ cup.

3 Add the milk to the potato water; you should have 1 cup liquid. Put the oats in a large bowl and stir in the liquid. Using a fork, mash up the potatoes a bit and add them to the oats. Stir in the celery, onion, carrot, parsley, egg, and salt. Add the sage, thyme, rosemary, and pepper; stir to combine.

4 Using the large holes on a box grater, grate the bread to make fine crumbs. Put ⅓ cup of these crumbs in a small bowl and add the baking powder. Mix well and add to the oat mixture. (Save any remaining crumbs for another use.) Mix in half of the Parmesan, then let the batter sit for 5 minutes.

5 On your stovetop, heat a 10-inch cast-iron skillet or other oven-safe skillet to medium heat. Add the olive oil and tilt the pan to spread it around. Scrape the batter into the pan, spreading it evenly with a fork. Sprinkle the remaining Parmesan on top and dot the top with small pieces of the butter.

6 Bake on the middle oven rack for 30 minutes. When done, the surface will be crusted over and browned. Transfer to a cooling rack and let cool for at least 10 minutes before serving. The best way to cut this is to score it with a fork; a knife tends to squish the bread. Refrigerate leftovers. Reheat slices in a buttered skillet on top of the stove.

MAKES 6 SERVINGS

- 1 slice hearty whole-wheat or white bread
- 1 medium russet potato, peeled and diced (about 1 cup)
- ½ cup milk
- 1 cup old-fashioned rolled oats (not quick or instant)
- ½ cup finely chopped celery
- ½ cup finely chopped onion
- 1 medium carrot, grated
- 2 tablespoons chopped fresh parsley
- 1 large egg, lightly beaten
- ½ teaspoon salt
- 1 teaspoon chopped fresh sage or ¼ teaspoon dried
- 1 teaspoon fresh thyme or ¼–½ teaspoon dried
- ½ teaspoon chopped fresh rosemary or ¼ teaspoon dried
- ⅛ teaspoon freshly ground black pepper
- 2 teaspoons baking powder
- ¼ cup grated Parmesan cheese
- 2 tablespoons light olive oil
- 2 tablespoons unsalted butter

SUMMER SQUASH LOAF WITH OLIVES AND CHEESE

You might not think you could make an exciting, tasty quick bread with summer squash, but this loaf will put any doubts to rest. It's a moist, all-purpose savory loaf that I've found more uses for than you can imagine: with pasta dishes in place of Italian bread; for finger sandwiches and bruschetta; at breakfast with cream cheese and sliced ham or scrambled eggs. Top it with pesto and fresh tomato slices in the summer. I've even cut the last of it into cubes and baked them up as croutons. A note of caution: summer squash contains quite a bit of moisture, so it's important to squeeze it well in step 3, or the loaf may come out too damp.

1 Preheat the oven to 375°F (190°C). Butter an 8½- by 4½-inch loaf pan.

2 Combine the flour, Parmesan, baking powder, salt, pepper, basil, and thyme in a large bowl. Whisk well to combine.

3 Grate the squash on the large holes of a box grater. Squeeze the gratings by hand to express most, though not all, of the liquid. Measure out 1½ cups of the squash. (Use any leftover gratings in soup, sautés, or other baked goods.)

4 Combine the eggs, milk, olive oil, ricotta, and about two-thirds of the grated squash in a blender. Process for several seconds, just long enough to make a slightly textured purée; it doesn't have to be perfectly smooth. Make a well in the dry ingredients. Add the liquid mixture and remaining squash; stir briefly, until everything is dampened. Add the feta cheese and olives. Continue stirring until everything is evenly mixed. The batter will be thickish, not pourable. Turn it into the prepared pan, smoothing it out and pushing it into the corners with the back of a spoon. Drizzle the melted butter over the top.

5 Bake the bread on the middle oven rack for about 60 minutes. When done, the loaf will be well risen and crusty. A tester inserted deep into the center of the bread will come out clean. Transfer the loaf to a rack and cool in the pan for 5 minutes; then run a thin knife blade or spatula around the edges and turn the loaf out. Continue to cool. Slice and serve warm or at room temperature. Refrigerate leftovers. Reheat slices, wrapped in foil, in a 300°F (150°C) oven for about 10 minutes.

MAKES ONE 8½- BY 4½-INCH LOAF

	Butter for the loaf pan
2	cups all-purpose flour
⅓	cup finely grated Parmesan cheese
2½	teaspoons baking powder
½	teaspoon salt
¼	teaspoon freshly ground black pepper
1	tablespoon chopped fresh basil or 1 teaspoon dried
2	teaspoons chopped fresh thyme or ½ teaspoon dried
2	medium-small yellow summer squash
2	large eggs
½	cup milk
⅓	cup olive oil
¼	cup ricotta cheese
½	cup crumbled feta cheese
½	cup pitted chopped olives
2	tablespoons unsalted butter, melted

BAKED STUFFED POTATO BREAD

What would happen if you took all the basic building blocks of a decked-out baked potato — butter, sour cream, chives, bacon bits, and cheese — and turned them into a quick bread? This is the stuff of harvest bakers' daydreams. This particular daydream led me to the kitchen and, not long after, to a crusty, cheesy, golden loaf that fulfilled my baked-potato flavor aspirations quite nicely. Serve with a big pot of soup or chili, and plan on polishing off most of it; like other soda breads, it's best served fresh (though this loaf fares better than most because the potatoes help keep it moist).

1 In a medium saucepan, combine the potato with enough water to cover it by an inch or so; add a big pinch of salt. Bring to a boil, lower the heat, and cook at a low boil for 10 to 12 minutes, until the potato is tender. Drain the potato (you can save the water for soup) and transfer it to a bowl. Cool briefly, then mash the potato well with a potato masher or ricer. Measure out 1 cup of mashed potatoes and set aside to cool in a mixing bowl. (Save any remaining mashed potato for another use.)

2 Cook the bacon in a large skillet until crisp. Cool. Crumble into a bowl.

3 Preheat the oven to 400°F (200°C). Oil a large baking sheet very lightly and dust it with cornmeal.

4 Combine the flour, baking powder, baking soda, and salt in a large bowl. Whisk well to mix.

5 Stir the milk and sour cream into the mashed potato, then stir in the melted butter and egg. Make a well in the dry ingredients and add the liquid mixture all at once. Stir with a wooden spoon until just a few dry streaks remain. Add the cheese, chives, caraway seeds, and crumbled bacon and mix until the dough pulls together.

6 Turn the dough out onto a well-floured work surface; flour your hands, too. Divide the dough in half. Gently knead each half for about 30 seconds. Shape the dough into two fat footballs. Place them on the sheet with plenty of space between them. Using a sharp serrated knife, make two ½-inch-deep diagonal slits on each loaf.

7 Bake the loaves for about 45 minutes, until they're deep golden and crusty. If you turn a loaf over and tap the bottom with a finger, it should sound hollow. Transfer the loaves to a cooling rack and cool for at least 30 minutes before slicing. Refrigerate leftovers in a plastic bag.

MAKES 2 MEDIUM LOAVES

Oil and cornmeal for the baking sheet

1 large russet potato, peeled and diced

1¼ teaspoons salt, plus a pinch for the potato water

6–8 bacon strips

3½ cups all-purpose flour

2 teaspoons baking powder

½ teaspoon baking soda

¾ cup milk

¾ cup sour cream

4 tablespoons unsalted butter, melted

1 large egg, lightly beaten

1¼ cups grated extra-sharp cheddar cheese or jalapeño cheddar cheese

2–3 tablespoons finely chopped chives

½ teaspoon caraway seed

SUN-DRIED TOMATO AND TARRAGON SODA BREAD

Here's a crusty quick bread that's got a lot going on. My initial aim here was to showcase the pleasant anise-like flavor of tarragon. Early attempts were good, but the tarragon tasted lonely, so over time the bread evolved into a repository for all sorts of things that taste good with tarragon, including tomatoes, cheddar cheese, and mustard. More isn't always better, but in this case it was, yielding a fragrant, savory loaf with sharp, mellow, and aromatic notes in every slice. You'll love how versatile it is. I'll toast my way through a loaf over the course of a week, dressing it up with cream cheese and a slice of ham for breakfast, or topping it with avocado mash and a poached egg, or serving it plain with a soup-and-salad dinner.

1 Preheat the oven to 400°F (200°C). Line a large baking sheet with parchment paper, or lightly oil the sheet and dust the middle of it with cornmeal.

2 Combine the flour, cornmeal, sugar, salt, baking powder, baking soda, and pepper in a large bowl. Using your hands, mix the dry ingredients thoroughly.

3 Combine the buttermilk, olive oil, and mustard in another bowl and whisk to blend. Make a well in the dry ingredients and add the liquid mixture. Using a wooden spoon, stir until everything is barely dampened. Sprinkle in 1 cup of the cheese, as well as the sun-dried tomatoes, walnuts, and tarragon. Continue stirring until the dough coheres and pulls away from the sides of the bowl. The dough will be quite dense. Let it rest in the bowl for 2 to 3 minutes.

4 Lightly flour your hands and your work counter. Turn the dough out onto the counter and knead gently for about 1 minute, dusting with flour as necessary to keep the dough from sticking. Shape the dough into a fat football and place it on the baking sheet. Brush the surface sparingly with the egg glaze. Using a sharp serrated knife, make three evenly spaced diagonal slits, about ½ inch deep, on top of the loaf. Sprinkle the loaf with the remaining ½ cup grated cheese.

5 Bake the bread for about 45 minutes, until the top is quite crusty and golden. When done, the loaf will sound hollow when you tap the bottom with a finger. Transfer the loaf to a cooling rack and cool thoroughly. Refrigerate leftovers in a plastic bag.

NOTE: For the sun-dried tomatoes, you can rehydrate dried ones (the most economical option) or buy them packed in water or oil; the latter, taste-wise, is my favorite option. Another option is to replace the sun-dried tomatoes with chopped roasted tomatoes (page 282).

MAKES 1 LARGE LOAF

Oil and cornmeal for the baking sheet (optional)

2¼ cups all-purpose flour

½ cup fine yellow cornmeal

1½ tablespoons sugar

1¼ teaspoons salt

1 teaspoon baking powder

1 teaspoon baking soda

¼ teaspoon freshly ground black pepper

1 cup buttermilk

3 tablespoons olive oil

1 tablespoon Dijon mustard

1½ cups grated extra-sharp cheddar cheese

¾ cup coarsely chopped sun-dried tomatoes (see note)

½ cup coarsely chopped walnuts

2 tablespoons chopped fresh tarragon or 1 tablespoon dried

1 egg beaten with 1 tablespoon water, for glaze

ROASTING PEPPERS

My favorite way to roast peppers, and the easiest, in my opinion, is outside on the grill. The process can be a bit messy and smoky, so keeping it out of the house isn't a bad idea. Your grill's intense heat and large surface area allow for more rapid charring, so it's faster than doing it over a gas burner (which we'll discuss in a moment).

Some cooks like to rub the surface of the peppers with a little olive oil first, but in my experience it doesn't seem to make much difference. Simply lay the whole peppers on your grill, in the hottest area you can find. The skins will very quickly begin to blacken and blister. Using long-handled tongs, keep turning the peppers so they char evenly all around. When they're more or less blackened all over, transfer them to a bowl and cover the bowl with a plate or plastic wrap. Allow to cool. Using dry paper towels, rub off the charred skins.

It's fine if little charred bits remain; they will add to the flavor. Don't run the peppers under water to remove the char; you'll wash away good flavor.

If you have a gas burner, you can roast them on your stovetop. Just crank up the flame, and place your peppers right on top of the grate above the flame. Turn and char as described.

One final option is to use your oven's broiler. Instead of roasting them whole, cut each bell pepper into three or four flat sections and place them on a baking sheet lined with aluminum foil, skin side up. This exposes all of the skin to the heat at the same time so you don't have to keep reaching into the oven to turn whole peppers. Slide the sheet under the broiler unit, very close to the heat, and broil until charred. Keep an eye on them, and adjust the position of the peppers as needed.

ROASTED BELL PEPPER BUTTERMILK CORNBREAD

With this cornbread the emphasis is on peppers — bell peppers and jalapeños. If you're in the habit of roasting peppers, then you're aware that the resulting flavor is quite distinct from that of a pepper that's been merely sautéed. It's a deeper, more primal flavor, which is what makes this cornbread unique and delicious. We do take one shortcut with the can of creamed corn. I use very few canned vegetables, but I make an exception here, frankly, to balance out the extra time required to roast the peppers. The pickled jalapeños give the cornbread a decided kick. I don't usually keep fresh jalapeños on hand, but if you want to use them, you probably already have a good feel for the amount of heat they pack, so add them accordingly. I think of this primarily as a fall and winter bread, a fine accompaniment for chili and stews.

1 Preheat the oven to 400°F (200°C). On the stovetop very gently melt the stick of butter over low heat in a 10-inch cast-iron skillet (if you don't have one, see the note below). When it's melted, turn off the heat.

2 Combine the flour, cornmeal, sugar, baking powder, baking soda, and salt in a large bowl.

3 In a separate bowl, whisk the eggs until frothy, then whisk in the buttermilk, creamed corn, jalapeño peppers, and melted butter. Make a well in the dry ingredients and add the liquid mixture. Stir briefly, just until everything is dampened. Add the chopped roasted peppers and the cheese, folding them in until the batter is evenly mixed. Scrape the batter into the skillet — the one you melted the butter in — and smooth the top.

4 Bake on the middle oven rack for 30 to 35 minutes, until the surface is golden brown. A tester inserted into the center of the bread should come out clean. Transfer the skillet to a cooling rack. Slice and serve warm. Refrigerate leftovers. Reheat leftovers, wrapped in foil, in a 300°F (150°C) oven for 10 to 12 minutes.

NOTE: If you do not have a cast-iron skillet, substitute a buttered 9- by 9-inch cake pan. Don't melt the butter in it on the stovetop, as you would for the skillet; melt the butter separately and pour it into the pan.

MAKES 8 TO 10 SERVINGS

- ½ cup (1 stick) unsalted butter
- 1 cup all-purpose flour
- 1 cup yellow cornmeal
- ⅓ cup sugar
- 2 teaspoons baking powder
- ½ teaspoon baking soda
- ½ teaspoon salt
- 2 large eggs
- 1 cup buttermilk
- 1 (8-ounce) can cream-style corn
- ¼ cup finely chopped pickled jalapeño peppers (or fresh jalapeños, to taste)
- 2 green or red bell peppers, roasted and chopped
- 1 cup grated extra-sharp cheddar cheese or pepper jack cheese

CORN-OFF-THE-COB SOUR CREAM CORNBREAD

I like all sorts of cornbreads — coarse grainy ones, bacon-and-cheese-laced versions (page 29), and moist, tender ones like this, chock-full of fresh-cut corn kernels. The interior isn't quite as moist as a Southern-style spoonbread (page 68), but the dense texture almost requires a fork. No matter how you eat it, it's a great way to incorporate fresh corn kernels into your harvest baking. Off corn season, I've been known to boil up some frozen corn so I can have this in the middle of winter, because it's the perfect accompaniment for cold-weather soups and stews. In summer try it with ratatouille or baked stuffed tomatoes.

1 Put the corn kernels in a medium saucepan and add water to cover. Bring to a boil and boil gently for 5 minutes. Drain the corn and set it aside to cool.

2 Preheat the oven to 350°F (180°C). Butter a 9- by 5-inch loaf pan, and dust it with cornmeal.

3 Combine the cornmeal, flour, sugar, baking powder, baking soda, and salt in a large bowl. Whisk well to mix.

4 Combine the sour cream, milk, melted butter, and egg in a separate bowl. Whisk until evenly blended. Make a well in the dry mixture and add the liquid mixture and corn. Stir well with a wooden spoon until evenly mixed. Transfer the batter to the prepared pan and smooth the top.

5 Bake on the middle oven rack for 40 to 45 minutes, until the bread is light golden and feels slightly springy when you press on the top. Transfer to a cooling rack and cool the bread in the pan for 10 to 15 minutes before slicing and serving. Refrigerate leftovers. Reheat slices in the microwave or wrapped in foil and placed in a 300°F (150°C) oven for 10 minutes.

MAKES ONE 9- BY 5-INCH LOAF

Butter and cornmeal for loaf pan

1½ cups corn kernels, preferably freshly cut (about 3 medium ears)

¾ cup yellow cornmeal

⅔ cup all-purpose flour

3 tablespoons sugar

1 teaspoon baking powder

½ teaspoon baking soda

¾ teaspoon salt

¾ cup sour cream

½ cup milk

½ cup (1 stick) unsalted butter, melted and partially cooled

1 large egg

CUTTING THE KERNELS OFF THE COB

There's a wide variety of sharp gizmos that make short work of cutting kernels off an ear of corn. I use a handy device called a Corn Zipper, made by Kuhn Rikon, and I've seen OXO's Corn Stripper in action. You just slide these little gadgets down the ear, and they slice the kernels right off. The old-school approach still works fine, too: Using a sharp chef's knife, cut about 1 inch off the pointy end of the shucked ear so you have a stumpy end to steady it. Holding the ear vertically, by the stem if it's still attached, slice downward to cut off the kernels. If your knife is good and sharp, they'll fall right off. If not, the kernels will probably fly around a bit. Take it slow and easy; a measure of caution is advised.

SWEET POTATO AND CORN SPOONBREAD

Spoonbread is a type of Southern cornbread that's too moist to be eaten out of hand, so it's spooned up instead. I've had many versions over the years, but this sweet potato one, which reminds me of a very moist Thanksgiving stuffing, is the best. As in a soufflé, beaten egg whites are typically added to spoonbread, allowing it a nice rise in the oven. This one gets an additional boost from baking powder. There's plenty here to serve a crowd, typically with a nice roast or other special meat dish and an array of vegetables. It would be perfect with the Thanksgiving feast. Time it so this is coming out of the oven when everyone is sitting down to dinner, so they can appreciate the soufflé-like drama.

1 Scoop out the sweet potato flesh and transfer to a bowl. Using a hand masher, mash the potatoes well. Put the corn in a small saucepan with enough water to cover by an inch or so. Bring to a boil and boil the corn for 5 minutes. Drain.

2 Preheat the oven to 375°F (190°C). Butter a large shallow casserole dish (about 2½ quarts) or other baking dish well.

3 Melt the butter in a large saucepan, preferably nonstick. Add the onion and cook for 7 to 8 minutes over medium heat. Stir in the garlic and cook another minute. Add the half-and-half, chicken stock, sage, thyme, rosemary, salt, pepper, and sugar. Gradually whisk the cornmeal into the liquid. As the mixture starts to thicken, switch to a wooden spoon and cook for 2 minutes, until the mixture has a thick, porridge-like consistency. Transfer to a large bowl and cool briefly. Stir in the baking powder, mashed sweet potatoes, and corn. Add the egg yolks, sausage, and cheese; stir well.

4 Put the egg whites in a large, clean, dry bowl. Using an electric mixer, beat the whites until they hold soft peaks. Add to the cornmeal mixture and fold them in gently with a rubber spatula until just a few streaks of whites remain. Transfer the batter to the buttered casserole dish and smooth the top with a spoon. Bake the spoonbread for 35 to 45 minutes, until it is puffed up and light golden brown. Serve as soon as possible.

NOTE: Almost any cooked sausage works just fine here, from crumbled sage breakfast sausage to diced hot Italian sausage. You could always leave out the sausage if meat is not your thing. But it really does help make the dish.

MAKES 8 TO 10 SERVINGS

Butter for the casserole

2 large sweet potatoes, baked and partially cooled (for instructions, see box on page 246 and follow steps 1–3)

1 cup corn kernels, fresh or frozen

3 tablespoons unsalted butter

½ large onion, finely chopped

2 garlic cloves, minced

1½ cups half-and-half or milk

1 cup chicken stock

1 tablespoon chopped fresh sage or 1½ teaspoons dried

2 teaspoons fresh thyme or 1 teaspoon dried

1 teaspoon chopped fresh rosemary or ½ teaspoon dried

1½ teaspoons salt (a bit more if you're using no- or low-sodium chicken stock)

¼ teaspoon freshly ground black pepper

1 tablespoon sugar

1 cup fine yellow cornmeal

1 teaspoon baking powder

4 large eggs, separated

1½ cups cooked sausage, diced or crumbled (see note)

1–1½ cups grated sharp or extra-sharp cheddar cheese

COTTAGE CHEESE SLICING LOAF WITH DILL AND CHIVES

You've probably seen a lot of recipes for cottage cheese breads over the years; I certainly have. And I've noticed that many of them have several things in common: most are no-knead loaf breads; they usually contain herbs; and they tend to be savory, rather than sweet. This one is all of the above. It has blue cheese and walnuts, which I love together, and olive oil, too, which contributes to the creamy, moist interior. (You can use other cheeses in place of the blue cheese; see the ingredients list.) I make this bread year-round, but I especially like it in the summer spread with fresh herb cream cheese and topped with sliced tomatoes. A good keeper, it will do fine in the fridge for a week or so.

1 Preheat the oven to 375°F (190°C). Butter an 8½- by 4½-inch loaf pan.

2 Combine the flour, sugar, baking powder, salt, and pepper in a large bowl. Whisk well to mix.

3 Whisk the eggs in a separate bowl until frothy. Whisk in the cottage cheese, olive oil, milk, chives, and dill.

4 Make a well in the dry mixture and add the liquid mixture. Stir gently, until everything is dampened and only a few dry streaks remain; then stir in the cheese and walnuts. Transfer the batter to the loaf pan and even out the top with a fork (not a spoon — a fork will leave you with lots of crusty little peaks that add to the bread's charm).

5 Bake the loaf for 30 minutes, then lower the heat to 350°F (180°C) and bake for another 15 to 20 minutes, until the top is a rich, crusty golden brown. Transfer the pan to a cooling rack. Cool for 20 minutes, then slide the loaf out of the pan and cool thoroughly. Store the loaf in the refrigerator, in a plastic bag.

MAKES ONE 8½- BY 4½-INCH LOAF

Butter for the loaf pan

1¾ cups all-purpose flour

1 tablespoon sugar

2½ teaspoons baking powder

½ teaspoon salt

⅛ teaspoon freshly ground black pepper

2 large eggs

¾ cup cottage cheese

¼ cup olive oil

2 tablespoons milk

2–3 tablespoons chopped chives

2–3 tablespoons chopped fresh dill

1 cup crumbled blue cheese or grated sharp cheddar cheese, fontina, Havarti, or other favorite melting cheese

¾ cup chopped walnuts (preferably toasted)

SAVORY SHORTBREAD THUMBPRINTS WITH TOMATO JAM

This is, and is not, what it appears to be: a sweet, jam-filled thumbprint cookie. Except that the cookies — Rosemary Lemon Shortbread Cookies (page 215) — are not very sweet, and our homemade tomato jam has a decidedly sweet-tart edge. So what looks to be your typical jam-filled thumbprint cookie turns out to be a savory appetizer, the crumbles of feta cheese on top of the jam leaving little doubt. Believe me when I tell you that it's an appetizing little package, though it does take a second or two for the palate to sort out the various flavors at play and register its full approval. These are great for an adult dinner party, but the flavor scheme might be a stretch for children.

1 Prepare the shortbread cookie dough as instructed, substituting ¼ cup finely grated Parmesan for the ¼ cup confectioners' sugar. Turn the dough out onto your work surface and shape into 1¼-inch-diameter balls. Place the balls about 2½ inches apart on a large baking sheet, preferably lined with parchment. (Use a shiny sheet, not a dark one, to prevent the cookies from overbrowning.)

2 Place a sheet of plastic wrap over the cookies. Using the flat bottom of a glass, press gently to flatten each ball into a disk about ½ inch thick. With your thumb, press the center of the disk to make a deep crater; be careful not to press all the way through the dough. Refrigerate the sheet for 1 to 2 hours.

3 Preheat the oven to 350°F (180°C). Carefully remove the plastic from the cookies if you haven't already. Bake for about 15 minutes, then check on them: the craters will have started to relax and fill in. Slide out the cookies, and using the rounded surface of a melon baller or another small rounded object, gently press each crater to reestablish its original crater shape. Continue to bake for 5 to 7 more minutes — a total of 20 to 22 minutes — until the bottoms of the cookies turn golden brown. (Since there is less sugar in these than in the original recipe, you may not see much if any browning on the top surface of the cookies.) Transfer to a rack and cool the cookies on the sheet for several minutes. Using a thin spatula, carefully move the cookies off the sheet and onto the rack to finish cooling.

4 When you're ready to assemble the shortbreads, preferably within an hour of serving them, spread about ½ teaspoon cream cheese in each crater, smearing it in with the back of a spoon to keep the crater shape. Then spoon a generous ½ teaspoon of tomato jam into each crater. Top the jam with a few little crumbles of feta cheese. Arrange on a platter and serve.

MAKES ABOUT 2 DOZEN SHORTBREAD APPETIZERS

Rosemary Lemon Shortbread Cookie dough (page 215), modified as described in step 1, replacing ¼ cup confectioners' sugar with ¼ cup finely grated Parmesan cheese

¼ cup cream cheese, slightly softened

Food Processor Tomato Jam (page 283)

¼ cup crumbled feta cheese

POTATO-STUFFED INDIAN FLATBREAD (*ALOO PARATHA*)

Indian cuisine has many wonderful breads, but the ones I like best are the various parathas, thin unleavened breads filled with all sorts of well-seasoned ingredients, from meats to vegetables and more. Among my favorites is aloo paratha, basically just spicy mashed potatoes sealed inside the dough and rolled thin before being toasted in a skillet. Getting the potatoes inside the bread is a fun trick, and you'll look like something of a culinary magician. The other trick is in how the potatoes are handled; you'll want to keep them as dry as possible so they don't dampen the dough, which is why we steam instead of boil them. Plan to make the filling and dough in the morning or day before, and assemble them when you're ready to eat. Serve these with your favorite Indian dishes, accompanied by chutney, raita, or the Curried Yogurt Dipping Sauce on page 285 for dipping.

1 Scrub the potatoes well. If they're large, cut them into several good-size chunks. Place them in a steamer basket inside a large saucepan. Add enough water to reach the bottom of the basket. Bring to a low boil, then cover and steam the potatoes until they feel tender when pierced with a toothpick or cake tester, about 10 minutes. Transfer the potatoes to a large plate and cool thoroughly. Put the carrots in the steamer and steam them for 7 to 8 minutes, until tender. Set aside to cool.

2 When the potatoes have cooled, peel them and place them in a large bowl. Add the steamed carrots, onion, cilantro, chiles, and ½ teaspoon salt. Add the curry powder, chili powder, and cumin, and season generously with pepper. Grate the ginger on the small holes of a box grater and add that also. Stir well to distribute the spices.

3 Using a pastry blender or potato masher, thoroughly mash the filling mixture until everything is well broken up and there are no big chunks that will puncture the dough when you roll out the bread. Give it a taste and see if you need more salt. Transfer the mixture to a bowl; cover and refrigerate for at least 2 to 3 hours.

4 Prepare the dough, which can be made a day in advance if desired. Combine the all-purpose flour, whole-wheat flour, and salt in a large bowl. Drizzle 2 tablespoons oil over the flour. Using your fingers, rub the oil thoroughly into the flour until it has a somewhat sandy texture. Add the water in three installments, working it in with one of your hands after each addition; it will be a sticky mess at first. Continue to add water and squeeze the dough until it coheres. Add about a teaspoon of oil to the bowl and knead the dough in the bowl for a minute or two; the oil will reduce the stickiness. Cover the dough and set it aside. Refrigerate if not using until the next day.

MAKES 6 FLATBREADS

FILLING

- 1½ pounds potatoes (3 to 4 medium ones; see note)
- 1 cup finely diced carrot or whole green peas, fresh or frozen
- ½ cup very finely chopped red onion
- ¼ cup finely chopped fresh cilantro or parsley
- 1–2 tablespoons chopped green chiles, to taste
- ½ teaspoon salt, plus more to taste
- 1½ teaspoons curry powder
- ½ teaspoon chili powder
- ½ teaspoon ground cumin
- Freshly ground black pepper
- Fresh ginger, peeled (a piece about the size of a small thumb)

NOTE: I almost always use red-skinned potatoes when I make these. I've also used Yukon Gold potatoes, but I typically don't use starchy russet potatoes. I could not find a single source that made a specific recommendation, so I'm not sure it makes a difference.

DOUGH

- 1 cup all-purpose flour, plus some for rolling out the dough

- 1 cup whole-wheat flour

- ½ teaspoon salt

- 2 tablespoons plus 1 teaspoon vegetable oil, plus some for brushing the dough

- ⅔ cup water (approximately)

5 When you're ready to assemble and cook the parathas, divide the dough into six equal pieces. Working with one piece of dough at a time — and keeping the others covered as you work — flour the dough lightly and roll it into a 5-inch circle on your counter. Brush the flour from the surface of the dough.

6 Measure out approximately ⅓ cup of the filling and mound it right in the center of the dough circle. Grasp the dough on opposite sides of the circle and pull them together over the filling, pinching the edges together. Continue pulling up opposite edges of the dough and pinching them together tightly at the top. When you're done, your filling will be enclosed in what looks like a pleated pincushion. Be sure that the filling is totally enclosed, or it will squeeze out when you roll the flatbread. Set aside on a lightly floured surface. Repeat for the other pieces of dough.

7 Begin preheating one or two large skillets (preferably nonstick or cast iron) on your stovetop over medium heat. Place one paratha, pinched side up, on a lightly floured surface. Using your rolling pin, gently and gradually roll the paratha into a 6½- to 7-inch circle. Go about it slowly, so you don't tear the dough. Dust with flour as needed to prevent sticking. You can roll out the other breads while you're cooking the first ones.

8 Place one paratha at a time in the hot skillet. Cook for about 2 minutes, then turn it over and cook for about 2 minutes on the second side. After you flip it once, use a pastry brush to lightly coat the top with a little oil; you don't need much. Flip again and cook for about 30 seconds. Brush the second side with oil, flip again, and cook for another 30 seconds. Please note that your breads will likely develop crispy little charred spots, and that's fine as long as it doesn't get out of hand. Also, they'll likely puff up quite a bit as they cook, so keep a paring knife nearby and poke them as they do to deflate them. You can serve these as they come off the heat, or you can transfer them to a baking sheet and hold them in a 300°F (150°C) oven while you cook the rest. Slice in half or into wedges and serve.

3

Yeast Breads, Rolls, and Buns

There was a time when, by necessity, nearly every home cook made her own yeast bread. But times have changed, and more and more, making bread at home seems to be limited to a few dedicated hobbyists unwilling to give up the tactile pleasures, measured pace, and incredible flavor of handmade, homemade bread. If you need a good reason to master the basics of yeast bread baking, I can offer none more compelling than this category of harvest breads. Here you'll find breads laced with herbs, highlighted with carrots, tenderized by potatoes, and otherwise elevated by the harvest.

Yeast Isn't Scary

Please don't be deterred if you've never made yeast bread before. Sure, there's a bit of a learning curve, as there is with any worthwhile endeavor. The only tricky part — and it's not really all that tricky — is learning how to knead your dough. But there are countless videos on YouTube that can show you how to do that, so no worries.

Here are some pointers that will help you get off to a good start.

- Yeast bread shouldn't be hurried, so pick a day when you plan to be around the house most of the morning or afternoon. Allow for 3 to 4 hours from start to finish. That said, much of the time you'll be waiting for your dough to rise, and you can do other things in the meantime. It's not like you're putting half your day on hold.

- If you start making yeast bread on a regular basis, purchase your active dry yeast in bulk jars rather than packets. It's more economical.

- Use unbleached all-purpose flour. Unbleached flour has an off-white hue that makes yeast breads look more natural and appealing. And bleaching can alter the strength of the flour, resulting in a dough that's not as elastic or responsive as one made with unbleached flour.

- When you begin kneading your dough, push on it gently with your palms so it doesn't stick to your hands. As the dough becomes bouncier and absorbs more flour, you can push a little harder.

- Let your dough rise in a warm, draft-free spot. Cover the bowl snugly with plastic wrap to keep out drafts and dust A tea towel draped over the top adds an extra blanket to keep your dough warm.

- Most doughs will take 45 minutes to 1½ hours to double in bulk. If a dough is very rich — with eggs, butter, and milk — it will often take longer.

- Make sure your oven is thoroughly preheated before your loaves go in. I like to turn my oven on a good 20 minutes before putting in my loaves.

- One fairly reliable way to tell that your loaves are done is the "tap test." Slip your loaf out of the pan — or simply turn it over if it's a free-form loaf — and tap the bottom with your finger. It should feel crusty and make a hollow sound. (Exception: Potato or winter squash breads won't give a nice crisp retort. Total elapsed baking time is the best indicator for them.)

CINNAMON-RAISIN CARROT LOAF

From the gorgeous carrot-flecked crumb to the dramatic dark swirl of cinnamon and brown sugar, this loaf is almost too pretty to eat, but eat it you will. (I love it toasted and spread with cream cheese and honey.) As with other harvest breads in this collection, I like to roast, rather than boil, the vegetable in question; roasting concentrates the color, flavor, and sweetness, rather than washing them away. With the carrot-and-sugar purée, you get a lovely and responsive dough that's a pleasure to knead and handle. Your home will smell cinnamon-and-brown-sugar fabulous for hours after you've baked this loaf, a good trick to have up your sleeve when company is coming.

1 Preheat the oven to 400°F (200°C). Tear off a sheet of aluminum foil about 12 inches long and stack the carrot slices in the middle. Drizzle with a little of the oil; add a pinch of salt. Close the carrots up tight in the foil and roast for about 45 minutes, until tender. Open up the foil and set the carrots aside to cool.

2 When the carrots have cooled, cut them into small chunks and measure out ¾ cup (save the remaining carrots for another use). Put the ¾ cup chunked carrots and the granulated sugar in a food processor and process to a very fine texture — not quite a smooth purée, but almost.

3 Pour the lukewarm water into a small bowl and sprinkle on the yeast. Set aside for 5 minutes to dissolve. Combine the milk and egg yolk in a separate large bowl. Stir in the salt, dissolved yeast, and processed carrots. Add 1½ cups of the flour and stir well. Stir in the softened butter and the raisins. Let the dough rest for 5 minutes.

4 Using a wooden spoon, stir in enough of the remaining flour, about ¼ cup at a time, to make a kneadable dough that pulls away from the sides of the bowl. Turn the dough out onto a floured work surface and knead with floured hands for 8 to 10 minutes, until the dough is supple and elastic. Smear a teaspoon or two of cooking oil in a large ceramic or glass bowl. Add the dough, turning it to coat the entire surface with oil. Cover the bowl with plastic wrap and set it aside in a warm, draft-free spot until the dough has doubled in bulk, about 1½ hours.

5 When the dough has doubled, punch it down and turn it out onto a lightly floured surface. Knead for 1 minute, then shape into a ball. Let the dough rest for 5 to 10 minutes, loosely covered with plastic wrap. In the meantime, combine the brown sugar and cinnamon in a small bowl, and mix well with your fingers. Butter a 9- by 5-inch loaf pan.

6 Lightly flour your work surface, and roll the dough into an oblong about 10 inches wide and 14 inches long, making it a little wider on the end furthest from you. Brush the surface of the dough with water, sparingly, then spread

MAKES ONE 9- BY 5-INCH LOAF

Butter for the pan

4 medium carrots, peeled, trimmed, and cut into 3-inch sections

1–2 teaspoons light olive oil or other cooking oil, plus a drizzle for roasting the carrots

1¼ teaspoons salt, plus a pinch for roasting the carrots

¼ cup granulated sugar

⅓ cup lukewarm water (105 to 110°F [41–43°C])

1 packet (¼ ounce) active dry yeast

⅔ cup lukewarm milk (105 to 110°F [41–43°C])

1 egg yolk

3 cups unbleached all-purpose flour

2 tablespoons unsalted butter, softened

¾ cup dark raisins

⅓ cup packed light brown sugar

½ teaspoon ground cinnamon

1 egg beaten with 1 tablespoon water, for glaze

the cinnamon and brown sugar mixture evenly over the surface, leaving a ½-inch border all around. Starting at the narrower end close to you, roll the dough up snugly, like a carpet. Pinch the dough at the seam to seal and tuck the ends under. Place the loaf, seam down, in the pan. Cover loosely with plastic wrap and set aside in a warm, draft-free spot until almost doubled in bulk, about 40 minutes to 1 hour. Adjust the oven rack so it is one position below the middle. Preheat the oven to 400°F (200°C).

7 When the dough is fully doubled, gently brush the surface with the egg glaze. Bake the loaf for 15 minutes, then reduce the heat to 375°F (190°C) and bake for an additional 35 to 45 minutes. When done, the top will be a very rich golden brown. If you turn the loaf out and tap the bottom with your finger, the loaf should sound hollow.

8 Turn the dough out of the pan and place it on a cooling rack. You can slice the loaf when it is still barely warm. Seal the thoroughly cooled loaf in a plastic bag. Store at room temperature for a couple of days, but if you'll be keeping it longer, refrigerate the loaf.

GREAT AMERICAN POTATO BREAD

I learned a good deal about bread baking from the late James Beard, champion of great American food and a cooking celebrity before everyone was. In 1973 he published his now classic *Beard on Bread*, which I promptly purchased upon returning from one of my overseas deployments with the navy. (As you can imagine, my fellow Seabees thought it pretty odd that I was buying cookbooks instead of stereo systems and Springsteen albums . . . until they tasted the results.) Beard was clearly a fan of potato breads — he has six in his bread book. Like me, he must have appreciated the subtle flavor potatoes add to bread, and the way they function as a natural dough conditioner. This loaf closely resembles a favorite of mine from his *James Beard's American Cookery*. It's a moist, classic, all-purpose bread, and my go-to loaf for grilled cheese sandwiches.

1 In a small saucepan, bring the diced potato and water to a boil. Cook at a low boil for 10 to 12 minutes, until the potato is very tender. Drain, reserving the potato water. Set the potatoes and water aside to cool.

2 When the potato water is lukewarm, measure out 1 cup and pour it into a large bowl. Sprinkle on the yeast and mix briefly with a fork. Set aside for 5 minutes to let the yeast dissolve.

3 Using a hand masher, mash the potatoes in a medium bowl until they're fairly smooth and lump-free; they don't need to be perfectly smooth. Measure out ¾ cup of mashed potato, saving the rest for another use.

4 Stir the milk, softened butter, sugar, salt, and ¾ cup mashed potato into the potato water. Add 3 cups of the flour. Using a wooden spoon, beat well by hand for about 100 strokes. The dough will be thick and shaggy, but it will smooth out a bit by the time you're done mixing. Let the dough rest for 5 minutes.

5 Using your wooden spoon, stir in enough of the remaining flour, adding ¼ to ⅓ cup at a time, to make a kneadable dough that pulls away from the sides of the bowl. Turn the dough out onto a floured work surface and knead with floured hands for 8 to 10 minutes, until the dough is supple and elastic, dusting with more flour as needed. Be aware that the mashed potatoes soften the dough and may make it a bit sticky. You don't have to baby the dough while you knead it, but don't be too rough, either. Smear a teaspoon or two of cooking oil in a large ceramic or glass bowl. Add the dough, turning it to coat the entire surface with oil. Cover the bowl with plastic wrap and set it aside in a warm, draft-free spot until the dough has doubled in bulk, 1 to 1½ hours.

6 When the dough has doubled, punch it down and turn it out onto a lightly floured work counter. Knead for 1 minute. Divide the dough in half, shaping each half into a ball. Let the dough balls rest, loosely covered with plastic wrap, for 10 minutes. Butter two 8½- by 4½-inch loaf pans.

MAKES TWO 8½- BY 4½-INCH LOAVES

	Butter for the pans
1	large russet potato, peeled and cut into small cubes
2½	cups water
1	packet (¼ ounce) active dry yeast
1	cup lukewarm milk (105 to 110°F [41–43°C])
4	tablespoons unsalted butter, softened
1	tablespoon sugar
2½	teaspoons salt
5¼–5¾	cups unbleached all-purpose flour
1–2	teaspoons cooking oil for the bowl
1	egg beaten with 1 teaspoon water, for glaze

7 Shape the dough into loaves (see How to Shape a Loaf, below) and place them in the pans. Cover loosely with plastic wrap and set the loaves aside in a warm, draft-free spot until they have almost doubled in bulk, about 30 to 45 minutes. Adjust the oven rack so it is one setting below the middle. As the loaves are nearing the end of their rise, preheat the oven to 400°F (200°C).

8 When the loaves have doubled, gently and sparingly brush them with the egg glaze. Bake for 10 minutes, then reduce the heat to 375°F (190°C) and bake for another 30 to 40 minutes, until they're a rich golden brown. Slip one of the loaves out of its pan and tap the bottom crust; if the loaf is done, it will sound hollow. Remove the loaves from the pans and cool them directly on a rack.

How to Shape a Loaf

For a yeast bread to get a good rise, there has to be enough tension in the dough so it expands upward, not just outward. Without that tension your bread will be squatty and might even droop over the sides of your pan when it rises.

Here's a simple way to create that tension when shaping your dough. Let your ball of dough relax for a few minutes, then press or roll it into an oblong about ½ inch thick. It will probably be 10 to 12 inches long. Make the end that's farthest away from you slightly wider than the end that's pointing toward you. Starting at the end closest to you, roll the dough up like a rug, keeping tension on the dough as you roll but not so much tension that the dough tears. When you reach the end, firmly pinch the dough together at the seam. Pinch the ends together as well, and tuck them under the loaf. Place the loaves in your pans, seam side facing down. Let rise and bake as directed.

SHAKER FRESH HERB BREAD WITH WALNUTS

During the 20 years I lived in New Hampshire, one of my favorite places to visit was the Shaker Village in Canterbury, New Hampshire. It's well documented that the Shakers were wonderfully inventive cooks, and they loved using fresh herbs in so much of what they prepared, including their breads. This rustic farmhouse loaf is modeled after Shaker-style loaves I've had over the past decades. It's a great all-purpose bread for savory sandwiches, and it would be hard to find a better toasting loaf for breakfast. Use a combination of herbs; no one herb should dominate. I like to snip three or four different ones, such as thyme or lemon thyme, dill, maybe some chives, oregano, and always a bit of rosemary. If fresh herbs aren't available, use about 2 tablespoons of dried herbs.

1   Pour the hot milk into a large bowl. Add the sugar and salt; stir to dissolve. Stir in the olive oil and set aside until the milk is lukewarm. Meanwhile, pour the water into a small bowl and sprinkle on the yeast. Stir once or twice with a fork and set aside for 5 minutes to let the yeast dissolve.

2   Stir the dissolved yeast and the egg yolk into the lukewarm milk. Add 4 cups of the flour. Beat vigorously with a wooden spoon for about 100 strokes. Cover the bowl with plastic wrap and set aside for 10 to 15 minutes.

3   Stir the walnuts, herbs, and celery seed into the dough. Stir in enough of the remaining flour, adding ¼ to ⅓ cup at a time, to make a kneadable dough that pulls away from the sides of the bowl. Turn the dough out onto a floured work surface, and knead with floured hands for 8 to 10 minutes, until the dough is supple and elastic. Smear a teaspoon or two of olive oil in a large ceramic or glass bowl. Add the dough, turning it to coat the entire surface with oil. Cover the bowl with plastic wrap and set it aside in a warm, draft-free spot until the dough has doubled in bulk, about 1 to 1½ hours.

4   Punch the dough down and turn it out onto a floured work surface. Divide it in half and knead each half for a minute, shaping it into a ball. Let the dough rest on a lightly floured surface for 5 to 10 minutes, loosely covered with plastic wrap. Butter two 8½- by 4½-inch loaf pans. Shape the dough into loaves and place them in the pans. Cover with plastic wrap and set them aside in a warm, draft-free spot until they have almost doubled in bulk, about 40 minutes to 1 hour. When they're almost doubled, position your oven rack so it is one setting below the middle. Preheat your oven to 375°F (190°C).

5   Remove the plastic and lightly brush the loaves with the egg glaze. Sprinkle with the sesame seeds. Bake the loaves for 45 to 50 minutes, until they're a rich golden brown. To see if they're done, slip one out of the pan and tap the bottom of the loaf with a finger; it should sound hollow. Remove the loaves from the pans and transfer them to a cooling rack. When the loaves are completely cool, transfer to plastic bags for storage.

MAKES TWO 8½- BY 4½-INCH LOAVES

Butter for the pans

2¼   cups hot milk

3   tablespoons sugar

2½   teaspoons salt

¼   cup light olive oil, plus a little for the bowl

⅓   cup lukewarm water (105 to 110°F [41–43°C])

1   packet (¼ ounce) active dry yeast

1   egg yolk

6¼–6¾   cups unbleached all-purpose flour

1   cup chopped walnuts

⅓–½   cup chopped fresh herbs

1   teaspoon celery seed

1   egg beaten with 1 tablespoon milk, for glaze

1   tablespoon sesame seeds

POTATO PAN BREAD WITH CHERRY TOMATOES

Part tomato focaccia, part soft potato sandwich bread, this is one hybrid you'll get plenty of mileage from. You'll be delighted with the way the potato tenderizes the bread and adds an earthy flavor, too. The dough is pressed into a pan, dimpled with cherry tomato halves, and topped with a generous coating of olive oil, rosemary, and kosher salt. The warm loaf can be cut into squares and served with your favorite Italian meal. Or you can halve the squares horizontally and build your favorite sandwiches. It's an especially good choice for grilled cheese and panini.

1 Combine the water and potato in a large saucepan. Bring to a boil and cook at a low boil for 10 to 12 minutes, until the potato is quite soft. Remove from the heat. Using a slotted spoon, remove the potatoes, reserving the potato water. Measure out ¾ cup of the potatoes and put them through a ricer or mash them very fine with a potato masher or large fork. (Reserve the rest of the potatoes for another use.)

2 Measure out 1⅔ cups of the potato water (if you're a little short, add tap water). Pour the water into a large bowl. When it has cooled to lukewarm, stir in the sugar. Sprinkle on the yeast. Stir once or twice and set aside for 5 minutes to let the yeast to dissolve.

3 Stir the riced potatoes into the liquid. Add 2 cups of the flour and stir vigorously with a wooden spoon for 100 strokes. Set aside for 5 to 10 minutes.

4 Add 2 tablespoons of the olive oil and the salt to the dough. Stir well. Stir in enough of the remaining flour, about ⅓ cup at a time, to make a firm, kneadable dough that pulls away from the sides of the bowl.

5 Turn the dough out onto a floured surface and knead, gently at first — the potatoes make a delicate dough — for about 8 minutes, adding flour as necessary to keep the dough from sticking. The potatoes make the dough a little lazy, so don't be surprised if it doesn't have as much bounce as other yeast doughs. Smear 2 teaspoons of the olive oil in a large bowl. Add the dough, turning it to coat the entire surface with oil. Cover the bowl with plastic wrap and set aside in a warm, draft-free spot until the dough has doubled in bulk, 45 minutes to 1 hour. Punch down the dough gently and pummel it lightly several times, but don't turn it out and knead it.

6 Using your fingers, spread 2 tablespoons of the olive oil on the bottom and sides of a 13- by 9-inch baking pan. Using your oily hands, place the dough in the pan and press it out as evenly as possible. Let the dough rest for 10 minutes, then press again, making a point to push the dough into the corners. Cover the pan with plastic wrap and set aside for 20 minutes.

MAKES AT LEAST 12 SERVINGS

- 3 cups water
- 1 medium baking potato, peeled and diced
- 1 teaspoon sugar
- 1 packet (¼ ounce) active dry yeast
- 4–4½ cups unbleached all-purpose flour
- 6 tablespoons plus 2 teaspoons olive oil
- 2 teaspoons salt
- 12–15 cherry tomatoes or grape tomatoes, halved lengthwise
- 2 tablespoons chopped fresh rosemary

  Kosher salt, for sprinkling

7 Remove the plastic and gently press the tomato halves into the dough, flat sides down, making four or five rows across and six rows lengthwise. Drizzle 2 more tablespoons of the olive oil over the dough. Sprinkle with the rosemary and, lightly, with the kosher salt. Set the dough aside, uncovered, until it has doubled its original bulk, 20 to 25 minutes. While the dough rises, preheat the oven to 425°F (220°C).

8 When the dough has doubled, put the pan in the oven and lower the heat to 400°F (200°C). Bake for 35 to 40 minutes, until golden brown and crusty. Transfer the pan to a cooling rack. Cool for 5 minutes, then slide the bread out of the pan and continue to cool. Serve warm, if possible. Wrap leftovers in foil and refrigerate. This freezes beautifully, too. Slip the foil-wrapped leftovers into plastic freezer bags.

HERB AND VEGGIE FLOWERPOT BREAD

Did you know that you can bake bread in a terra-cotta flowerpot? Indeed you can, and it's only fitting that loaves baked in flowerpots be a showcase for good stuff from the soil. Here we begin by finely chopping and grating a handful of vegetables and drying them out in the oven. This process concentrates the flavors, which in turn permeate the loaves as they bake. This recipe uses carrots, celery, and onions, but don't be shy about going off script and substituting some parsnips, winter squash, a clove or two of sliced garlic — whatever sounds appealing. Fresh or dried herbs round out the garden-fresh profile, and a bit of cheddar cheese adds richness and tang. It all adds up to one fragrant loaf that's especially good for sandwiches. There are a few little tricks for baking in flowerpots, outlined on pages 86–87; heed, and your loaves will turn out beautifully from the start. Remember to allow enough time early in the day, or the day before, to "season" your flowerpots.

1 Preheat the oven to 300°F (150°C). Oil a large rimmed baking sheet very lightly. Spread the carrots, celery, and onion evenly in a single layer on the sheet. Place in the oven and roast for 45 minutes to an hour. When they're ready, they'll look shrunken and shriveled — especially the carrots — and take up about half as much room on the sheet. You don't want them to get brittle dry. Transfer the sheet to a cooling rack and allow the vegetables to cool.

2 Pour the water into a large bowl. Stir in the sugar and sprinkle on the yeast. Stir once or twice with a fork and set aside for 5 minutes.

3 Add the cornmeal and 3 cups of the flour to the water. Using a wooden spoon, stir well for 100 strokes. Set aside for 10 minutes.

4 Add the softened butter, salt, sage, and thyme to the dough. Stir well. Stir in the veggies and cheese. Add enough of the remaining flour, about ¼ cup at a time, to make a firm dough that pulls away from the sides of the bowl. Using your wooden spoon, work the dough vigorously against the sides of the bowl for a minute or so.

5 Flour your work surface and turn the dough out. Using floured hands, knead the dough for about 8 minutes, dusting with flour as necessary to keep the dough from sticking. Rub a teaspoon or two of cooking oil in a large ceramic or glass bowl. Add the dough, rotating it to coat the entire surface with oil. Cover the bowl with plastic wrap and set aside in a warm, draft-free spot for 1 to 1½ hours, until the dough has doubled in bulk.

6 While the dough rises, prepare your two flowerpots using one of the options outlined in the box on the next page.

RECIPE CONTINUED ON NEXT PAGE

MAKES 2 LOAVES

- 1–2 teaspoons cooking oil for the baking sheet and bowl
- 1½ cups grated carrots
- 1 celery stalk, finely chopped
- ½ medium onion, finely chopped
- 2 cups lukewarm water (105 to 110°F [41–43°C])
- 1 tablespoon sugar
- 1 packet (¼-ounce) active dry yeast
- ¼ cup fine yellow cornmeal
- 4¼–4½ cups unbleached all-purpose flour
- 2 tablespoons unsalted butter, softened, plus a little melted butter for brushing
- 2 teaspoons salt
- 2 tablespoons chopped fresh sage or 2 teaspoons dried
- 2 teaspoons fresh thyme or ¾ teaspoon dried
- 1 cup grated sharp cheddar cheese

7 When the dough has doubled, punch it down and turn it out onto a floured surface. Knead the dough for 1 minute, then divide it in half. Shape each half into a ball and place them in the pots. Cover the pots with plastic wrap and put them aside in a warm, draft-free spot until the loaves have almost doubled in bulk, about 40 minutes to 1 hour. As they approach this point, move one of your oven racks to the lowest position. If you have a second rack, move it up high or take it out of the oven. These are tall loaves, and you don't want them bumping into the rack. Preheat the oven to 400°F (200°C).

8 As soon as the loaves appear to have doubled, brush the top of each one with a little melted butter. Use a sharp serrated knife to make a shallow slash right across the middle of each loaf. Bake the loaves for 30 minutes, then reduce the heat to 375°F (190°C) and bake for an additional 15 to 20 minutes. The tops of the loaves will be a rich golden brown. Transfer the pots to a cooling rack. Cool the breads for about 5 minutes, then slide them out of the pots. Slide a knife down the sides if you need to loosen them. Lay the loaves on their sides and cool thoroughly. Store, refrigerated, in plastic bags.

FLOWERPOT BREAD BASICS

You can bake yeast bread in clay flowerpots of any size, but I think the best ones for the home baker measure 5½ to 6 inches in diameter and about 5 inches tall. These will yield a medium-size (if somewhat cone-shaped) loaf that you can slice up for sandwiches and toast.

Buy a couple of new terra-cotta pots just for this purpose. You'll have to "season" them, like you would a cast-iron skillet, before their initial use. Wash and dry them well. Rub the insides thoroughly with cooking oil; safflower oil and light olive oil are good because they have a high smoke point. Put the pots on a baking sheet and place in a preheated 450°F (230°C) oven for 1 hour. Don't be surprised if a strong odor develops as the pots heat; open the windows if it becomes bothersome. Remove the pots after an hour and set them aside on a cooling rack. Cool thoroughly. Some say that you should repeat this process a second time, but I never did with my own pots, and I've had no problems.

Until you've baked in your pots several times, and even after you have, it's a good idea to take extra measures to keep your loaves from sticking. The easiest way is to butter your pots well with softened butter and line them with strips of parchment paper brushed with melted butter. By the way, if your pots have a hole in the bottom — most do — cover it with a little circle of buttered aluminum foil.

For an attractive, wholesome-rustic look, butter the inside of the pots thickly with soft butter and put a generous little pile of sunflower seeds in the bottom. Lean the pot way over and slowly rotate it so the seeds coat the sides thoroughly. You can sprinkle on a second layer of smaller seeds, such as sesame or poppy seeds, once the sunflower seeds are in place. Handle the pots carefully after the seeds go on so you don't knock them off.

When you're done baking, clean your pots like you would any other pan, soaking them if anything gets stuck on.

CHEDDAR AND VEGETABLE BREAD-A-SAURUS

This outsized loaf is almost too big to handle and so awe inspiring and impressive of stature that I'm reluctant to downsize it (though I will tell you how to in the variation at right, if you want to make two loaves). What we have here is essentially a "whole meal bread," your veggies and starch all rolled up, literally, into one tasty package. (We often will make a meal of this, with nothing more than warm pasta sauce on the side for dipping.) There's a certain amount of flexibility with the vegetable filling so long as you exercise discipline, adhere to good taste, and don't try to turn this into an edible free-for-all. Stay in the ballpark with regard to quantity, and you can substitute other vegetables, such as finely diced carrots or celery, or chopped Swiss chard instead of spinach. A bit of smoked sausage or pepperoni would be nice, too. Just make sure nothing is cut too big or undercooked. You'll need a large baking sheet, at least 17 or 18 inches long.

1 If you haven't already, prepare the potato bread dough and set it aside to rise.

2 Melt the butter in a large skillet or pot. Add the onions and cook for 3 to 4 minutes over medium heat. Add the zucchini and green pepper and cook for 5 to 6 minutes, then stir in the mushrooms, garlic, and spinach. Salt and pepper the vegetables to taste. Cook for several minutes more, until the spinach is completely wilted and any liquid in the pan has cooked off. Transfer the mixture to a large plate and cool thoroughly.

3 When the dough has doubled in bulk, punch it down and turn it out onto a floured work surface. Knead the dough for 1 minute, then shape it into a ball. Loosely cover the dough with plastic wrap and let rest for 10 minutes. Meanwhile, lightly oil a large baking sheet — probably the largest one you have — and dust it with cornmeal.

4 Dust your work area with more flour and then pat, roll, and gently stretch the dough into a large 15- by 20-inch rectangle. Cover evenly with the cheese, leaving a 1-inch border all around. Scatter the herbs over the cheese, followed by the tomatoes. Finally, distribute the cooled vegetables evenly over everything.

5 Starting along one of the short sides, roll up the dough like a rug; a second set of hands is a big help. (Don't try to roll it too tightly; leave a little "expansion room" for the dough.) Pinch the dough together along the seam and at the ends, tucking the ends under. Lift the loaf onto the baking sheet — again, a second set of hands helps — and lay it diagonally across the sheet so the loaf has more room. Using a sharp serrated knife, make seven or eight deep, slightly angled cuts about halfway through the loaf. Loosely cover the loaf with plastic wrap and set aside in a warm, draft-free spot. After about 25 minutes, preheat the oven to 400°F (200°C). After 35 to 45 minutes in total, when the dough feels very soft and yields to gentle finger pressure, it is ready to bake.

MAKES 10 OR MORE SERVINGS

BREAD

Oil and cornmeal for the baking sheet

Great American Potato Bread dough (page 78)

FILLING

3 tablespoons unsalted butter

1½ large onions, chopped

1 small zucchini, quartered lengthwise, then cut in thin slices

½ green bell pepper, finely chopped

1–1½ cups thinly sliced white mushroom caps

3 garlic cloves, minced

4–6 cups packed baby spinach

Salt and freshly ground black pepper

2 cups grated extra-sharp cheddar cheese

2–3 tablespoons chopped fresh herbs (thyme, basil, parsley, rosemary)

3–4 roasted tomato halves, sliced (page 282), or about ¼ cup chopped sun dried tomatoes packed in oil

1 egg beaten with 1 teaspoon water, for glaze

6 Lightly brush all the exposed areas of dough with the egg glaze. Bake the loaf for 20 minutes, then reduce the heat to 375°F (190°C) and bake for 20 minutes more. Turn the baking sheet 180 degrees and bake for another 20 minutes, for a total of about 60 minutes. The best indicator of doneness is total elapsed baking time, so use that as your gauge.

7 Slide the bread off the baking sheet and onto a cooling rack. Cool until it is barely lukewarm, an hour or so, before slicing.

TWO SMALLER LOAVES

To make two loaves instead of one large one, divide the dough in half after you've kneaded it. Shape each half into a ball and let rest for 10 minutes. Working with one piece of dough at a time, press, roll, and stretch it into an oblong 11 to 12 inches long and 9 to 10 inches wide. Top as for the larger loaf, then roll it up, starting at one of the narrow ends. Pinch the dough together at the seams and tuck the ends under. Place in two 9- by 5-inch buttered loaf pans. Preheat the oven to 400°F (200°C). Let rise until almost doubled, about 30 to 40 minutes, then make several 1-inch-deep diagonal slits in the bread with a serrated knife. Brush with the egg glaze. When the loaves have doubled, bake for 30 minutes, then reduce the heat to 375°F (190°C) and bake for another 25 minutes, until the loaves are done.

If you don't have two large loaf pans, you could bake two loaves on one or two baking sheets. Press or roll each half into a rectangle about ⅓ inch thick and divide the filling between them. Roll, shape, and score the loaves as above and place them on the sheets. Let rise and bake as above; they won't take quite as long to finish baking.

MUSHROOM, SPINACH, AND BLUE CHEESE-STUFFED BAGUETTE

This version of a stuffed French-style bread is nearly a meal in itself, or at least enough of one that you need little more than a big, colorful salad and a glass of wine to accompany it. You'll begin by making a basic baguette-style yeast dough, which you'll then stuff with delicious sautéed veggies and blue cheese; Gruyère or fontina also works nicely, if you want something milder. It's probably not the first recipe I'd recommend if you're a yeast bread novice, but if you're an old hand, you'll find this one hard to resist.

1 Pour the lukewarm water into a large bowl and sprinkle on the yeast. Give it a stir with a fork and set aside for 5 minutes to let the yeast dissolve. Add 2 cups of the flour. Using a wooden spoon, beat well for 100 strokes. Let the mixture rest for 5 minutes. Add the salt and another 1 cup of the flour, about ¼ cup at a time, beating well with your spoon after each addition. As the dough starts to cohere, work it vigorously against the sides of the bowl with your spoon for a minute or so.

2 Turn the dough out onto a floured work counter and knead it for about 8 minutes, until the dough is smooth and elastic, dusting with flour as needed to keep the dough from sticking. Smear a teaspoon of olive oil into a glass or ceramic mixing bowl. Add the dough, turning it to lightly coat the entire surface with oil. Cover the bowl with plastic wrap and set the dough aside in a warm, draft-free spot until it has doubled in bulk, about 1 hour.

3 While the dough rises, melt the butter in a large skillet. Add the onions and sauté for 5 minutes over moderate heat. Stir in the mushrooms, garlic, and Worcestershire sauce. Cover and let the mushrooms sweat for a couple of minutes; then uncover and cook until there's just a little liquid left in the pan. Stir in the spinach and cook, continuing to stir, until it has wilted. Season with salt and pepper to taste, then remove from the heat. Set aside to cool.

4 When the dough has doubled, punch it down and turn it out onto a lightly floured work surface. Knead for 1 minute, then divide it in half. Shape each half into a ball and let rest, loosely covered with plastic wrap, for 5 to 10 minutes. Meanwhile, oil a large baking sheet very lightly and dust it with cornmeal.

MAKES 2 LOAVES

BAGUETTE

1	teaspoon olive oil for the bowl
1⅓	cups lukewarm water (105 to 110°F [41–43°C])
1½	teaspoons active dry yeast (a little more than half a packet)
3¼–3½	cups unbleached all-purpose flour
1½	teaspoons salt

FILLING

	Oil and cornmeal for the baking sheet
3	tablespoons unsalted butter
½	onion, finely chopped
1	pound sliced white mushrooms (5 to 6 cups)
3	garlic cloves, minced
1½	teaspoons Worcestershire sauce
4	cups loosely packed baby spinach
	Salt and freshly ground black pepper
1½	cups crumbled blue cheese

5 Working with one piece of dough at a time, press or roll the dough into an oblong about 12 inches long and 8 inches wide. Scatter half of the blue cheese over the dough, leaving a 1-inch border all around. Cover evenly with half of the sautéed mixture. Using a pastry brush, lightly moisten the long side farthest from you. Starting from the long side close to you, turn the edge of the dough over the filling and roll up the filled dough like you would a rug. When you reach the opposite edge, pinch the dough together along all the seams and tuck the ends under. Place the baguette on the prepared sheet, seam side down. Repeat for the other baguette. Cover the loaves loosely with plastic wrap and set aside in a warm, draft-free spot for 20 minutes. Preheat the oven to 425°F (220°C).

6 After 20 minutes, use a sharp serrated knife to make three diagonal slits, about ½ inch deep, on the top of each loaf. Lightly brush the tops with water. Bake for 25 to 30 minutes, until the tops are a rich golden brown. The bottoms of the loaves should sound hollow when tapped with a finger. Transfer the loaves to a cooling rack and cool to lukewarm before slicing. Refrigerate leftovers. Reheat, wrapped in foil, in a 350°F (180°C) oven for 15 to 20 minutes.

WHEATEN ROASTED GARLIC BAGUETTES

Roasting works wonders on garlic, mellowing its rough edges, deepening the flavor, and leaving one with a whole new appreciation for a bulb we often take for granted. Mashed with a little salt and olive oil, it makes a great spread on toast, but here's another way to team it up with good bread — bake it into a wheaten baguette. It makes for a loaf that smells indescribably good and tastes even better. Serve it with pasta or halve it lengthwise and use it for your favorite veggie sandwiches. I love to top it with tapenade, fresh sliced onions, and mozzarella.

1 If you haven't already, roast the garlic. When it is cool enough to handle, squeeze the cloves out of their skins into a small shallow bowl. Sprinkle with the rosemary and a big pinch of salt. Mash the mixture well with a fork or the back of a spoon to make a garlicky paste. Use a few drops of water, if necessary, to make it more pasty. Set aside.

2 Pour the water into a large bowl. Stir in the sugar and sprinkle the yeast on top; stir with a fork. Set aside for 5 minutes to let the yeast dissolve. Add the whole-wheat flour and 1 cup of the all-purpose flour. Beat well with a wooden spoon for 100 strokes. Cover the bowl with plastic wrap and set aside at room temperature for 1 hour.

3 Stir 2 teaspoons salt into the dough. Stir in the remaining all-purpose flour about ¼ cup at a time, until the dough coheres and pulls away from the sides of the bowl. When it does, start working the dough vigorously against the sides of the bowl with your wooden spoon; this will reduce your overall kneading time when you turn the dough out.

4 Turn the dough out onto a lightly floured surface. Dust your hands with flour, and knead the dough for about 8 minutes, using just enough additional flour to keep the dough from sticking. Smear a teaspoon or two of olive oil in a glass or ceramic mixing bowl. Add the dough, turning it to coat the surface thoroughly with oil. Cover the bowl with plastic wrap and set the dough aside in a warm, draft-free spot until it has doubled in bulk, about 1 hour. While the dough rises, oil a large baking sheet very lightly and dust it with cornmeal. Adjust your oven racks so one is in the middle and another one is in the lowest position.

5 Punch the dough down and turn it out onto a lightly floured work surface. Knead for 1 minute, then divide the dough in half. Shape each half into a ball and let rest, loosely covered with plastic wrap, for 10 minutes.

MAKES 2 BAGUETTES

1–2	teaspoons oil for the bowl
	Oil and cornmeal for the baking sheet
2	whole garlic heads, roasted (see box)
1	teaspoon minced fresh rosemary or ¼ teaspoons dried
2	teaspoons salt, plus a pinch for the garlic
1½	cups lukewarm water (105 to 110°F [41–43°C])
½	teaspoon sugar
1½	teaspoons active dry yeast (a little more than half a packet)
1	cup whole-wheat flour
2⅓–2½	cups unbleached all-purpose flour

6 Working with one piece of dough at a time on a lightly floured surface, press or roll the dough into an oval about 12 inches long and 7 inches wide. Spread half of the garlic paste over the dough, leaving a 1-inch border all around. Starting on one of the long sides, roll the dough up like a rug, pinching the dough firmly along the edge to seal. Pinch the ends and tuck them under. Place the dough log on the sheet, seam side down, leaving plenty of room for the second one. Repeat for the other half of the dough. Cover the loaves very loosely with plastic wrap. Set aside in a warm, draft-free spot for 30 minutes. Midway into the rising, preheat your oven to 475°F (245°C). Put about ¾ inch of water in a shallow baking dish or pie pan and place it on the middle rack while the oven heats.

7 After 30 minutes, remove the plastic from the loaves. Using a sharp serrated knife, make three evenly spaced, ½-inch-deep diagonal slashes on top of each loaf. Place the baking sheet on the bottom shelf. Bake for 20 minutes; then quickly open the door, remove the water, and move the loaves up to the middle rack. Bake for another 5 to 7 minutes, just long enough to darken the tops a bit. Transfer the loaves to a cooling rack. Cool for at least 15 minutes before slicing.

HOW TO ROAST GARLIC

Preheat the oven to 400°F (200°C). Tear off a sheet of aluminum foil about 12 inches long. Rub the papery outer skins off one or more whole heads of garlic. Then, using a sharp chef's knife, slice off the top quarters of the heads, exposing the insides of the cloves. Place the garlic heads on the foil and drizzle 1 to 2 teaspoons olive oil over the cut area. Close up the garlic tightly in the foil. Bake on the middle oven rack for 50 to 60 minutes, until the cloves are tender-soft and several shades darker. Cool thoroughly, then squeeze the cloves out of their skins. Use as directed.

POTATO AND ONION-CRUSTED BURGER BUNS

I've often said that if you're going to make a world-class burger — beef, veggie, or anything in between — the buns shouldn't be an afterthought. They usually are, sadly, and the moment the burger and bun make contact, the latter starts to disintegrate. The world hungers for a bun of substance, and the best way to get one is to make it yourself. Ours are just the right combination of softness, thanks to the potato, and sturdiness, thanks to the whole-wheat flour. They'll hold their own with anything you can throw at them, from the juiciest of burgers to the slatheriest of sauces. Those sautéed onions on top are a harvest baker badge of pride, and the first indication that these aren't your run-of-the-mill buns. They will keep just fine for several days, but for a real treat use as least some of them on the day they're baked.

1 Combine 1½ cups of the water and the potato in a medium saucepan with a big pinch of salt. Bring to a boil, and cook at a low boil for 10 to 12 minutes, until the potato is soft. Drain, reserving the potato water. Pour the potato water into a glass measuring cup and add just enough milk, if needed, to make 1 cup. Transfer the liquid to a large bowl.

2 Rice the potatoes in a potato ricer, or transfer them to a bowl and mash them very fine with a large fork. Whisk them into the liquid along with the sugar, egg yolk, and 2 tablespoons softened butter.

3 Heat the remaining ¼ cup water to slightly warmer than body temperature. Transfer to a small bowl and sprinkle on the yeast. Stir with a fork. Set aside for 5 minutes to dissolve, then stir the yeast into the potato mixture.

4 Add the whole-wheat flour and 1 cup of the all-purpose flour to the liquid. Stir well with a wooden spoon for about 100 strokes. Cover the bowl with plastic wrap and set aside for 10 minutes.

5 After 10 minutes, stir 1¾ teaspoons salt into the dough. Gradually stir in enough of the remaining all-purpose flour, ¼ to ⅓ cup at a time, to make a firm, kneadable dough that pulls away from the sides of the bowl. (Note: Because of the potato, the dough may be a little stickier than others you've worked with. That's fine.)

6 Turn the dough out onto a floured surface and knead — gently at first because the potatoes make a delicate dough — for 7 to 8 minutes, adding flour as necessary to keep the dough from sticking. Smear a teaspoon or two of cooking oil in a large glass or ceramic bowl. Add the dough, turning it to coat the entire surface with oil. Cover the bowl with plastic wrap and set aside in a warm, draft-free spot until the dough has doubled in bulk, 45 minutes to 1 hour.

MAKES 9 LARGE BUNS

1–2	teaspoons cooking oil for the bowl, baking sheet, and plastic wrap
	Cornmeal for the baking sheet, if needed
1¾	cups water
¾	cup peeled and diced baking potato
1¾	teaspoons salt, plus a pinch for the potatoes
	Milk, as needed
1½	tablespoons sugar
1	egg yolk
4	tablespoons unsalted butter (2 of them softened), plus a bit for the baking sheet
1	packet (¼ ounce) active dry yeast
1	cup whole-wheat flour
2¼–2½	cups unbleached all-purpose flour
1	medium onion, finely chopped
1	egg beaten with 1 tablespoon milk, for glaze

7 While the dough rises, melt the remaining 2 tablespoons butter in a medium skillet. Add the onions and sauté over medium heat, stirring often, until they are light golden in color, about 10 minutes. Set aside to cool.

8 Line a large baking sheet with parchment paper, if you have some, and butter lightly. Otherwise, lightly oil the sheet and dust it with cornmeal.

9 When the dough has doubled, punch it down and knead for 1 minute on a lightly floured surface. Divide into nine equal pieces and shape them into balls. Place the balls on the sheet, evenly spaced, leaving 3 inches between them. Lightly oil a long sheet of plastic wrap and lay it over the buns. Let them rise for 15 minutes. Then gently press on the plastic and flatten each bun so it's about 3½ inches in diameter. Let rise 20 minutes more.

10 Preheat the oven to 375°F (190°C) at the beginning of this final rise. After 20 minutes — when the buns are good and puffy — lightly brush them with the egg glaze. Spoon some of the onions over each one and gently smooth them onto the surface. Bake the buns on the center oven rack for 25 to 30 minutes, until the tops and bottoms are a rich golden brown. Transfer the buns to a cooling rack and cool before slicing.

FROM BIG BUNS TO DINNER ROLLS

Company coming and you need a big batch of dinner rolls? This recipe will work nicely. Instead of dividing the dough into 9 pieces, divide it into 16 or 18. Shape into balls and place them, not quite touching, on a lightly buttered 13- by 9-inch baking pan. Cover with oiled plastic, as above. *Do not* flatten the rolls after 15 minutes. Instead, let them rise until swollen and nearly doubled in bulk, 30 to 40 minutes. Brush with the egg glaze and spoon on the onions. Bake for 25 to 30 minutes.

PESTO, WALNUT, AND CHEESE PINWHEEL ROLLS

Now here's a fragrant, savory roll that'll stand out even in the best of company, alongside your family's heirloom lasagna recipe or cheesy chicken Parmesan. It's an offshoot of my favorite potato bread (page 78), whose softness makes for a very appealing dinner roll. The dough is rolled out, coated thickly with pesto and cheese, and rolled up and cut into thick slices, the same way you'd make sticky buns. Serve them warm and fresh, and there won't be any leftovers. Note that you will only be using a little more than half of the potato bread dough for this recipe. That will leave you enough to shape and bake a plain smaller loaf in an 8½- by 4½-inch bread pan.

1 Make the potato bread as instructed, but stir in 1 cup chopped walnuts at the beginning of step 5 in the recipe, before adding the remaining flour. If you prefer, you can scatter the chopped walnuts over the dough during the assembly of these rolls, along with the pesto and cheese. Set the dough aside to rise until it is doubled in bulk.

2 When the dough has doubled, punch it down and turn it out onto a floured surface. Knead for 1 minute. Divide the dough into not-quite-equal halves; you'll need the larger half for this recipe. Shape the larger half of dough into a ball and let it rest on a floured work surface for 10 minutes, loosely covered with plastic wrap. Butter a 9- by 9-inch cake pan.

3 Press or roll the dough into an approximate 13- by 10-inch rectangle. Spread the pesto evenly over the surface of the dough, leaving a ½-inch border all around. Sprinkle the cheese over the pesto. (If you didn't add the walnuts to the dough itself and you still want to use them, distribute them evenly over the cheese.) Starting at one of the long sides, roll the dough up snugly, like a rug, pinching the dough at the seam to seal. Pinch and seal the ends; you'll have a log of filled dough. Using a sharp serrated knife, cut the log into nine equal slices and place them swirl side up in the pan, making three rows of three. Loosely cover the pan with plastic wrap and set aside in a warm, draft-free spot, until almost doubled in bulk, about 30 to 45 minutes. Preheat the oven to 375°F (190°C).

4 When the rolls have doubled, remove the plastic and brush the melted butter liberally over the tops of the rolls. Bake for about 40 minutes, until the rolls are nicely browned. Transfer the pan to a cooling rack and cool for 5 minutes. Run a spatula around the sides and remove the rolls. Transfer them to a cooling rack. As soon as possible, place them in a cloth-lined basket and serve. Refrigerate leftovers. Rewarm them, wrapped in foil, for about 10 minutes in a 300°F (150°C) oven.

MAKES 9 LARGE DINNER ROLLS

BREAD

Butter for the baking pan

Great American Potato Bread dough (page 78), modified by adding 1 cup chopped walnuts (see step 1)

FILLING

⅓   cup pesto (see page 98)

1½   cups grated Italian cheeses (at least half mozzarella, with some Asiago and Parmesan cheese, if possible)

3   tablespoons unsalted butter, melted

A Passion for Pesto

I can't tell you exactly how much pesto I use in a year, but it's a lot — jars and jars' worth. I use it on pastas, of course. But I also add it to tomato pies (page 154) and pizza (page 112), slather it on grilled cheese sandwiches and appetizer toasts, and use it to season tomato sauces and soups. I even smear it on corn on the cob before grilling. It's an addiction I have no interest in kicking.

Come summer I like to grow basil and make my own pesto. I'm a container gardener, so I plant seedlings in pots.

You'll need at least half a dozen plants if you plan to make pesto on a semi-regular basis. Basil does best in a sunny location and likes well-drained soil. It doesn't like the cold, so plant it well after the last frost.

To prepare homemade pesto, you'll need about 3 loosely packed cups of freshly picked basil leaves. Combine them in a food processor with 2 or 3 crushed garlic cloves, ½ cup olive oil, ½ cup freshly grated Parmesan cheese, ¼ cup pine nuts or coarsely chopped walnuts, ⅛ teaspoon salt, and a bit of ground black pepper. Pulse the

machine repeatedly to make a smooth sauce, scraping down the sides of the bowl several times. Taste, then adjust the ingredients as needed, adding a little more oil, salt, or cheese if you think the pesto needs it. Transfer the pesto to a jar, seal, and refrigerate it for up to a week. It can also be frozen.

GOLDEN DELICATA SQUASH DINNER ROLLS

A good dinner roll is soft, mildly sweet, and irresistibly fragrant; this one is all that, with a gorgeous golden hue from the delicata squash. Of course, you can use another winter squash, but I love how the intense, sweet flavor of the delicata enhances this Thanksgiving staple of ours. Not only are these rolls perfect with turkey, gravy, and all the fixings, they're just the right size for making sandwiches, too.

1 Preheat the oven to 400°F (200°C). Line a large rimmed baking sheet with aluminum foil or parchment paper. Halve the squash lengthwise and scoop out the seeds. Place the squash on the sheet, cut side up, and drizzle a little of the 2 tablespoons olive oil in each half. Brush the flesh with the oil. Bake the squash on the middle oven rack for 50 to 60 minutes, until tender, rebrushing the pooled oil over the flesh once or twice as it bakes. Transfer the baking sheet to a cooling rack and cool the squash thoroughly.

2 When the squash has cooled, scrape out the flesh and put it through a potato ricer or press it through a sieve to smooth it out. Set aside 1 cup of the squash. (Refrigerate any leftovers and use in soups, stews, or quick breads.)

3 Pour the lukewarm water into a large bowl; sprinkle in the yeast and stir briefly with a fork. Wait 5 minutes for the yeast to dissolve, then stir in the milk, sugar, 3 tablespoons softened butter, egg yolk, and salt, along with the 1 cup reserved squash. Stir in 3 cups of the flour. Using a wooden spoon, beat vigorously for 100 strokes. Set aside for 5 to 10 minutes.

4 Stir in enough of the remaining flour, ¼ to ⅓ cup at a time, to make a firm, kneadable dough that pulls away from the sides of the bowl. Turn the dough out onto a floured work surface. Knead the dough, gently at first — the squash makes the dough a little sticky — for 8 to 10 minutes, until smooth and supple, using enough additional flour to keep the dough from sticking. Smear a teaspoon or two of olive oil in a large bowl and add the dough, turning it to coat the surface with oil. Cover the bowl with plastic wrap and set aside in a warm spot until the dough has doubled in bulk, about 1 hour.

5 Butter a 13- by 9- by 2-inch baking pan with a little of the melted butter. When the dough has doubled, punch it down and turn it out onto a lightly floured surface. Knead for 1 minute, then divide the dough into thirds. Divide each third into six equal pieces. Shape them into balls and set them in the pan, making three rows of six balls. Lightly brush the dough balls with melted butter. Cover the pan with plastic wrap and set it aside until the rolls are nearly doubled in bulk, 35 to 45 minutes. Preheat the oven to 400°F (200°C).

6 When the rolls have doubled, remove the plastic and bake for about 30 minutes, until golden brown and crusty. If you tap the top of a roll with your fingertip, it should sound hollow. Transfer the pan to a rack and cool the rolls in the pan for 5 minutes. Then transfer the rolls directly onto the rack and continue to cool. Serve warm.

MAKES 18 DINNER ROLLS

- 2 medium-size delicata squash
- 2 tablespoons light olive oil, plus 1 to 2 teaspoons for the bowl
- ⅓ cup lukewarm water (105 to 110°F [41–43°C])
- 1 packet (¼ ounce) active dry yeast
- 1 cup lukewarm milk (105 to 110°F [41–43°C])
- ⅓ cup sugar
- 3 tablespoons unsalted butter, softened, plus a little extra melted butter for brushing the rolls and the pan
- 1 egg yolk
- 2 teaspoons salt
- 5½–6 cups unbleached all-purpose flour

HOT FOCACCIA SANDWICHES FOR A CROWD (WITH POTATO PAN BREAD)

This is not a recipe per se but a blueprint for making delicious and creative hot oven sandwiches with all manner of cheeses, meats, and vegetables. They're like oven panini. You will start by making the Potato Pan Bread with Cherry Tomatoes (page 82) but without the tomatoes. Do this at least a couple of hours ahead; the day before is fine. Be sure to have plenty of each sandwich filler on hand, including at least 1 to 1½ pounds of your selected cheese (this is a party-size recipe, though you can easily scale it down). You could assemble this as one big sandwich, but smaller sections are much easier to manage and give you the flexibility for making multiple kinds. The suggested variations are simply a springboard for your own creations.

1 Prepare and bake the bread as usual, but instead of adding the tomatoes, simply poke the bread with an oiled finger, making several rows of dimples. Drizzle with the oil. Sprinkle with rosemary, if desired, and the salt. Let rise, then bake as directed. Remove from the pan and cool on a rack.

2 When you're ready to assemble the sandwiches, preheat the oven to 400°F (200°C). Cut the bread crosswise, in half or thirds, and "butterfly" each section, cutting it in half horizontally to get a top and bottom. Stack the pieces back together and wrap the pairs, individually, in foil. Place in the oven for 12 to 15 minutes. (Only use as many sections as you'll need for your meal. The bread will keep for several days.)

3 Working with one section at a time, unwrap the bread and place the pieces on your work surface, the insides of the bread facing you. Spread both halves generously with your choice of condiments — mustard, mayo, ranch dressing, pesto, or whatever. Cover the bottom half generously with grated cheese and stack on your remaining ingredients. Top with more grated cheese and put the bread lid back on. Brush the top with olive oil. Wrap the sandwich up snugly in the foil. Repeat for the other bread sections. Put them back in the oven and heat for about 15 minutes, until the cheese is melted.

4 Unwrap the sandwiches and cut them into serving-size pieces with a serrated knife. Serve hot. A full recipe should make at least 16 to 20 servings, depending on the portion size.

MAKES 16 TO 20 SERVINGS, DEPENDING ON PORTION SIZE

Potato Pan Bread with Cherry Tomatoes (page 82), modified as in step 1

Sandwich toppings as desired (condiments, cheese, and meat and/or vegetables)

PANINI VARIATIONS

All-Veggie: Ranch dressing or pesto; grated cheddar or other melting cheese; sautéed onions; sautéed or marinated bell peppers; sautéed or steamed broccoli (al dente); sliced tomatoes

Bacon, Tomato, and Onion: Mustard and mayonnaise; grated cheddar, fontina, or other melting cheese; several thin slices of tomatoes and onions; lots of crisp fried bacon

Chicken, Bacon, and Ranch: A fusion of the first two variations, with ranch dressing and thinly sliced roast chicken, bacon, and veggies of your choice

Spinach, Artichoke, and Sun-Dried Tomato: Plenty of grated Havarti cheese and thinly sliced marinated artichoke hearts; a thin layer of baby spinach and oil-packed sun-dried tomatoes

Eggplant Parmesan: Eggplant slices fried like you would for eggplant Parmesan; spread tomato sauce on the bread, and add plenty of freshly grated Parmesan and mozzarella cheeses

Reuben: Thousand Island dressing; drained (and gently squeezed) sauerkraut; corned beef; Swiss cheese

PART 2
CRUSTY ENTRÉES

4

HARVEST PIZZAS, FLATBREADS, CALZONES,
and Other Stuffed Breads

Most of us grew up on pizza, but chances are it rarely veered too far from the standard red sauce and cheese variety. That's precisely why I love this category: it explores an unexpectedly rich area of opportunity for the harvest baker. Here you'll find pizza topped with crusty cauliflower, and another with winter squash and kale. We slather a pizza with smooth broccoli and cheese sauce and stuff a calzone with garlicky, smoky collards. It's food you're familiar with, decked out in delicious new ways.

To get you off on the right foot, I include a couple of easy pizza dough recipes — one made by hand and one with the food processor.

HAND METHOD PIZZA DOUGH

Before there were food processors, KitchenAid mixers, bread machines, and bread machine apps, there were the good old days of making yeast bread by hand. That's how I learned to make bread, and at the risk of sounding like an old crank who walked 10 miles to school in a snowstorm when I was a boy, you should, too. This is a good recipe to start with if you've never made yeast bread before. The dough is responsive — you can feel it spring to life in your hands — and you only have a relatively small quantity of dough to work with. As you add flour, you get to experience how a living dough evolves from raw ingredients into a cohesive mass. This sort of hands-on learning transmits valuable messages to the brain that a machine can't.

1 Pour the water into a large bowl. Stir in the sugar. Sprinkle the yeast over the water. Let it sit for a minute, then give it a little ruffle with a fork to stir it up. Set it aside for 5 minutes. As it sits, you'll see the mixture begin to bubble up and come alive.

2 Add 1¾ cups of the flour to the water. Using a wooden spoon, stir vigorously for 100 strokes; the dough will be quite thick at this point but not firm enough to pull away from the sides of the bowl. Set the dough aside for 5 minutes.

3 Add the salt and 2 tablespoons olive oil to the dough. Stir well. Start adding the remaining flour to the dough, no more than ¼ cup at a time — less as the dough gets firmer. Before long, the dough will begin to pull away from the sides. When it does, work the dough vigorously against the sides of the bowl with your wooden spoon for a minute or two.

4 Dust your work surface with some of the remaining flour and turn out the dough. Dust the dough and your hands with flour and start kneading, gingerly at first because it will be sticky. The usual way of kneading is to push the dough down and away from you, bring the dough back toward you, fold it over, give it a quarter turn, and repeat. (The easiest way to learn this skill is by watching someone else do it. If you don't have an experienced kneader in your life, find one on YouTube.) Continue dusting your dough with flour as required.

5 After 8 tor 9 minutes of kneading, your dough should be smooth, supple, and elastic. If tears develop in the dough, you're pushing too hard. Smear a teaspoon or two of olive oil in a large ceramic or glass bowl, add the dough, and turn it to coat the surface with oil. Cover the bowl with plastic wrap. Place the bowl in a warm, draft-free spot until the dough is doubled in bulk, 45 minutes to 1 hour. Once it has doubled, punch down the dough and proceed with your recipe.

MAKES ENOUGH DOUGH FOR 2 MEDIUM PIZZAS OR 2 OR MORE CALZONES

1	cup plus 3 tablespoons lukewarm water (105 to 110°F [41–43°C])
1	teaspoon sugar
1	packet (¼ ounce) active dry yeast
3–3¼	cups unbleached all-purpose flour
1½	teaspoons salt
2	tablespoons olive oil, plus a little for the bowl

WHOLE-WHEAT PIZZA DOUGH

Before you start, combine 1¾ cups whole-wheat flour and 1½ cups unbleached all-purpose flour in a bowl and whisk well to mix. Use this custom flour mixture to prepare your dough.

DOUGH MATH AND MECHANICS

Both the Hand Method Pizza Dough and the Food Processor Pizza Dough recipes yield roughly 1½ pounds of pizza dough. That's enough dough for two medium-size pizzas or calzones, or more if you make them smaller.

By design, some of the recipes in this section require only half of the dough. This leaves you half to make a traditional red sauce and cheese pizza in case there are less adventurous pizza eaters in the house, or another kind altogether. If you're a single or a couple, you can keep half of the dough in the fridge and use it a day or two later. Or freeze it for up to a month.

To refrigerate the dough for a day or two, punch it down and leave it in the original rising bowl. Cover the bowl with plastic and place it in the fridge. The cold will eventually stop the dough from rising, but check on it every couple of hours at first, punching it down to expel the carbon dioxide gas that builds up. When you're

ready to use the dough, remove it from the fridge, place it on a flour-dusted surface, and knead for a minute or so to wake it up. Run some hot water into a fresh bowl to warm the bowl, then dry and oil it. Put your dough in the bowl, cover it with plastic wrap, and let it rise until doubled in bulk. This could take several hours.

To freeze the dough, first refrigerate it like we did above, punching the dough down as required. When the dough stops rising, put it in a plastic freezer bag and place it in the freezer. A good 4 to 6 hours before you plan to use the frozen dough, take it out of the plastic bag and put it into a warm bowl as above. When the dough has thawed, knead it briefly to wake it up and put it back in the bowl until it has doubled in bulk.

Once you've experienced homemade pizza dough, you'll be sold. It's really convenient to have extra pizza dough on hand, and the quality will always be superior to that of any pizza dough you buy.

FOOD PROCESSOR PIZZA DOUGH

I love making yeast dough by hand, but there are always times when it's more convenient to use a food processor. Being a hands-on traditionalist, using the processor took some getting used to, but it wasn't long before I became a real fan. Here's the basic recipe and a whole-wheat variation for those who like their crust to have a wholesome profile. This recipe is a boon for anyone who wants to make pizza more often but feels pressed for time.

1 Pour the water into a spouted 2-cup measuring cup. Stir in the sugar. Sprinkle in the yeast and mix with a fork. Set aside for 5 minutes.

2 Combine the flour and salt in a large food processor — a 10- to 12-cup-capacity machine is ideal — outfitted with the standard cutting blade. Pulse several times to mix.

3 Stir 2 tablespoons olive oil into the yeast water. With the machine running, pour the liquid through the feed tube in a continuous 10-second stream. When the mixture forms a ball, continue to run the processor nonstop for 8 to 10 seconds of machine kneading.

4 Turn the dough out onto a lightly floured counter; work carefully because the dough will probably be stuck to the blade. Knead the dough by hand for 30 seconds or so, until the surface of the dough feels smooth and supple. Smear a teaspoon of olive oil in a large bowl. Place the dough in the bowl, turning it to coat the entire surface with oil. Cover the bowl with plastic wrap and set aside in a warm, draft-free spot until the dough has doubled in bulk, 45 minutes to 1 hour. Once it has doubled, punch the dough down and proceed with your recipe.

MAKES ENOUGH DOUGH FOR 2 MEDIUM PIZZAS OR 2 OR MORE CALZONES

- 1 cup plus 2 tablespoons lukewarm water (105 to 110°F [41–43°C])
- 1 teaspoon sugar
- 1 packet (¼ ounce) active dry yeast
- 3 cups plus 2 tablespoons unbleached all-purpose flour
- 1½ teaspoons salt
- 2 tablespoons olive oil, plus a little for the bowl

WHOLE-WHEAT PIZZA DOUGH

Increase the water to 1¼ cups. Replace 1½ cups of the all-purpose flour with 1½ cups whole-wheat flour. Mix and handle as above.

YEASTED OLIVE OIL DOUGH

This dough differs from the two preceding pizza doughs in that it has a larger proportion of oil, as well as an egg and some milk. Depending on how it's handled and baked, it can yield a tender, bread-like crust (as with the Cabbage and Sausage Stuffed Buns on page 142) or a crisp, cracker-like crust when it's used to make a pizza (page 123). Whatever the application, this dough gets high marks for its ease of handling, flavor, and utility. I like how fast and simple it is to make in the food processor, but I've also included instructions for preparing it by hand if that's your preference.

1 Pour the lukewarm milk into a spouted 1- or 2-cup measuring cup; stir in the sugar. Sprinkle the yeast over the milk and stir it in with a fork or small whisk. Set aside for 5 minutes to let the yeast dissolve.

2 Combine the flour and salt in a food processor; pulse the machine several times to mix. With the machine running, pour the olive oil, in a thin stream, into the feed tube. Stop the machine when all the oil is added.

3 Stir the beaten egg into the yeast liquid. Add the liquid to the processor in a 7- to 10-second stream, giving the machine a series of 1-second pulses as you add it. When all the liquid has been added, run the machine nonstop for 10 seconds to "knead" the dough. If the dough sticks to the sides of the processor, stop the machine and shake a tablespoon or two of flour over the dough before you continue to run the processor.

4 Turn the dough out onto a floured surface and knead it by hand for about 1 minute; the dough should quickly become soft and supple. Put a teaspoon or two of olive oil in a bowl and smear it around. Add the dough, turning it to coat the entire surface with oil. Cover the bowl with plastic wrap and let it rise until doubled in bulk, about 1 hour. Proceed as directed in your recipe.

Hand Method: Follow step 1 as instructed. Instead of using the food processor in step 2, combine the flour and salt in a large bowl and whisk to mix. Pour the olive oil over the dry ingredients and whisk it in. Rub with your fingers if the mixture becomes clumpy. Make a well in the middle of the dry mixture and add the liquid all at once. Stir well, until the dough coheres. Sprinkle with a little additional flour if the dough sticks to the sides of the bowl. Turn the dough out onto a lightly floured surface and knead for 3 to 4 minutes, until smooth and supple. Dust with additional flour to keep the dough from sticking. Transfer the dough to an oiled bowl and allow to rise as in step 4.

MAKES ENOUGH DOUGH FOR 1 LARGE STUFFED BREAD OR SEVERAL SMALLER ONES

- ½ cup lukewarm milk (105 to 110°F [41–43°C])
- 1 teaspoon sugar
- 1½ teaspoons active dry yeast (a little more than half a packet)
- 1 large egg, at room temperature, lightly beaten
- 2 cups plus 2 tablespoons unbleached all-purpose flour
- ¾ teaspoon salt
- ¼ cup olive oil, plus a teaspoon or two for the rising bowl

WHOLE-WHEAT YEASTED OLIVE OIL DOUGH

Substitute 1 cup whole-wheat flour for an equal amount of all-purpose flour.

ITALIAN SAUSAGE AND BROCCOLI RABE PIZZA

Compared to kale, chard, and spinach, broccoli rabe doesn't get nearly the attention it deserves. Part of the reason might be appearance: it looks a little like undernourished broccoli . . . but with its mild bitterness, it doesn't taste anything like broccoli. The only way to get to the bottom of this is to try broccoli rabe for yourself and see just how delicious it can be. I can think of no better way to get acquainted than this pizza. Combining broccoli rabe with the richness of the sausage and cheese is an excellent way to temper its agreeable bite, and drizzling it with balsamic vinegar mellows it even more.

1 Prepare the pizza dough and set it aside to rise. You'll need half of the dough for this recipe. The other half can be refrigerated, frozen, or used to make a second pizza (see page 106) by doubling all of the topping ingredients. Lightly oil a large baking sheet and dust it with cornmeal.

2 Before you unbunch it, cut the ends off the stems of the broccoli rabe and discard them. Rinse the broccoli rabe thoroughly, but leave it dripping wet so you have some moisture in the skillet. Cut the stem sections into 1-inch pieces. Coarsely chop the remaining broccoli rabe.

3 Gently heat the oil in a large skillet or sauté pan. Stir in the broccoli rabe stems. Cover and cook over gentle heat for 3 to 4 minutes, stirring on occasion. Stir in the garlic and remaining broccoli rabe. Add salt and pepper to taste. Cook, stirring, for 1 minute, then stir in a tablespoon or two of water. Cover and cook over gentle heat for 5 to 7 minutes, until the broccoli rabe is tender. Keep an eye on the skillet, and add another tablespoon or two of water if it starts to become dry. Add more salt and pepper if needed. Drizzle on the balsamic vinegar and stir well. Remove from the heat.

4 When your dough has doubled and you're ready to bake the pizza, preheat the oven to 450°F (230°C). Punch the dough down and knead for 1 minute on a lightly floured surface. Divide the dough in half. (Save half of the dough for another use.) Cover your dough loosely with plastic wrap and let it rest for 10 minutes on a lightly floured surface.

5 Once it has rested, roll the dough into a large, thin circle or oblong. Transfer to the baking sheet. Lightly brush the surface with olive oil, especially around the edges. Let the dough rest for 10 minutes.

6 Scatter the diced tomato over the dough (or spread the tomato sauce). Distribute the sautéed broccoli rabe and sausage evenly over the dough. Bake on the middle oven rack for 15 minutes. Slide out the pizza and top it with the cheese. Bake for another 5 to 6 minutes, until the cheese is fully melted and the crust is golden brown. Slide the pizza onto a rack and cool for 5 to 10 minutes before serving. Refrigerate leftovers. Reheat slices directly on a baking sheet, in a 300°F (150°C) oven, for 8 to 10 minutes.

MAKES 3 TO 4 SERVINGS

Oil and cornmeal for the baking sheet

Food Processor Pizza Dough (page 107) or Hand Method Pizza Dough (page 105)

1 bunch broccoli rabe (1 pound or a little less)

¼ cup olive oil, plus a little extra for brushing the dough

5 garlic cloves, minced

Salt and freshly ground black pepper

1 tablespoon balsamic vinegar

1 medium-size ripe tomato, seeded and diced, or ½ cup tomato sauce

2 links (6 to 8 ounces) fully cooked hot or mild Italian sausage, thinly sliced

1½ cups grated mozzarella cheese or a mix of Italian cheeses

WHITE BEAN, SPINACH, AND BACON PIZZA

I love a traditional red-sauce pizza — who doesn't? — but the pizza revolution of the past decades has opened wide the doors of creativity with delicious results, like this pizza topped with garlicky white bean mash, spinach, onions, and bacon. When all these flavors come together on a crispy crust, you get a harvest pizza that's indescribably satisfying.

1 Prepare the pizza dough and set it aside to rise. You'll only need half of the dough for this recipe. The other half can be refrigerated, frozen, or used to make a second pizza (see page 106). Lightly oil a large baking sheet and dust it with cornmeal.

2 Cook the bacon in a large skillet until crisp. Remove the bacon and set it aside to cool. Add the onion to the skillet and cook in the bacon fat for 1 minute. Add all of the spinach and, using tongs, mop it around in the pan for no more than 30 seconds, just long enough to barely wilt it. Remove the spinach from the skillet and set it aside on a plate.

3 Cool the skillet off a bit, then add 2 to 3 tablespoons of the olive oil. Stir in the garlic and heat for about 15 seconds over medium heat. Stir in the white beans and water, scraping the skillet well with a wooden spoon to pick up any flavorful bits from the surface. Heat briefly, then remove from the heat and mash the beans with a large fork or potato masher. Don't try to mash them too thoroughly; they should be rough but a little saucy, with a good mix of whole and mashed beans. Season with salt and pepper to taste.

4 When your dough has doubled and you're ready to bake the pizza, preheat the oven to 450°F (230°C). Punch the dough down and knead for 1 minute on a lightly floured surface. Divide the dough in half. (Save half of the dough for another use.) Cover your dough loosely with plastic wrap and let it rest for 10 minutes on a lightly floured surface.

5 Once it has rested, press or roll the dough into a large, thin circle or oblong. Transfer it to the baking sheet. Lightly brush the surface with the remaining tablespoon or two of olive oil, especially around the edges. Let the dough rest for 10 minutes.

6 Dollop the bean mixture evenly over the surface of the dough, but don't smooth it. Cover evenly with the cooked spinach. Crumble about half of the bacon over the top. Bake on the middle oven rack for 15 minutes.

7 Slide the pizza out of the oven and sprinkle the cheese and rosemary on top. Bake for another 5 to 7 minutes, just long enough to melt the cheese thoroughly. The crust should be golden brown. Slide the pizza onto a rack and cool for 5 to 10 minutes. Crumble the remaining bacon over the top and serve. Refrigerate leftovers. Reheat slices directly on a baking sheet, in a 300°F (150°C) oven, for 8 to 10 minutes.

MAKES 3 TO 4 SERVINGS

Oil and cornmeal for the baking sheet

Food Processor Pizza Dough (page 107) or Hand Method Pizza Dough (page 105)

4–6 bacon strips

½ medium red onion, very thinly sliced

3–4 cups packed baby spinach (5 to 6 ounces)

3–4 tablespoons olive oil

4 garlic cloves, minced

1½ cups (one 15- or 16-ounce can) soft-cooked white beans

¼ cup water

Salt and freshly ground black pepper

1 cup grated mozzarella or provolone cheese

2 teaspoons chopped fresh rosemary or thyme

PESTO PIZZA WITH MIXED BABY GREENS

Here's a fun idea for your next dinner party, and a wonderful show-off dish if you grow your own greens: a pesto pizza "plate" with a salad of mixed greens and fresh herbs served on top. To be clear, the greens aren't baked on the pizza or even wilted; they're simply piled on, all fresh and dressed. (I love the peppery bite of some arugula in the mix.) Think of it as your bread and salad course all in one, more of a knife-and-fork dish than something eaten out of hand like traditional pizza. We saturate these small pizzas with oil and pesto to keep them soft and bake them at a slightly lower temperature so the bread doesn't get too crunchy and become a nuisance to cut. Top them with cheese, if you like. You can't go wrong.

1 Prepare the dough and set it aside to rise. Very lightly oil two large baking sheets and dust them with cornmeal. Mix the pesto and 4 tablespoons of the olive oil in a small bowl; you'll spoon this over the pizzas before baking them.

2 To make the dressing, combine ⅓ cup olive oil, vinegar, onion, mustard, garlic, and 1 teaspoon brown sugar in a large bowl. Whisk well. Whisk in salt and pepper to taste, and adjust the seasonings as desired. Add the feta cheese and olives. Stir gently to coat the cheese.

3 When the dough has doubled, punch it down and turn it out onto a lightly floured surface. Knead for 1 minute, then divide the dough into six equal pieces. Shape the pieces into balls and let them rest for 10 minutes, loosely covered with plastic wrap.

4 Take one piece of dough and press it out into an approximate 6-inch circle, thoroughly dimpling the surface with your fingertips. Transfer it to one of the baking sheets. Repeat for the remaining pieces of dough, arranging three on each sheet. Spoon the pesto mixture evenly over them, dividing it equally and smearing it right up to the edge. Set the pizzas aside for 15 minutes. Position one of your oven racks in the middle of the oven and the other in the lowest position. Preheat the oven to 425°F (220°C).

5 Bake the pizzas for 18 to 20 minutes, until light golden brown, switching the positions of the sheets about halfway through. If you're using the cheese, slide the pizzas out after 15 minutes, sprinkle some over each one, and bake for 5 minutes more, until the cheese melts.

6 Add the greens and fresh herbs to the dressing bowl with the feta and olives and toss well. Put one pizza on each plate and top with the greens. Serve right away.

MAKES 6 SERVINGS

Oil and cornmeal for the baking sheets

Food Processor Pizza Dough (page 107) or Hand Method Pizza Dough (page 105)

⅓ cup pesto (page 98)

⅓ cup plus 4 tablespoons olive oil

2 tablespoons red wine vinegar

1 tablespoon minced red onion

2–3 teaspoons Dijon mustard

1 garlic clove, minced

1–2 teaspoons brown sugar

Salt and freshly ground black pepper

1 cup diced or crumbled feta cheese

½ cup pitted olives, chopped

2 cups grated mozzarella, fontina, or other melting cheese (optional)

6–8 ounces (several good-size handfuls) baby salad greens

2–3 tablespoons mixed chopped fresh herbs, including basil, dill, thyme, and lemon thyme

PEPPERONI AND VEGGIE PULL-APART PIZZA

Part pizza, part monkey bread (or pull-apart bread), this informal loaf goes great with your favorite Italian dishes or whole-meal salads, and it makes a fine snacking loaf, too, on its own or with individual bowls of tomato sauce for dipping. In case you've never made one before, it's called a "pull-apart" bread because the dough is divided into lots of smaller pieces, like irregular rolls, instead of being baked in one solid loaf. The pieces pull apart easily, in this case with bits and pieces of sautéed vegetables and cheese attached. This is another loaf kids love to help with, especially with shaping the dough and coating it with butter and cheese.

1 Prepare the pizza dough and set it aside to rise. Meanwhile, oil a 13- by 9-inch cake pan liberally with olive oil.

2 Heat 3 tablespoons olive oil in a large skillet. Add the onion and bell pepper. Cook over medium heat, stirring occasionally, for 8 to 10 minutes. Stir in the garlic and cherry tomatoes; season the vegetables with salt and pepper to taste. Cook, stirring often, for about 2 minutes; you want to soften the tomatoes but not turn them into sauce. Stir in the rosemary and remove from the heat.

3 Put the melted butter and Parmesan in separate shallow bowls in your work area. Put your oiled pan nearby, too. When the dough has doubled, punch it down and turn it out onto a floured work surface. Knead for 1 minute. Using a dough scraper or knife, cut off small pieces of dough and roughly shape them into golf ball–size rounds. They don't have to be perfectly sized or shaped. Dip the balls in the butter and then roll them in the Parmesan, coating lightly. Place all the dough pieces in the pan, somewhat randomly but more or less evenly spaced. Scatter the pepperoni over and between the pieces of dough, followed by the cooked vegetables. Loosely cover the pan with plastic wrap and set it aside in a warm, draft-free spot for about 30 minutes, until the dough has swollen quite a bit. Preheat the oven to 375°F (190°C).

4 When the dough looks pretty much doubled (it will be hard to tell with the topping), bake for 30 minutes. Slide out the pan and sprinkle the bread with the mozzarella. Bake for another 10 minutes, until the mozzarella is melted and the rolls are golden brown. Transfer the pan to a cooling rack and cool for 5 to 10 minutes. Then remove the rolls and serve as soon as possible. Refrigerate leftovers. Reheat leftovers, wrapped in foil, in a 300°F (150°C) oven for about 10 minutes.

MAKES 8 OR MORE SERVINGS

Food Processor Pizza Dough (page 107) or Hand Method Pizza Dough (page 105)

3 tablespoons olive oil, plus some for the pan

½ large onion, finely chopped

½ bell pepper, finely chopped

2–3 garlic cloves, minced

1½ cups halved or quartered cherry tomatoes

Salt and freshly ground black pepper

2 teaspoons chopped fresh rosemary

3 tablespoons unsalted butter, melted

1–1¼ cups finely grated Parmesan cheese

1 cup diced pepperoni

1½ cups grated mozzarella cheese (may be part Asiago or provolone)

ROASTED BEET, SPINACH, AND FETA CHEESE FLATBREAD

You're to be forgiven if you've never considered using beets as a topping for pizza or flatbread; they're not the first vegetable that comes to mind. After you try this flatbread, they won't be the last, either. The feta cheese and, to a lesser extent, the vinegar add the right amount of sharpness to perk up the beets' mild flavor (if you prefer, you can substitute goat cheese). More often than not, beets are sold without their greens attached, or the greens are not in good enough shape to use. If, however, your beets are homegrown or the greens happen to be in good condition, you can mix some of them in with the spinach.

1 Prepare the dough and set it aside to rise. Meanwhile, lightly oil two large baking sheets, and dust with cornmeal. Adjust your oven racks so one is in the bottom position and the other one is in the middle. (If you don't have two racks, you'll have to bake these one at a time.) Preheat the oven to 400°F (200°C).

2 If the beet stems and leaves are still attached, trim them off where they meet the root. Trim off most of the skinny tail, too. Tear off a 12- to 14-inch piece of aluminum foil and drizzle the middle with a little olive oil. Place the beets in the center and sprinkle with 2 tablespoons water. Close up the foil, place the foil packet on a baking sheet, and bake until the beets are tender all the way through when pierced with a cake tester or paring knife. This could take anywhere from 50 to 75 minutes, depending on the size of the beets. Open the foil so the beets can cool and set them aside.

3 When the beets are cool enough to handle, peel off the skins — or rub them off with dry paper towels — and cut them into ¼-inch-thick slices.

4 When the dough has doubled, punch it down and turn it out onto a lightly floured work surface. Knead for 1 minute, then divide the dough in half. Shape each half into a ball. Let the dough rest on a floured surface, loosely covered with plastic wrap, for 10 minutes. Preheat the oven to 425°F (220°C).

5 As the dough rests, heat the olive oil in a large pot or deep skillet. Add in the onion and cook over moderate heat for 5 minutes. Remove from the heat and add all of the spinach to the still-hot pan. Mix thoroughly; the aim is to soften the greens and wilt them a bit, not cook them down. Season with a bit of salt and pepper.

MAKES 5 TO 6 SERVINGS

Oil and cornmeal for the baking sheets

Yeasted Olive Oil Dough (page 108)

1 pound beets (3 to 4 medium ones), scrubbed

⅓ cup olive oil, plus a little more for the dough and for drizzling

1 large onion, finely chopped

1 pound baby spinach

Salt and freshly ground black pepper

4 teaspoons red wine vinegar

2 cups crumbled feta cheese

6 Working with one piece of dough at a time on a floured surface, press or roll the dough into a large, thin circle or oblong. Transfer to one of the baking sheets. Repeat for the other dough. Brush both lightly with olive oil. Let rest for 10 minutes.

7 Divide the spinach between the two doughs, spreading it around as evenly as possible. Top with the sliced beets, and drizzle each pizza with about 2 teaspoons of red wine vinegar. Dust the top with a bit more salt and pepper. Sprinkle the feta cheese on top, dividing it equally between them.

8 Place one pizza on each of the two oven racks, and bake for 12 minutes. Switch the position of the sheets, moving the bottom one up and the other one down, and bake for another 12 to 13 minutes. When done, the pizzas should be very crusty on the bottom and some of the feta cheese will be golden and crusted. Slide the pizzas onto cooling racks. Slice and serve without delay. Refrigerate leftovers. Reheat, wrapped in foil, in a 300°F (150°C) oven for 10 to 12 minutes.

TOMATO JAM PIZZA WITH CARAMELIZED ONIONS

This wonderful pizza is yet another reason to make sure summer doesn't come and go without cooking up a batch or two of tomato jam. It looks like a traditional red-sauce pizza, but the spiced, sweet-tart tomato jam makes it into something else entirely. The tanginess of the goat cheese — especially if combined with the salty feta — makes the perfect counterpoint. While this recipe yields one pizza, a full batch of tomato jam will yield enough to make two pizzas, if that's what you want. (If so, double all of the topping ingredients.)

1 Prepare the pizza dough and set it aside to rise. You'll need half of the dough for this recipe. The other half can be refrigerated, frozen, or used to make a second pizza (see page 106). Lightly oil a large baking sheet and dust it with cornmeal.

2 Melt the butter in a large skillet. Add the onions and cook them over medium heat for about 12 minutes, until golden, stirring often. Salt and pepper the onions lightly and remove from the heat.

3 When your dough has doubled and you're ready to bake the pizza, preheat the oven to 450°F (230°C). Punch the dough down and knead for 1 minute on a lightly floured surface. Divide the dough in half. (Save half for another use.) Shape the dough into a ball. Cover loosely with plastic wrap and let it rest for 10 minutes on a lightly floured surface.

4 Once it has rested, press or roll the dough into a large, thin circle or oblong. Transfer to the baking sheet and let it rest for 10 minutes.

5 Spread the tomato jam over the surface of the dough, leaving a ½-inch border all around. Drizzle with 1 to 2 tablespoons of olive oil. Distribute the onions evenly over the jam. Top with the cheese. Bake the pizza for 20 to 22 minutes, until the edge has browned and the cheese has blistered. Slide the pizza onto a rack and cool for 5 to 10 minutes before serving. Refrigerate leftovers. Reheat slices directly on a baking sheet, in a 300°F (150°C) oven, for 8 to 10 minutes.

MAKES 3 TO 4 SERVINGS

Oil and cornmeal for the baking sheet

Food Processor Pizza Dough (page 107) or Hand Method Pizza Dough (page 105)

3 tablespoons butter

1½ large onions, thinly sliced

Salt and freshly ground black pepper

¾ cup Food Processor Tomato Jam (page 283)

1–2 tablespoons olive oil

6–8 ounces goat cheese (or a combination of goat cheese and feta cheese)

TOMATO BREADS

The name "Tomato Breads" doesn't begin to do justice to these outsize rounds of sautéed onions, balsamic-glazed tomatoes, cheeses, and pesto (if you please). These breads are like fat little pizzas, and at almost 6 inches across, they're large enough to be halved and served with your favorite pasta dishes. Or serve one per person with a big, colorful salad.

1 Prepare the dough and set it aside to rise. Lightly oil a large baking sheet and dust it with cornmeal.

2 Melt 3 tablespoons of the butter in a large sauté pan. Add the onions; salt and pepper them to taste. Cook the onions over moderate heat, stirring often, until they begin to caramelize, about 15 minutes. Transfer the onions to a plate and set aside. Combine the feta and Parmesan in a small bowl and set that aside also.

3 Reheat the skillet and add the remaining 1 tablespoon butter. Add the tomato slices — or as many as you can — and cook over medium heat for 30 seconds. Turn the slices over and cook for another 30 seconds. Drizzle the balsamic vinegar over the tomatoes, but reserve a little bit of it if you have more tomato slices to cook. If so, repeat the process for the remaining slices; you probably won't need more butter. Remove from the heat, leaving the tomatoes right in the pan.

4 When the dough has doubled in bulk, punch it down and knead briefly on a lightly floured surface. Divide it in half, then divide each half into three equal pieces, totaling six pieces. Shape each one into a ball. Set the balls on a floured surface, loosely covered with plastic wrap, and let rest for 15 minutes.

5 Preheat the oven to 400°F (200°C). Working with one piece of dough at a time, press it out into an approximate 5½-inch-diameter circle; use a rolling pin if you need help keeping it round and even. Transfer to the baking sheet. Repeat for the remaining pieces of dough, making two evenly spaced rows of three dough circles. Cover with the plastic wrap and let the dough rest for 15 minutes.

6 Smear 1 tablespoon pesto (or olive oil, if you prefer) over each dough circle. Cover each with 3 or 4 tomato slices, a handful of the feta and Parmesan mixture, and some of the onions, dividing them up equally. If you didn't use the pesto, top each one with some of the chopped basil. If there's glaze left in the pan, drizzle some over each bread. Brush the edges of the dough with the egg glaze. Bake on the middle oven rack for about 25 minutes, until the breads are big, puffy, and golden brown. Cool briefly on a rack, but serve as soon as possible. Reheat leftovers, wrapped in foil, in a 300°F (150°C) oven for about 12 minutes.

MAKES 6 OR MORE SERVINGS

Oil and cornmeal for the baking sheet

Food Processor Pizza Dough (page 107) or Hand Method Pizza Dough (page 105)

4 tablespoons unsalted butter

2 large onions, quartered and thinly sliced

Salt and freshly ground black pepper

1½ cups crumbled feta cheese

½ cup grated Parmesan cheese

3 large plum tomatoes, cut into ⅓-inch-thick crosswise slices

2 tablespoons balsamic vinegar

6 tablespoons pesto (page 98) or olive oil

⅓ cup chopped fresh basil (if you're not using the pesto)

1 egg yolk, lightly beaten, for glaze

GRILLED HARVEST PIZZA, BASIC AND BEYOND

The grilled pizza craze had been around for more than 20 years before I finally got the bug and decided to give it a try. I wasn't exactly quaking in my boots, but I did have what seemed like some reasonable doubts: What if the dough decided to ooze between the grates and stick, unceremoniously, to the grill? Would I be able to gauge and regulate the heat well enough on a device whose heat is famously irregular? And would there be a sufficient flavor payoff to make the effort worthwhile? Well, there is a learning curve (see the Grilled Pizza Primer), and you're not likely to master it on your first go-round. But once you get the hang of it, you'll be sold. And you can grill your favorite summer veggies and add them right to your pizza. Here's a basic version to acquaint you with the technique, but I hope you'll soon be making personalized pizzas topped with veggies you and yours adore.

1 Prepare the dough and set it aside to rise. When the dough has doubled, punch it down, divide it in half, and knead each half into a ball on a lightly floured surface. Cover one piece of dough with plastic wrap and let it rest on the floured surface for 10 minutes. Loosely wrap the other piece with plastic wrap, and put it in the fridge. Start heating your grill. If yours is large enough, get one zone of the grill good and hot and have another that's slightly less so.

2 Using your fingers, flatten the nonrefrigerated piece of dough into a 7- or 8-inch circle on a floured surface. Let it rest for 4 to 5 minutes. Drizzle 2 tablespoons of the olive oil on a large rimmed baking sheet and spread it around with your fingers. Place the flattened dough on the oiled sheet and press it out a little more. Turn the dough over, and keep flattening and gently stretching it with your fingers and palms until you have about a 13-inch oblong.

3 In one fluid and uninterrupted movement, gingerly lift the dough off the baking sheet, taking care not to stretch it, and place it on the grill in the "hot zone." *Don't try to move the dough for the first few minutes.* After 3 to 4 minutes, when the dough has firmed up a bit and started to blister, use tongs to lift the sides here and there to see how it's doing. You should see browning and grill marks, but if you see a lot of scorching, slide your pizza dough over to the moderate zone.

4 After about 5 minutes, your dough should be ready to turn. There are several ways to do this, but the easiest way is to lift a corner with your tongs, grab the pizza with oven mitts on, and turn it over by hand. Smaller pizzas can probably be flipped with nothing more than a wide spatula.

5 As soon as you flip the crust, brush the surface, particularly the edges, with more of the olive oil. Spoon about 1½ cups of the sauce onto the pizza and spread it evenly. Scatter half of the sliced onion and bell pepper over the sauce and top with half of the pepperoni or sausage. Cover with half of the cheese mix and herbs.

MAKES 2 PIZZAS, 3 TO 4 SERVINGS EACH

Oil for the baking sheet

Food Processor Pizza Dough (page 107) or Hand Method Pizza Dough (page 105)

¼–⅓ cup olive oil

3 cups Quick Summer Tomato Sauce (page 281) or your favorite tomato sauce

1 medium onion, thinly sliced

1 medium green bell pepper, thinly sliced

2–3 ounces pepperoni slices or 2 cups fully cooked and sliced Italian sausage

1 pound grated pizza cheeses (a mix of mozzarella, Colby, provolone, and so on)

2 small handfuls coarsely chopped, fresh Italian herbs, such as parsley, basil, and oregano

6 Cover the grill and cook the pizza 4 to 5 minutes in the moderate zone of the grill (or the hot zone, if that's what the pizza needs — it's easy enough to slide it from one side to the other). Slide the pizza off the grill, onto a baking sheet, then onto a cutting board. Slice and serve. Or if you prefer, you can keep the pizza warm in your oven for a few minutes before cutting so you have time to start the second pizza and get it on the grill before the first one is served.

GRILLED PIZZA PRIMER

Here are some tips as you set out on your grilled pizza adventure:

• Unless you want to take your own cooking cred down a notch of two, don't make grilled pizza for company if you've never tried it before. The first time won't be your shining moment, and the last thing you want is a photo of you — crying over the charred wreckage of a gooey pizza disk — making the rounds on Facebook. Practice first.

• Clean your grill. I know; I hate doing it, too. But those petrified remnants of blue cheese burgers and barbecued chicken will tear up your crust and make it difficult to slide it around.

• Have all your toppings ready and waiting, well ahead, on a tray in the fridge. Appoint someone as your toppings runner so you don't have to leave your crust as it cooks. Bad things can happen in your absence.

• For extra insurance some cooks like to brush their grill surface with oil before laying on the dough. But applying oil directly to the dough when you shape it (in step 2) has always been enough for me.

• The bigger the pizza, the harder it is to handle. Turning the dough on the grill becomes particularly tricky. To make it more manageable, consider dividing the dough into thirds rather than halves and grilling three smaller pizzas.

• It's a little too nontraditional for my taste, but some cooks like to reverse the order of the toppings on grilled pizza and put the cheese down first, on the crust, instead of last. They say it helps the cheese melt faster, and it does. But so long as you get the toppings on soon after you flip the crust, and then you close the lid, the cheese will be perfectly melted when your pizza is done.

• Don't worry about charred areas on your crust; you're going to have them. The good news is, charred things always taste better when they're cooked outdoors, and better yet if they're served outdoors.

GRILLED FLATBREAD WITH HUMMUS AND VEGGIES

For our purposes there's virtually no difference between a pizza and a flatbread. I've read that flatbreads are sometimes made with unleavened dough, but it's a distinction that few seem to be concerned with. Flatbreads do, however, often come with a license to experiment with toppings outside the box — hummus and grilled veggies, for instance. This flatbread is sensational for summer grilling, when we have fresh peppers and eggplant in abundance. Crispy, colorful, and full of grilled charm, it's a showpiece appetizer that will put regular old hummus and crackers to shame.

1 Prepare the dough and set it aside to rise. Meanwhile, preheat your grill. Cut off the stem end of the eggplant. Cut the eggplant lengthwise into ½-inch-thick slabs and set them aside on a large rimmed baking sheet. Put the peppers on the sheet also. Cut three or four ½-inch-thick rings of the onion. Peel and place on the baking sheet. Brush all the vegetables lavishly with olive oil and season with salt and pepper. Grill the veggies until they're tender and pleasantly charred, brushing with more olive oil when you turn them. Put them back on the baking sheet to cool. When they're cool enough to handle, peel the blistered skin off the peppers. Cut everything into big, bite-size pieces and set aside.

2 Once the dough has risen, punch it down, divide it in half, and knead each half into a ball on a lightly floured surface. Cover one piece of dough with plastic wrap and let it rest on a floured surface for 10 minutes. Loosely wrap the other piece in plastic wrap and put it in the fridge. If your grill is large enough, get one zone of the grill good and hot and have another that's slightly less so.

3 Using your fingers, flatten the nonrefrigerated piece of dough into a 7- or 8-inch circle on a floured surface. Let it rest for 4 to 5 minutes. Drizzle 2 tablespoons of the olive oil on a large rimmed baking sheet and spread it around with your fingers. Place the flattened dough on the oiled sheet and press it out a little more. Turn the dough over, and keep flattening and gently stretching it with your fingers and palms until you have a 13- to 14-inch oblong.

4 In one smooth movement, gingerly lift the dough off the baking sheet, trying to not stretch it, and drape it on the grill in the "hot zone." *Don't try to move the dough for the first few minutes.* After 3 to 4 minutes, when the dough has firmed up a bit and started to blister, use tongs to lift the sides here and there to see how it's doing. You should see browning and grill marks, but if you see a lot of scorching, slide your pizza dough over to the moderate zone.

MAKES 2 PIZZAS, 3 TO 4 SERVINGS EACH

Food Processor Pizza Dough (page 107) or Hand Method Pizza Dough (page 105)

1   large eggplant

2   large bell peppers, halved and cored

1   large sweet onion

⅓   cup (or more) olive oil, for brushing the veggies and crust

Salt and freshly ground black pepper

2   cups (about 1 pound) hummus, store-bought or homemade

2   cups crumbled feta cheese

3   tablespoons chopped fresh parsley

RECIPE CONTINUED ON NEXT PAGE

5 After about 5 minutes, your dough should be ready to turn. There are several ways to do this, but the easiest way is to lift a corner with your tongs, grab the pizza with oven mitts on, and turn it over by hand. Smaller pizzas can probably be flipped with nothing more than a wide spatula.

6 As soon as you flip the crust, liberally brush the surface, particularly the edges, with more of the olive oil. Cook on the second side for 2 minutes, then spread 1 cup of the hummus over the surface. Top with half of the veggies and half of the cheese.

7 Cover the grill and cook the pizza another 4 to 5 minutes. Slide the pizza onto a baking sheet and then onto a cutting board. Sprinkle with half the parsley, then slice and serve. Or if you prefer, you can keep the pizza warm in your oven for a few minutes, before cutting, so you have time to start the second pizza and get it on the grill before the first one is served.

CRACKER BREAD PIZZA WITH RED ONIONS, PESTO, AND PARMESAN

The Yeasted Olive Oil Dough (page 108) makes a terrific pizza crust. Like a traditional pizza dough, it's made with yeast; that's evident. But when it's rolled good and thin, it ends up with a distinctive cracker-like crunch. This cracker-like quality is best appreciated when your pizza isn't topped too heavily or blanketed with red sauce, which is why I like this onion and pesto version, which shows off the crust rather than turning it into a mere vehicle for the toppings. Since this recipe makes two pizzas, feel free to give one of them a personal signature. How about a handful of blue cheese crumbles instead of all Parmesan? A dusting of freshly chopped garden herbs? You get the idea.

1 Prepare the dough and set it aside to rise. Very lightly oil two large baking sheets and dust them with cornmeal. Adjust your oven racks so one is in the bottom position and the other one is in the middle. (If you don't have two racks, you'll have to bake the pizzas one at a time.)

2 When the dough has doubled, punch it down and turn it out onto a lightly floured work surface. Knead for 1 minute, then divide the dough in half. Shape each half into a ball. Let the balls rest on a floured surface, loosely covered with plastic wrap, for 10 minutes. Preheat the oven to 425°F (220°C).

3 Combine the sliced onions, pesto, and olive oil in a mixing bowl. Add the spinach, if using. Mix well.

4 Working on a floured surface with one piece of dough at a time, press or roll the dough into a large, thin circle or oblong. Transfer to one of the baking sheets. Repeat for the other piece of dough. Let rest for 5 minutes.

5 Divide the onion mixture evenly between the rolled doughs; use a fork to rake it around so it's evenly distributed. Salt and pepper the pizzas to taste.

6 Place one pizza on each of the two shelves and bake for 12 minutes. Switch the position of the sheets, moving the bottom one up and the other one down, and bake for another 12 to 13 minutes. When done, the pizzas should be very crusty on the bottom and blistered on top. Remove the pans and immediately sprinkle plenty of the Parmesan over each one. Top each one with olives, if using. Slide the pizzas onto cooling racks. Slice and serve without delay. Refrigerate leftovers. Reheat, wrapped in foil, in a 300°F (150°C) oven for about 10 minutes.

MAKES 2 PIZZAS, 2 TO 3 SERVINGS EACH

Oil and cornmeal for the baking sheets

Yeasted Olive Oil Dough (page 108)

1½ large red onions, halved and thinly sliced

¼ cup pesto, store-bought or homemade (page 98)

¼ cup olive oil

Large handful baby spinach (optional)

Salt and freshly ground black pepper

¾–1 cup grated Parmesan cheese

Large handful pitted cured black olives, coarsely chopped (optional)

POTATO, BACON, AND BLUE CHEESE PIZZA

I've made my share of potato pizzas, so I know this to be true: unless you layer on a few very bold flavors, it can be pretty boring. Enter blue cheese and bacon, a salty, satisfying pair that provides plenty of oomph to turn these spuds into a pizza to be reckoned with. The potatoes are moistened with ranch dressing and cream, so you've got a little bit of a *potatoes au gratin* vibe going on here, too.

1 Prepare the dough and let it rise. You'll need half of the dough for this recipe. The other half can be refrigerated, frozen, or used to make a second pizza (see page 106) by doubling all of the filling ingredients. Lightly oil a large baking sheet and dust it with cornmeal.

2 Peel the potatoes and cut them into ⅛-inch-thick slices. Transfer to a large saucepan and add enough water to cover. Salt lightly. Bring to a boil, then lower the heat and boil gently for 3 to 4 minutes, until the potatoes are almost tender. Drain. Oil a large plate, so the potatoes don't stick, and spread the potato slices out on the plate to cool.

3 Cook the bacon strips in a large skillet until crisp. Transfer the bacon to a plate to cool. Spoon off some of the fat in the pan, leaving 2 to 3 tablespoons, and add the onion. Cook the onion over moderate heat for 10 to 12 minutes, until it begins to caramelize. Add the garlic, cook for 30 seconds, and remove from the heat.

4 Preheat the oven to 450°F (230°C). When the dough has doubled, punch it down, knead for 1 minute on a floured surface, and let it rest for 5 to 10 minutes. Once it has rested, press or roll the dough into a large, thin circle or oblong. Transfer to the baking sheet. Lightly brush the surface with olive oil, especially around the edges.

5 Combine the blue cheese, ranch dressing, cream, and Parmesan in a shallow bowl. Mash thoroughly with a large fork to combine.

6 To assemble, scatter the onions here and there over the dough. Dollop with about half of the blue cheese mixture, then arrange the potato slices randomly over the surface. Salt the potatoes lightly and add pepper to taste. Crumble the bacon over the potatoes. Dollop the surface with the remaining blue cheese mixture and sprinkle with the rosemary.

7 Bake the pizza on the middle oven rack for 22 to 25 minutes, until the topping is golden brown and bubbly. Slide the pizza to a rack and cool for 5 to 10 minutes before serving. Refrigerate leftovers. Reheat slices directly on a baking sheet, in a 350°F (180°C) oven, for 8 to 10 minutes.

MAKES 3 TO 4 SERVINGS

Oil and cornmeal for the baking sheet and potato plate

Food Processor Pizza Dough (page 107) or Hand Method Pizza Dough (page 105)

4 or 5 medium-size red-skinned potatoes (about 1 pound)

Salt

4 bacon strips

1 large onion, halved and thinly sliced

3 garlic cloves, thinly sliced

Drizzles of olive oil, for the baking sheet and pizza

1¼ cups crumbled blue cheese

¼ cup ranch dressing

¼ cup heavy cream

3 tablespoons finely grated Parmesan cheese

Freshly ground black pepper

1½ tablespoons chopped fresh rosemary

ROASTED CAULIFLOWER PIZZA

Cauliflower has been the darling of the produce aisle for some time now, as evidenced by the price it's fetching these days. It probably helped when cooks stopped boiling it to death and started getting creative, smoothing it into sauces, working it into veggie burgers and grilled cheese sandwiches, and even shaping it into pizza crust (the jury is still out on that one). One of my favorite uses for cauliflower is as a pizza topping. I roast it up with garlic and paprika and pile it on my dough with onions, rosemary, olives, and cheese. It's seriously good.

1 Prepare the pizza dough and set it aside to rise. You'll need half of the dough for this recipe. The other half can be refrigerated, frozen, or used to make a second pizza by doubling all of the filling ingredients (see note below). Lightly oil a large baking sheet and dust it with cornmeal.

2 Preheat the oven to 425°F (220°C). Coat a large baking sheet with oil, or line it with parchment paper. Cut the cauliflower into bite-size florets, and place them in a colander. Rinse well. Transfer to a large bowl and drizzle with 3 tablespoons of the olive oil. Sprinkle on the garlic, paprika, and salt and pepper to taste. Mix well with your hands until everything is coated. While your hands are messy, lift the cauliflower onto the baking sheet and spread it around so it's not piled up. Roast for 20 to 22 minutes, until it's cooked but still has some crunch to it. Transfer the sheet to a cooling rack.

3 Heat the remaining 3 tablespoons olive oil in a large skillet. Add the onion and sauté over moderate heat for about 10 minutes, until it begins to caramelize. Stir in the rosemary, cook for another minute, and remove from the heat.

4 When your dough has doubled and you're ready to bake the pizza, preheat the oven to 450°F (230°C). Punch the dough down and knead for 1 minute on a lightly floured surface. Divide the dough in half. (Save half of the dough for another use.) Cover your dough loosely with plastic wrap and let it rest for 10 minutes on a lightly floured surface.

5 Once it has rested, press or roll the dough into a large, thin circle or oblong. Transfer to the baking sheet. Lightly brush the surface with olive oil, especially around the edges. Let the dough rest for 10 minutes.

6 Spoon the sautéed onion evenly over the dough. Top with the cauliflower. Bake on the middle oven rack for 15 minutes. Slide out the pizza and top it with the olives, feta, and cheddar. Bake for another 5 to 6 minutes, until the cheese is fully melted and the crust is golden brown. Slide the pizza onto a rack and cool for 5 to 10 minutes before serving. Refrigerate leftovers. Reheat slices directly on a baking sheet, in a 300°F (150°C) oven, for 8 to 10 minutes.

MAKES 3 TO 4 SERVINGS

Oil and cornmeal for the baking sheets

Food Processor Pizza Dough (page 107) or Hand Method Pizza Dough (page 105)

1 medium-size head cauliflower

6 tablespoons olive oil, plus a little for the pizza

3 garlic cloves, minced

1 teaspoon paprika (use smoked paprika for a deeper flavor)

Salt and freshly ground black pepper

1 large onion, thinly sliced

1 tablespoon chopped fresh rosemary

Small handful of pitted olives, halved or quartered

1 cup crumbled feta cheese

1 cup grated sharp white cheddar, Gruyère, or fontina cheese

NOTE: To double the recipe, use both halves of dough and make two pizzas. Use one very large head of cauliflower, and roast it on two baking sheets instead of one. Double all other ingredients except the amount of olive oil: use ¼ cup to coat the cauliflower and another ¼ cup to sauté the onions.

CAULIFLOWER PARMESAN PIZZA

I can't take credit for inventing cauliflower Parmesan. But once I tried it — based on a straightforward recipe I clipped from the *New York Times* — it took me about 5 seconds to head for the kitchen, make some dough, and draw up plans for a Cauliflower Parmesan Pizza. I'm really glad I did. The assembly begins with breading and pan-frying thick cauliflower slices. The red sauce goes on the dough and then is covered with the cauliflower and cheese. It's best not to smother the cauliflower in sauce; the breading on the cauliflower will stay crisper. Vegetarians take note: there aren't many pizzas where I don't crave at least a bit of meat, but this one is so satisfying I don't miss it at all.

1 Prepare the pizza dough and set it aside to rise. You'll need half of the dough for this recipe. The other half can be refrigerated, frozen, or used to make a second pizza (see page 106). Lightly oil a large baking sheet and dust it with cornmeal.

2 Rinse the cauliflower well and dry with paper towels. Trim any questionable areas. Rest the cauliflower on its bottom surface and cut it in half, down through the core area. Cut the core section out of each half, but not too deeply; some core will help hold the cauliflower together. Lay the halves on their cut surfaces and cut into slices nearly ½ inch thick. You'll only need about three-quarters of the head. Set the slices aside on a plate.

3 Put the flour on a plate or in a shallow baking dish; season it well with salt and pepper. Whisk the eggs in a shallow bowl until frothy. Put the bread crumbs in a shallow container also. Position these three containers near your stove, along with the sliced cauliflower.

4 Heat about 3 tablespoons of the olive oil in a large skillet, preferably non-stick, over medium heat. Dredge both sides of a cauliflower slice in flour, dip it into the egg, coat both sides with the bread crumbs, and place it in the skillet. Repeat, placing the slices fairly close together. Fry the slices for about 3 minutes on each side, until golden brown. Transfer to a plate as they come off. Add a little more oil to the skillet and fry the remaining slices.

5 When your dough has doubled and you're ready to bake the pizza, preheat the oven to 450°F (230°C). Punch the dough down and knead for 1 minute on a lightly floured surface. Divide the dough in half. (Save half of the dough for another use.) Shape the dough into a ball. Cover loosely with plastic wrap and let it rest for 10 minutes on a lightly floured surface.

6 Once it has rested, press or roll the dough into a large, thin circle or oblong. Transfer to the baking sheet. Let the dough rest for 10 minutes.

MAKES 3 TO 4 SERVINGS

Oil and cornmeal for the baking sheet

Food Processor Pizza Dough (page 107) or Hand Method Pizza Dough (page 105)

1 medium-size head cauliflower

½ cup all-purpose flour

Salt and freshly ground black pepper

3 large eggs

1–1½ cups Italian-style bread crumbs

4–6 tablespoons olive oil

1 cup tomato sauce

⅓–½ cup finely grated Parmesan cheese

1–1¼ cups grated mozzarella cheese or 5 to 6 ounces sliced fresh mozzarella cheese

7 Spread about ¾ cup of the sauce evenly over the dough. Place the pieces of cauliflower on top; you'll cover much of the surface. Dollop the cauliflower with the remaining sauce, but don't smear it over the pieces. Sprinkle the Parmesan on top. Bake on the middle oven rack for 15 minutes.

8 Slide the pizza out of the oven and cover with the mozzarella. Bake for another 5 to 7 minutes, just long enough to melt or soften the cheese. Slide the pizza onto a rack and cool for 5 to 10 minutes before serving. Refrigerate leftovers. Reheat slices directly on a baking sheet, in a 300°F (150°C) oven, for 8 to 10 minutes.

BROCCOLI SAUCE AND CHEDDAR CHEESE PIZZA

There's nothing particularly novel about a pizza topped with broccoli; that's one way to make a broccoli pizza. Here's another: take your broccoli, stalks and all, and turn it into a textured purée to use as your pizza sauce. Vegetarians will love it — substitute vegetable stock for the chicken stock — and it's just plain good eating. The flavor of the sauce is what carries this pizza, so taste it and adjust the seasonings as you go. If you decide to double the recipe to make two pizzas and find that your processor isn't large enough to hold all the broccoli, make the sauce in two batches.

1 Prepare the pizza dough and set it aside to rise. You'll need half of the dough for this recipe. The other half can be refrigerated, frozen, or used to make a second pizza (see page 106). Lightly oil a large baking sheet and dust it with cornmeal.

2 Steam the broccoli in a large saucepan until it is just barely tender, 4 to 5 minutes. Immediately spread the broccoli out on a large plate and cool to room temperature.

3 Transfer the broccoli to a food processor. Add the Parmesan and butter. Using short bursts, pulse the machine several times, until the broccoli is roughly chopped. Add ½ cup of the stock and a bit of salt and pepper. Pulse again to smooth the purée a little more. Taste, adding more Parmesan, salt, and pepper to make a full-flavored mixture; the pizza will be bland if it isn't. Adjust the consistency, as needed, with some or all of the remaining stock. It should be thickish, moist, and slightly textured.

4 When your dough has doubled and you're ready to bake the pizza, preheat the oven to 450°F (230°C). Punch the dough down and knead for 1 minute on a lightly floured surface. Divide the dough in half. (Save half of the dough for another use.) Shape the dough into a ball. Cover loosely with plastic wrap and let it rest for 10 minutes on a lightly floured surface.

5 Once it has rested, press or roll the dough into a large, thin circle or oblong. Transfer to the baking sheet. Lightly brush the dough with olive oil. Let it rest for 10 minutes.

6 Spread the broccoli purée evenly over the dough. Drizzle the heavy cream here and there over the surface. Bake for 15 minutes, then slide the pizza out of the oven, and cover with the cheddar. Bake for another 5 to 7 minutes, until the cheese has melted. Slide the pizza onto a rack and cool for 5 to 10 minutes before serving. Refrigerate leftovers. Reheat slices directly on a baking sheet, in a 300°F (150°C) oven, for 8 to 10 minutes.

MAKES 3 TO 4 SERVINGS

Oil and cornmeal for the baking sheet

Food Processor Pizza Dough (page 107) or Hand Method Pizza Dough (page 105)

4 cups broccoli (whole florets and peeled, diced stalks)

½ cup finely grated Parmesan cheese, plus more to taste

2 tablespoons unsalted butter, very soft

½–¾ cup warm chicken stock or vegetable stock

Salt and freshly ground black pepper

Olive oil, for brushing the dough

3–4 tablespoons heavy cream

2 cups grated sharp or extra-sharp cheddar cheese

More Broccoli for Your Buck

Whether you grow it or buy it, cook it or bake with it, throwing away your broccoli stalks is like tossing away good money. There's flavor and good nutrition in those stalks, so please regard them as equals to the more popular florets. Depending on the size and age of your broccoli, the stalks may be thick or thin and more or less fibrous. Cut the stalks into manageable 1½- to 2-inch sections then peel the outer skin with a paring knife. The thicker the stems, the more skin you'll have to whittle off. The tender core is what you're after. Dice the core and cook it up with the florets. Cut it into matchsticks for stir-fries or bigger for dipping. Or add the stalks to soup.

FRESH FENNEL AND ITALIAN SAUSAGE PIZZA

Fresh fennel is one of those underutilized vegetables — such as broccoli rabe and parsnips — that cooks don't miss until they've tried it and then can't imagine how they lived without it. Harvest bakers will discover one of fennel's highest callings as a pizza topping. When fennel is sautéed with onion and garlic, the flavor mellows and creates a beautiful harmony with the Italian sausage and other toppings. (Use sausage that's seasoned with fennel seed for an added fennel hit.) In case you've never handled fennel before, don't be intimidated; the box (at right) will guide you through it.

1 Prepare the pizza dough and set it aside to rise. You'll need half of the dough for this recipe. The other half can be refrigerated, frozen, or used to make a second pizza (see page 106). Lightly oil a large baking sheet and dust it with cornmeal.

2 Heat the olive oil in a large skillet over medium heat. Add the sausage, breaking it into pieces. Let it brown for 7 to 8 minutes, until cooked through. Using a slotted spoon, remove the meat and set it aside. Stir the onion, fennel, and garlic into the pan; add salt and pepper to taste. Cook over medium heat, stirring, for 3 to 4 minutes. Cover, reduce the heat slightly, and cook the vegetables for about 10 minutes, until they're a light golden brown. Keep an eye on the vegetables, and if they seem to need liquid at any point, stir in a tablespoon of water. Remove from the heat.

3 When your dough has doubled and you're ready to bake the pizza, preheat the oven to 450°F (230°C). Punch the dough down and knead for 1 minute on a lightly floured surface. Divide the dough in half. (Save half of the dough for another use.) Shape the dough into a ball. Cover loosely with plastic wrap and let it rest for 10 minutes on a lightly floured surface.

4 Once it has rested, roll or press the dough into a large, thin circle or oblong. Transfer to the baking sheet. Lightly brush the surface with about 1 tablespoon of olive oil. Let the dough rest for 10 minutes.

5 Distribute the sautéed vegetables evenly over the dough. Sprinkle with the Parmesan and drizzle with more olive oil. Bake on the middle oven rack for 15 minutes.

6 Slide the pizza out of the oven. Sprinkle with the mozzarella and lay some of the fennel fronds on top. Bake for another 5 to 7 minutes, just long enough to melt the cheese thoroughly. The crust should be golden brown. Slide the pizza onto a rack, sprinkle with the chopped parsley, and cool for 5 to 10 minutes before serving. Refrigerate leftovers. Reheat slices directly on a baking sheet, in a 300°F (150°C) oven, for 8 to 10 minutes.

MAKES 3 TO 4 SERVINGS

Oil and cornmeal for the baking sheet

Food Processor Pizza Dough (page 107) or Hand Method Pizza Dough (page 105)

2 tablespoons olive oil, plus more for brushing and drizzling on the dough

6 ounces (approximately) bulk Italian sausage

1 large onion, halved and thinly sliced

1 large fennel bulb, sliced (see box), with fronds reserved

2 garlic cloves, thinly sliced

Salt and freshly ground black pepper

⅓ cup finely grated Parmesan cheese

1–1½ cups mozzarella cheese

2 tablespoons chopped fresh Italian parsley

Fennel 101

Fennel has a delicious crunch and delicate flavor — like celery, but with more personality. Its subtle anise flavor can brighten up a salad or antipasto tray; its refreshing crunch goes great with dips; and it imparts a delicate flavor to mild-tasting fish.

Fennel looks something like a flattened bunch of celery with a fist-like bulb at the base. It's typically sold with the stalks attached, but sometimes you'll find just the bulbs with an inch or so of the stalks remaining. Either way is fine, but if you buy stalkless bulbs, you won't have the fronds to dress up your pizza.

Rinse the fennel, and cut off the stalks where they meet the bulb. Reserve the feathery fronds for garnishing your pizza, but discard the stalks. With your chef's knife, trim off the bottom ⅛ inch of the bulb. Using a vegetable peeler, peel the outer surface of the bulb. If the outer layer looks damaged or tired, or if it is large and tough, you can take a knife, score down through it, and peel off the entire outer layer.

Hold the bulb with the trimmed base on your cutting board and cut down through the fennel with your knife, exposing the core in each half. If the core is large and tough, cut it out. Smaller bulbs will have smaller, more tender cores that you can simply leave in. Lay the halves down, and slice them crosswise into ¼-inch slices. That's all there is to it.

WINTER SQUASH PIZZA WITH BABY KALE

There are at least a couple of ways to top a pizza with your favorite winter squash. One way is to roast slices of squash, as in our Roasted Winter Squash Pizza (page 134). The other way, this one, is to simmer the squash and turn it into a velvety, savory sauce. The inspiration for this idea came from my daughter, Ali, an accomplished cook and caterer who lives in New Hampshire. In her signature lasagna, she uses a similar sauce to blanket layers of noodles, sautéed baby kale, and cheese. I'm here to tell you those same ingredients (minus the noodles) make one fine pizza. Though this recipe is written for one pizza, there's plenty of squash sauce for two pizzas, if you like.

1 Prepare the pizza dough and set it aside to rise. You'll need half of the dough for this recipe. The other half can be refrigerated, frozen, or used to make a second pizza (see page 106). Lightly oil a large baking sheet and dust it with cornmeal.

2 Halve the squash lengthwise, peel it, and scoop out the seeds. Cube the squash and measure out 5 cups' worth. (Reserve the remaining squash for another use.)

3 Melt the butter in a large sauté pan. Stir in the chopped onions and squash. Cook over medium heat for about 10 minutes, until the onions are mostly clear. Stir in the garlic and red pepper flakes and cook for another minute. Stir in 1½ cups of the stock, the thyme, ¼ teaspoon salt, and pepper to taste. Bring to a low boil. Cover the pan and cook at a low boil for about 25 minutes, until all of the squash is tender. For the most part the stock should just cover the squash, but if it's evaporating and seems to need a little more, add another ¼ cup stock to the pan. Remove from the heat, uncover, and let cool to lukewarm.

4 To make the sauce, transfer the squash and all of its cooking liquid to your food processor. (If your processor is on the small side, you may need to do this in two batches.) Add the Parmesan. Process to a smooth purée. You want to end up with a texture like thickish tomato sauce, so add a little milk, additional stock, or water if you need to. Taste, adding more salt and pepper if needed.

5 When your dough has doubled and you're ready to bake the pizza, preheat the oven to 450°F (230°C). Punch the dough down and knead for 1 minute on a lightly floured surface. Divide the dough in half. (Save half of the dough for another use.) Cover your dough loosely with plastic wrap and let it rest for 10 minutes on a lightly floured surface.

6 Once it has rested, press or roll the dough into a large, thin circle or oblong. Transfer to the baking sheet. Lightly brush the surface with a tablespoon of olive oil. Let the dough rest for 10 minutes.

MAKES 3 TO 4 SERVINGS

Oil and cornmeal for the baking sheet

Food Processor Pizza Dough (page 107) or Hand Method Pizza Dough (page 105)

2 pounds butternut squash (1 medium-large squash)

2 tablespoons unsalted butter

1½ large onions (the whole one chopped, the half thinly sliced)

3 garlic cloves, minced

Sprinkling of hot red pepper flakes

1½–1¾ cups chicken stock or vegetable stock

1 teaspoon fresh thyme leaves or ½ teaspoon dried

Salt and freshly ground black pepper

⅓ cup finely grated Parmesan cheese

Milk, additional stock, or water (up to about ½ cup), if needed

3 tablespoons olive oil, for the kale and dough

3 cups (packed) baby kale

1–1½ cups grated fontina cheese or mozzarella cheese

7 While the dough rests, combine the kale and the sliced onion in a mixing bowl. Drizzle with the remaining 2 tablespoons olive oil. Toss well.

8 Spread a thick layer of sauce over the dough. You'll probably need a little less than half. Scatter the kale and onions evenly over the sauce. Bake on the middle oven rack for 15 minutes.

9 Slide the pizza out of the oven and sprinkle the fontina or mozzarella on top. Bake for another 5 to 7 minutes, just long enough to melt the cheese thoroughly. The crust should be golden brown. Slide the pizza onto a rack and cool for 5 to 10 minutes before serving. Refrigerate leftovers. Reheat slices directly on a baking sheet, in a 300°F (150°C) oven, for 8 to 10 minutes.

NOTE: This squash sauce is also excellent on pasta; just reheat it the next day. Add additional seasoning if necessary, and don't be surprised if you have to thin it with a bit of water or stock to get the consistency just right. I might boil a few frozen peas in with the pasta, or toss in a handful of broccoli florets for the last couple of minutes. Top your dish with grated Parmesan.

On the other hand, if you want to make a second squash pizza, you'll already have plenty of sauce, but you'll need to double the amount of kale, onion, and melting cheese for the top.

ROASTED WINTER SQUASH PIZZA

Restraint is a quaint aspiration for me, but it has little hope of making it past my kitchen door. So what we have here is a layer of puréed ricotta and Parmesan cheese topped with roasted winter squash slices. While this might constitute "the works" elsewhere, for me it's just a starting point for a pizza party that also includes sliced sausage or pepperoni, baby greens, and more cheese on top. (I never said the recipe was endorsed by the American Heart Association, did I?) It's worth mentioning that the only thing standing between this pizza and a vegetarian feast is the pepperoni or sausage, so take it or leave it as you please.

1 Prepare the pizza dough and set it aside to rise. You'll need half of the dough for this recipe. The other half can be refrigerated, frozen, or used to make a second pizza (see page 106). Lightly oil a large baking sheet and dust it with cornmeal.

2 Preheat the oven to 400°F (200°C). Rinse and dry the squash. Cut off the neck of the squash where it meets the bulbous part. (The neck is all you'll need for this recipe, but since you'll have the oven on anyway, you may want to seed and bake the bulb area for another use.) Peel the neck with a vegetable peeler, and slice it in half lengthwise. Cut each half into ¼- to ⅓-inch-thick slices, and place them in a large bowl. Drizzle with 2 tablespoons of the olive oil. Add the sage and then salt and pepper to taste. Mix by hand, coating the slices well.

3 Line a large baking sheet with parchment paper or aluminum foil. If using the latter, lightly butter or oil the foil. Spread the squash slices on the sheet in a single layer. Bake on the middle oven rack for 25 to 30 minutes, until just tender. Set the sheet on a rack to cool briefly. Loosen the squash with a spatula, but leave it right on the sheet.

4 Combine the ricotta and Parmesan in a food processor. Add a bit of salt and pepper. Process to a smooth purée.

5 Put the greens in a mixing bowl and drizzle with the remaining 2 tablespoons oil. Mix well by hand.

6 When your dough has doubled and you're ready to bake the pizza, preheat the oven to 450°F (230°C). Punch the dough down and knead for 1 minute on a lightly floured surface. Divide the dough in half. (Save half of the dough for another use.) Cover your dough loosely with plastic wrap and let it rest for 10 minutes on a lightly floured surface.

7 Once it has rested, press or roll the dough into a large, thin circle or oblong. Transfer to the baking sheet. Lightly brush the surface with about a tablespoon of olive oil. Let the dough rest for 10 minutes.

MAKES 3 TO 4 SERVINGS

Oil and cornmeal for the baking sheet

Food Processor Pizza Dough (page 107) or Hand Method Pizza Dough (page 105)

1 large butternut squash (see note)

5 tablespoons olive oil, plus more for brushing the dough

1 tablespoon minced fresh sage or 1½ teaspoons dried

Salt and freshly ground black pepper

1 cup ricotta cheese

¼ cup finely grated Parmesan cheese

2–3 cups packed baby kale or spinach

⅓ cup thinly sliced pepperoni or 1 to 1¼ cups fully cooked, thinly sliced hot Italian sausage

1–1½ cups grated mozzarella cheese, provolone, or other melting cheese

8 Spread the puréed cheese mixture over the dough. Top with roasted squash slices; they can overlap slightly. Spread the greens and pepperoni on top. Bake on the middle oven rack for 15 minutes.

9 Slide the pizza out of the oven and sprinkle with the mozzarella. Bake for another 5 to 7 minutes, just long enough to melt the mozzarella thoroughly. The crust should be golden brown. Slide the pizza onto a rack and cool for 5 to 10 minutes before serving. Refrigerate leftovers. Reheat slices directly on a baking sheet, in a 300°F (150°C) oven, for 8 to 10 minutes.

NOTE: You don't necessarily have to use butternut squash, but the long, thick neck makes it perhaps the easiest and neatest winter squash to slice. Delicata squash is another popular choice, and many cooks believe that the skin is so unobtrusive that there's no need to peel it; I'm not one of them. (Be sure to rinse the squash thoroughly if you follow suit.) No matter the variety, the roasting/baking time remains the same — 25 to 30 minutes.

COLLARD GREENS AND SAUSAGE CALZONE

I love the sight of fresh collards stacked high at the farmers' market or, better yet, some makeshift roadside stand along a quiet stretch of country road. Even before my car has come to a complete stop, I'm planning meals around them for the coming week — these collard calzones, for instance. After we simmer the leaves in beef broth, onion, and garlic, they'll get tucked inside the dough with some cheese and sausage and then baked to perfection. Spiced chicken or turkey sausage is a good option, and you have a lot of leeway for the cheese, too; I've used mozzarella, smoked cheddar, and others.

1 Prepare the pizza dough and set it aside to rise. Lightly oil a large baking sheet and dust it with cornmeal. If you prefer, simply line the sheet with parchment paper.

2 Heat the oil in a large pot, one large enough to hold all the collards. Sauté the onion over moderate heat for 7 to 8 minutes, until mostly translucent. Stir in the garlic and cook for 30 seconds, then add the collards, water, bouillon cube, Worcestershire sauce, and a pinch or two of salt. Bring to a simmer, cover, and simmer for 40 to 50 minutes, until the collards are tender (they may take even longer if the leaves are very large). Taste the collards as they cook, adding a bit more salt if needed. Keep a close eye on the liquid, and if it gets too low, add a little more. If there's quite a bit of liquid still left when the collards are almost done, remove the lid during the last 10 minutes or so of cooking. When they're done, remove from the heat and pour the collards into a colander placed over a large bowl.

3 When the dough has doubled, punch it down, turn it out onto a floured surface, and knead briefly. Divide it into four equal pieces, and shape each piece into a ball. Cover the pieces with plastic wrap and let rest for 10 minutes. Meanwhile, preheat the oven to 425F° (220°C).

4 Press down lightly on the collards to express excess juice, but don't overdo it; a bit of moisture is ideal. (Save the accumulated juice and use it in soup.) Working with one piece of dough at a time, press or roll it into a thin oblong about 11 inches long and 8 inches wide. Leaving a ¾-inch border of uncovered dough, pile one-quarter of the collards on half of the dough. Top with one-quarter of the sausage and one-quarter of the cheese. Drizzle the filling with 1 tablespoon of the barbecue sauce, if using. Moisten the entire border with a wet fingertip, and fold the uncovered half of the dough over the filling. Press firmly along the edge to seal. Transfer to the baking sheet. Repeat for the other calzones.

5 Brush the calzones sparingly with the egg glaze. Bake on the middle oven rack for 25 to 30 minutes, until the calzones are a rich golden brown. Transfer the calzones to a cooling rack. Brush each one with a little olive oil if you want the bread casing to soften a bit. Cool for 10 minutes before serving.

MAKES 4 SERVINGS

Oil and cornmeal for the baking sheet

Food Processor Pizza Dough (page 107) or Hand Method Pizza Dough (page 105)

3 tablespoons olive oil or unsalted butter

1 large onion, quartered and sliced

3 garlic cloves, minced

10–12 cups coarsely chopped collard greens

2 cups water

1 beef bouillon cube, crumbled

1 teaspoon Worcestershire sauce

Salt

½ pound fully cooked smoked sausage (chicken, turkey, or other), in bite-size pieces

1½ cups diced or grated cheese (cheddar, smoked cheddar, mozzarella, Gouda, or fontina)

¼ cup mustard-based barbecue sauce (optional)

1 egg beaten with 1 teaspoon water, for glaze

Olive oil, for brushing on the calzones (optional)

THREE-CHEESE AND MUSTARD GREENS CALZONES

Mustard greens are a powerhouse of nutrition, but they come with a peppery bite that takes some getting used to. A great way to temper that sassiness is to balance it out with ricotta cheese, the way we do in these hearty calzones, with some feta and mozzarella thrown in for good measure. Ricotta can always use a little extra flavor, so zip it up with plenty of parsley, basil, and thyme. Don't forget the salt and pepper, too. A few chickpeas and chunks of tomato round out the filling. I've made this as one big calzone, and it's a lot to handle, so I suggest you divide the dough in half and make two instead.

1 Prepare the pizza dough and set it aside to rise. Lightly oil a large baking sheet and dust it with cornmeal, or simply line the sheet with parchment paper.

2 Rinse the mustard greens and transfer them to a colander to drain. Don't worry about drying them. Break off and discard any thick stems. Chop the leaves coarsely.

3 Heat 3 tablespoons olive oil in a large sauté pan or pot. Add the onion and cook over medium heat, stirring often, for about 10 minutes, until light golden in color. Stir in the garlic, greens, and a bit of salt and pepper. Cover the pan and cook for 10 minutes over medium heat, stirring from time to time. Keep an eye on the greens, and if they need a little additional moisture, add a few tablespoons of water as needed. Stir in the chickpeas, tomato, and a bit more salt and pepper, and cook for 5 minutes more. The greens should be tender and the tomatoes nicely softened. Cook off any puddles of liquid left in the pan. Transfer the mixture to a shallow casserole dish and set aside to cool.

4 Put the ricotta and feta in a mixing bowl. Stir in the parsley, basil, thyme, and salt and pepper to taste. Set aside.

5 When the dough has doubled, punch it down and turn the dough out onto a lightly floured work surface. Knead the dough for 1 minute, then divide it in half. Shape each half into a ball and place on a floured surface. Cover with plastic wrap and let rest for 10 minutes. Preheat the oven to 425°F (220°C).

6 Working on a floured surface with one piece of dough at a time, press or roll it into a thin oblong of about 13 by 8 inches. Spread half of the ricotta mixture lengthwise over half of the oblong, leaving a ¾-inch border. Top with half of the mozzarella and olives and half of the mustard greens mixture. Dampen the perimeter of the dough with a pastry brush, and fold the uncovered half of the dough over the filling. Line up the edges and press to seal. Roll up the edge slightly, so it looks like a rope. Place the calzone on the baking sheet. Repeat for the other calzone. Brush the tops with olive oil. Holding a pair of scissors almost parallel to the calzone, make several snips in the dough, running lengthwise, for steam vents. Let the calzones rest for 5 minutes.

7 Bake the calzones for 25 to 30 minutes, until browned and crusty. Slide them onto a baking sheet and brush the tops again with olive oil. Cool for 10 to 15 minutes, then slice and serve. (Be careful; the filling will still be hot.)

MAKES 4 TO 6 SERVINGS

Oil and cornmeal for the baking sheet

Food Processor Pizza Dough (page 107) or Hand Method Pizza Dough (page 105)

1 large bundle mustard greens (about ½ pound)

3 tablespoons olive oil, plus a little more for brushing on the dough and crust

1 large onion, halved and thinly sliced

5–6 garlic cloves, minced

Salt and freshly ground black pepper

1 cup canned chickpeas, well rinsed

1 large tomato, cored, seeded, and coarsely chopped

1 cup ricotta cheese

½ cup crumbled feta cheese

¼ cup chopped fresh parsley

2 tablespoons chopped fresh basil or 2 teaspoons dried

1 teaspoon fresh thyme or ½ teaspoon dried

1 cup grated mozzarella cheese

½ cup pitted and chopped olives

KALE, POTATO, AND SAUSAGE POCKETS

Whether you call them pockets or individual calzones, these personal pies in a pizza crust are a delicious handful. This version features one of my favorite garden greens, kale, with chunked potatoes for bulk, sausage for flavor, and cheese for richness. Straight from the oven they're pure bliss, but they're also rugged enough to take on a hike, rewarm in a campfire skillet, or freeze and reheat later in the oven for a quick dinner. You have lots of flexibility with your choice of cheese; crumbled feta is a good option. I don't put tomato sauce in these but instead serve it on the side.

1 Prepare the dough and set it aside to rise. Lightly oil a large baking sheet and dust it with cornmeal, or simply line the sheet with parchment paper.

2 Melt the butter in a large sauté pan. Add the onion and sauté for 10 minutes, until light golden. Stir in the garlic and cook for 1 minute, then stir in the kale and ⅔ cup of the chicken stock. Bring to a simmer, cover, and cook the kale for 5 minutes. Stir in the potatoes and season generously with salt and pepper. Add more of the remaining stock if there's very little left in the pan. Cover and cook for 5 to 6 minutes longer, until the potatoes are almost done. Add the sausage and continue to cook until the potatoes are just tender and the liquid is mostly gone. Remove from the heat and set aside to cool.

3 While the filling cools, punch the dough down and turn it out onto a floured surface. Knead for 1 minute, then divide the dough into six equal pieces. Shape each of the pieces into a ball and set them on a floured surface. Cover with plastic wrap and let rest for 10 minutes.

4 Preheat the oven to 425°F (220°C). Add the melting cheese, ricotta, and Parmesan to the cooled filling; mix them in gently so you don't mash the potatoes. Mix in the basil. Taste, and adjust the seasonings if necessary.

5 Working with one piece at a time, press or roll the dough into a thin 9- by 6-inch oblong. Moisten the entire edge with a damp fingertip or pastry brush. Draw an imaginary line across the center of the dough, crosswise, and mound one-sixth of the filling on half of the oblong, leaving a ¾-inch border all around. Fold the uncovered half over the filling, line up the edges, and press to seal. Leave the edge as is, or roll it into a rope. Place on the baking sheet. Repeat for the remaining pockets.

6 Brush the pockets lightly with the egg glaze. Bake on the center oven rack for 25 to 30 minutes, until the pockets are golden and crusty on the top and bottom. Transfer the pockets to a rack and cool for at least 10 minutes before serving with the tomato sauce on the side. Wrap leftovers in foil and refrigerate or freeze. Reheat in the foil, in a 350°F (180°C) oven, until heated through (15 to 20 minutes if refrigerated, 30 minutes or more if frozen).

MAKES 6 POCKETS

Oil and cornmeal for the baking sheets

Food Processor Pizza Dough (page 107) or Hand Method Pizza Dough (page 105)

2 tablespoons unsalted butter

1 large onion, halved and sliced

2 garlic cloves, minced

8 cups coarsely chopped kale (1 to 1¼ pounds)

⅔–1 cup chicken stock

1½ cups small-diced red-skinned potato

Salt and freshly ground black pepper

½ pound fully cooked Italian sausage, finely chopped

1 cup melting cheese, such as mozzarella, provolone, cheddar, or fontina

¾ cup ricotta cheese

½ cup grated Parmesan cheese

2 tablespoons chopped fresh basil or pesto (page 98)

1 egg, lightly beaten for glaze

Tomato sauce, heated, for serving

PANE RIPIENO (ITALIAN STUFFED BREAD)

Pane ripieno refers to an assortment of rolled, hollowed, and stuffed, not to mention scored and filled, Italian breads made with practically every ingredient under the sun. Like most of the versions I've encountered, ours is stuffed to overflowing with sautéed onions, green peppers, eggplant, tomatoes, and garlic. Cheese and pesto, too. All of it gets spread out on a round of pizza dough, topped with a second dough, and baked to golden brown. Serve up big slices with a crisp Greek or Italian-style salad.

1 Prepare the dough and set it aside to rise. Lightly oil a large baking sheet and dust it with cornmeal.

2 Once the dough has doubled, punch it down and knead briefly. Divide the dough in half and shape into balls. Smear a little oil in two medium bowls. Put one dough ball in each, rotating the dough to coat it with oil. Cover with plastic wrap and refrigerate while you make the filling.

3 Heat 3 tablespoons of the olive oil in a large sauté pan. Add the onion and bell pepper and sauté over medium heat for 5 minutes. Add the remaining 3 tablespoons olive oil, garlic, eggplant, ½ teaspoon salt, and pepper. Cook, partially covered, for 3 to 4 minutes, stirring occasionally, until the eggplant is tender but not mushy. Stir in the chopped tomatoes and cook, uncovered, for 2 minutes; you want to just soften the tomatoes, not turn them into sauce. Remove from the heat, stir in the sausage, and set aside to cool.

4 When the vegetables have cooled, preheat the oven to 425°F (220°C). Take one ball of dough and flatten it into a disk on a floured work surface. Press or roll it into a thin 12- to 13-inch circle, and transfer the circle to the baking sheet. Leaving a 1-inch border around the edge, cover the circle with half of the cheese. Dollop the cheese with the pesto, and distribute the vegetable and sausage mixture evenly over the cheese. Cover it with the remaining cheese.

5 Roll the other ball of dough into a circle the same size as the first one. Moisten the border of the first half with a wet fingertip or pastry brush. Drape the second circle of dough over the filling, lining it up with the edges. Press to seal, and pinch and roll the perimeter to make a ropelike edge.

6 Using a pastry brush, brush the top of the dough with the egg glaze. Make three short slits in the top with a serrated knife. Bake for about 35 minutes, until the top is a rich golden brown. Slide the stuffed bread onto a cooling rack and cool for 10 to 15 minutes. Slice into large wedges and serve. Refrigerate leftovers. Reheat directly on a baking sheet in a 300°F (150°C) oven for 15 to 20 minutes.

MAKES 6 TO 8 SERVINGS

Oil and cornmeal for the baking sheet and bowls

Food Processor Pizza Dough (page 107) or Hand Method Pizza Dough (page 105)

6 tablespoons-olive oil

1 large onion, quartered and thinly sliced

1 large green or red bell pepper, thinly sliced

3 garlic cloves, minced

3 cups peeled and cubed eggplant (1 medium-small)

½ teaspoon salt

Freshly ground black pepper

3 plum tomatoes, cored and coarsely chopped

½ pound fully cooked Italian sausage, in bite-size pieces

2 cups (8 ounces) grated sharp cheeses (any combination of mozzarella, provolone, Parmesan, and feta)

3–4 tablespoons pesto (page 98)

1 egg beaten with 1 teaspoon water, for glaze

NOTE: The reason we chill the dough here after it rises is to give the filling time to cool before stuffing the bread. The chilling slows the rising and makes the dough a little easier to handle. Alternatively, you could prepare and cool the filling during the dough's initial rising, then shape the bread as soon as the dough has doubled.

CABBAGE AND SAUSAGE STUFFED BUNS (BIEROCKS)

These irresistible filled buns are a pleasure to make and even more fun to eat. They're traditionally stuffed with sautéed green cabbage, but the filling can also include ground beef, sausage, mustard, and cheese; our version uses all of the above. I think the Yeasted Olive Oil Dough (page 108) makes the perfect casing, one that's not too thick or bready. This is great grab-and-go cuisine, perfect for busy weekends, tailgate parties, lunch on the run, hikes, and other activities.

1 Prepare the dough and set it aside to rise. Lightly oil a large baking sheet and dust it with cornmeal, or simply line the sheet with parchment paper.

2 Melt the butter in a large skillet. Add the onion and sauté over moderate heat for 5 minutes. Stir in the cabbage and continue to sauté for 3 to 4 minutes. Salt and pepper the cabbage lightly, then add half of the stock, cover, and reduce the heat to low. Braise the cabbage for 10 minutes. Add the remaining stock and the sausage, cover, and continue to braise until the cabbage is soft and tender. Keep an eye on the liquid in the pan. Remove the lid during the last few minutes to cook off any excess liquid. Or add a little extra, if necessary. Remove the pan from the heat, stir the vinegar and mustard into the cabbage, and set aside to cool.

3 When the dough has risen and you're ready to assemble the buns, preheat the oven to 375°F (190°C). Punch the dough down and turn it out onto a lightly floured work surface. Knead for 1 minute and divide the dough into six equal pieces. Shape them into balls and let the balls rest, loosely covered with plastic wrap, for 10 minutes.

4 Working with one piece of dough at a time, roll it into a 6½- to 7-inch circle. Place ¼ cup of the cheese in the center of the circle, leaving an approximate 1¼-inch border of dough all around. Place one-sixth of the filling on top of the cheese. Using a pastry brush, lightly moisten the outer portion of the dough border.

5 Grasp the dough on opposite side of the circle and pull two edges together over the filling, slightly stretching the dough and pinching them together at the top. Repeat in several more places, pinching opposite edges together at the top. The dough will sort of self-pleat as you go, and you'll be left with a bun that looks something like a pleated pincushion or pillow. Place it, pleated side up, on the baking sheet (see note). Repeat for the remaining buns.

MAKES 6 SERVINGS

Oil and cornmeal for the baking sheet

Yeasted Olive Oil Dough (page 108)

3 tablespoons unsalted butter

1 large onion, chopped

6 cups very thinly sliced green cabbage

Salt and freshly ground black pepper

½ cup chicken or beef stock

¼ pound fully cooked smoked sausage (beef, pork, or turkey), cut into small dice

2 teaspoons white vinegar

1 tablespoon Dijon mustard

1½ cups grated sharp cheddar cheese

1 egg beaten with 1 teaspoon milk, for glaze

Poppy or sesame seeds, for sprinkling

6 Brush the buns lightly with the egg glaze and sprinkle with seeds. Bake for 30 minutes, until golden brown. Transfer the buns to a cooling rack and cool for at least 15 minutes before serving. Refrigerate or freeze leftovers. To reheat, wrap individually in foil and place in a 350°F (180°C) oven for 15 to 20 minutes. If frozen, they'll take about twice as long to reheat.

NOTE: Filled buns like these are often baked with the pleated side down, not up the way I describe. My method might be less common, but I just love the way the pleats separate slightly as these bake, forming golden-brown ridges. Having the seam facing up also keeps them from leaking juice onto your baking sheet. Try it both ways, and see which you like best.

5

SAVORY HARVEST PIES
Quiches, Tarts, Pot Pies, and More

If you're one of those cooks who starts hyperventilating at the mere mention of making pie dough, take a deep breath and forget about any mishaps that haunt your past. You can do this. Mastering pie doughs, and by extension the pies they go with, is often less about technique than it is about (a) confidence and (b) the understanding that even if your crust isn't perfect every time, the outcome will always taste delicious. As I often tell people, some of my favorite pies have been my ugliest ones.

So proceed boldly in the knowledge that all of these pies are accessible and attainable, dishes you can serve family and friends this very week. You won't be sorry.

GOOD BASIC PIE DOUGH

Learning to make a good, basic pie dough is essential for anyone who aspires to be a well-rounded harvest baker. You always need one for sweet pies and savory ones, not to mention galettes and more. This recipe is written for a food processor, not only because that's the way I do it most often but also because it's quick and often less intimidating than doing it by hand. (For those who prefer, I do give directions, after the main recipe, for making this by hand.) If you need a top and a bottom crust for a pie, or if you want to make two deep-dish pie shells, use the Slab Pie Dough recipe on page 148.

1 Combine the flour, cornstarch, and salt in a food processor. Pulse several times to mix. Remove the lid and scatter the butter over the dry ingredients. Pulse the machine 8 to 10 times, until all of the butter is broken into small pieces, none larger than the size of a split pea.

2 Add the water through the feed tube in a 5- to 10-second stream, pulsing the machine as you add it. Stop pulsing the machine when the mixture is still fairly crumbly but starting to form larger clumps. Turn the mixture out onto your work surface and shape it into a ¾- to 1-inch-thick disk. The best way to do this and keep your hands off the dough (the warmth from your hands will make the dough sticky) is to place two long pieces of plastic wrap on your work surface, overlapping them by several inches. Dump the dough mixture in the middle, grasp and scrunch up the edges of the plastic, lift the plastic, and pull the mixture toward the center. When your hands meet in the middle, press down on the dough with your fists, to flatten it out somewhat; then move your hands around the plastic and repeat several times to make a round disk. If this sounds confusing, just remember that all you're trying to do is form a dough disk without actually touching the dough.

3 Wrap up the dough in a fresh sheet of plastic, and refrigerate for 1½ to 2 hours before rolling.

NOTE: To make this dough by hand, see page 146.

TIP: Especially in warm weather, I'll often chill the cubes of butter on a plate, and the flour, too, for about 20 minutes before mixing the dough. Starting with cold ingredients results in a dough that is less sticky and easier to work with, and it yields a crust with a flakier texture. Of course, if you have room you can store your flour right in the freezer, in which case it would already be chilled. If you store it in the paper bag it comes in, be sure to put it in a second (plastic) bag and seal it tightly so the flour doesn't absorb excess humidity. Better yet, transfer your flour to an airtight plastic container with a wide mouth. One caveat: For yeast bread, don't use flour straight from the freezer; it will inhibit the rising. Measure out what you need, and allow it to come to room temperature first.

MAKES ONE 9- TO 9½-INCH REGULAR OR DEEP-DISH PIE SHELL

- 1½ cups all-purpose flour
- 1½ teaspoons cornstarch
- ½ teaspoon salt
- ½ cup (1 stick) plus 2 tablespoons cold unsalted butter, cut into ½-inch cubes
- ⅓ cup ice-cold water

WHOLE-WHEAT PIE DOUGH

An all-whole-wheat pie dough can be tricky to work with because the coarseness of the flour makes it crumbly and difficult to roll and get into the pan. A half-whole-wheat version is much less finicky. Once you become familiar with the dough, you can start tilting the balance of flours to include more whole wheat, if you want. I sift out the coarse pieces of wheat, which might seem to contradict the whole idea of using whole-wheat flour. But it does so only marginally, since the sifter is likely to winnow out only a tablespoon or two of the really coarse stuff.

Sift or sieve 1 cup whole-wheat flour into a bowl. Measure out ¾ cup of the sifted flour, and substitute it for ¾ cup of the all-purpose flour. Proceed as above. (Save the coarse particles you sifted out, and the extra flour, and add them back to the flour bag.)

TO MAKE GOOD BASIC PIE DOUGH BY HAND

Chill the butter (see tip on page 145). Combine the flour, cornstarch, and salt in a large bowl. Mix by hand or with a whisk. Scatter the butter over the dry ingredients, tossing lightly to coat everything. Using a pastry blender, cut in the butter until it's reduced to the size of split peas or smaller. Sprinkle in the water, a tablespoon at a time, tossing with a large fork to mix. Continue adding water until everything has been dampened enough to hold together when you press the mixture between your fingers. Turn the mixture out onto your work surface, shape into a disk, and refrigerate for 1½ to 2 hours before rolling.

OAT AND CORNMEAL PIE DOUGH

I don't mean to sound like an ancient relic, but about 25 years after this recipe first appeared in one of my early books, I got a message — through LinkedIn, no less — from a woman who told me that this was her favorite piecrust recipe of all time. Seems she once owned a bakery and had used this dough to make all of her pies. I was glad to be reminded what a very good crust this is — grainy, wholesome, and delicious. It's adaptable, too, as suitable for summer fruit pies as it is for savory pies. Be advised that whole-grain pie doughs are typically a little trickier to work with than those made entirely from all-purpose flour. The grittiness of the grain can cause cracking, but you can minimize it if you don't chill the dough too long before rolling it. The basic recipe makes enough for a single crust (one large pie shell). Instructions for a double crust follow.

1 Put the oats and cornmeal in a food processor. Pulse the machine, repeatedly, until the oats are very finely ground. It will never look like fine flour, more like a gritty meal. Still, get it fairly fine, then add the flour, sugar (if desired), and salt. Pulse again several times to mix.

2 Remove the lid and scatter the butter over the dry ingredients. Pulse the machine six to eight times, until the butter is broken into split pea–size pieces.

3 Put the egg yolk in a 1-cup glass measure, and add enough cold water to equal ⅓ cup. Blend with a fork. Add the liquid through the feed tube, in a 6- to 8-second stream, pulsing the machine as you add it; once all the water has been added, you'll only need to process for another few seconds. The dough should come together in clumps but not ball up around the blade. It will probably seem a bit moister than other food processor doughs you've made, which is fine.

4 Turn the dough out onto a large sheet of plastic wrap and form it into a thick mound. Grab the sides of the plastic and use it to help you shape and flatten the dough into a disk about ½ inch thick. Wrap the dough up in the plastic, and refrigerate for about 1 hour before rolling. If the dough becomes too cold-firm, it will have a tendency to crack. It's fine to make the dough and refrigerate it for several hours, or even a day ahead, but you'll need to remove it from the fridge about 15 minutes before you plan to roll it.

To make a double crust: Double all of the ingredients. Grind the oats and cornmeal as above. Add the flour, sugar (if desired), and salt, and pulse to mix. Add all of the butter (1 cup) at once, and pulse until the fat is broken into split pea–size pieces. Add both egg yolks to your measuring cup, and add enough cold water to equal ⅔ cup liquid; blend with a fork. Add as above, in an 8- to 10-second stream. After turning the dough out, divide it in half before shaping into disks. If you're using the dough to make a double-crust pie, and not two pie shells, make one of the halves — for the bottom crust — slightly larger than the other.

MAKES ONE 9- TO 9½-INCH REGULAR OR DEEP-DISH PIE SHELL

- ¼ cup old-fashioned rolled oats or quick oats
- ¼ cup fine yellow cornmeal
- 1 cup all-purpose flour
- 2 teaspoons sugar (optional); omit if you're making a savory pie
- ½ teaspoon salt
- ½ cup (1 stick) cold unsalted butter, cut into ½-inch cubes
- 1 egg yolk
- ¼ cup (approximately) cold water

SLAB PIE DOUGH (AND SHELL)

Slab pies, which can be sweet or savory, have caught on in popularity over the last few years. I don't know who first coined the term *slab pie*, but it's a fitting description for a pie that looks more like a board or plank and less like your basic wheel. If there's a bit of a challenge to assembling a slab pie, it's getting the oversized dough rolled out and into the pan without incident. If you prefer, this can be done in two stages by halving the dough and rolling the pieces separately (see Tip #1). It's important to use the right jelly roll pan here, one that's 15 by 10 inches and 1 inch high. Unless the sides are a full 1 inch, your fillings are likely to spill over the sides.

1 Combine the flour, confectioners' sugar (or cornstarch), and salt in a mixing bowl. Whisk briefly to combine, then refrigerate for 20 to 30 minutes. Put the butter cubes on a plate, and refrigerate along with the flour mixture. Butter a 15- by 10- by 1-inch jelly roll pan very lightly with soft butter. If it is a nonstick pan, no buttering is necessary.

2 When you're ready to mix the dough, transfer the dry ingredients to a food processor; pulse several times to mix. Remove the lid and scatter all the butter over the dry ingredients. Pulse the machine 10 to 12 times, until the butter is broken into split pea–size pieces.

3 Add half of the water through the feed tube in an approximate 5-second stream, pulsing the machine repeatedly as you pour. Stop the machine, remove the lid, and fluff the mixture with a fork, pulling it up from the bottom. This loosens the mixture; the machine tends to compact it. Replace the lid, and add most of the remaining liquid in the same manner, pulsing as you add it. When you still have a couple of tablespoons of water left, remove the lid and check the dough; it should hold together easily when you press it between your fingers. If it's still quite crumbly, add the remaining water and pulse a few more times. By now the dough should be coming together in good-size clumps.

4 Dump the mixture out onto a lightly floured work surface. Shape and compact the dough into a rectangle roughly 1¼ inches thick. Tear off a sheet of plastic wrap about 24 inches long. Flour it lightly, and put the dough in the center of it. Dust the top of the dough with flour, and gently — because the dough will be soft — roll it out a little bit to increase the size of the rectangle. It should still be pretty thick, perhaps ¾ inch. This is simply a preliminary rolling/shaping to take the dough a step in the right direction. Square up the sides and corners as best you can to make it easier to roll out a rectangle later. Wrap the dough up in the plastic, slide it onto a small baking sheet, and refrigerate for at least 2 hours. Longer is fine.

MAKES 1 LARGE SLAB PIE SHELL

Butter for the pan

3 cups all-purpose flour

2 tablespoons confectioners' sugar (for sweet pies) or 2 tablespoons cornstarch (for savory pies)

1 teaspoon salt

1¼ cups (2½ sticks) cold unsalted butter, cut into ½-inch cubes

½–⅔ cup cold water

5 When you're ready to roll the dough, unwrap it and dust the top lightly with flour. Invert the dough onto a 24-inch-long sheet of waxed paper; you could also use a fresh piece of plastic wrap or parchment paper if you prefer. Roll out the dough into an 18- by 13-inch rectangle. Invert it into the pan, or slide it in. Center it, and tuck the dough into the pan so it fits like a glove. If you have excess dough hanging over, fold it and press it against the sides to beef up the edge of the pastry. Refrigerate the shell for at least 1 hour, or freeze for 30 minutes, before filling and baking. Keep it cold until right before filling.

To make a double crust for a 9- to 9½-inch deep-dish pie: Do not prepare the jelly roll pan. Chill the ingredients as described in step 1, then follow the recipe through step 3. Empty the dough mixture onto your work counter and shape into two thick disks, one of them — for the bottom crust — slightly larger than the other. Wrap in plastic wrap and refrigerate for at least 1½ to 2 hours before rolling.

To make the dough by hand: If you would rather make the dough by hand, proceed as above, but refrigerate the flour mixture and butter for only 15 minutes. Add the butter to the dry ingredients. Using a pastry blender, cut in the butter until it is broken into split pea–size pieces. Sprinkle in half of the water and lightly mix it in with a fork. Repeat, adding another 2 tablespoons of water. Add the remaining water, about 1 tablespoon at a time, as needed, mixing the dough until it forms crumbs that just hold together when pressed between your fingers. Shape, refrigerate, and roll as above.

TIP #1: If you'd rather not work with such a big piece of dough all at once, divide the dough in half and shape each half into a thick rectangle. Using the same approach as in step 4, lightly roll the dough into two thick rectangles. Wrap, and refrigerate them for 1½ to 2 hours. Roll each one into an 11- by 8½-inch rectangle. Place them in the pan so that they overlap in the middle; press to seal, and proceed as above.

TIP #2: For slightly easier rolling, and a more tender dough, substitute 4 tablespoons cold Crisco for the ½ stick of butter. Use spoonful-size pieces and add them to the processor along with the butter.

CRISCO AND LARD

A little Crisco or lard can do nice things for a piecrust. I often replace a little of the butter with one or the other, and I like the result very much. Both act like muscle relaxants for the dough and make it easier to roll. They also improve the texture of the crust, adding a bit of durability and desirable flakiness. If you want to experiment, start by substituting 2 tablespoons cold Crisco or lard for an equal amount of butter. Add it when you add the butter, and proceed with the recipe.

TURNOVER DOUGH

We use this dough to make a variety of savory hand pies or turnovers, including the Vegetable and Beef Hand Pies (page 208) and Spiced Eggplant and Lentil Turnovers (page 201). It's an anomaly within the greater pie pastry genre in that the ingredients are more thoroughly combined than normal, and therefore the dough can tolerate, and indeed benefits from, a bit of handling. (It's actually kneaded.) The majority of the fat here is lard, for flaky texture, with a smaller proportion of butter for flavor. It's a combination that's hard to beat.

1 Combine the flour and salt in a large bowl. Add the lard and butter and toss everything by hand to coat the fat with flour. Using a pastry blender, cut the fat thoroughly into the flour until the mixture resembles a coarse meal or cracker crumbs.

2 Whisk the egg, water, and vinegar in a separate small bowl until frothy. Make a well in the middle of the dry mixture and add the liquid. Using a large fork, start mixing from the center out, until everything is dampened, lifting and gently tossing with your fork and scraping along the bottom of the bowl. When the dough is still a shaggy mass, dive in with your hands and begin to gently squeeze and knead the dough until it coheres and forms large clumps.

3 Turn the dough out onto your work counter and continue to work it, pressing it together and kneading lightly for a couple of minutes, until the dough is smooth and holds together easily without cracking. Place the dough on a sheet of plastic wrap and wrap it up snugly.

4 Refrigerate the dough for at least an hour; it will behave better, when you roll it, if it has had time to chill and rest.

MAKES ENOUGH FOR 5 OR 6 LARGE HAND PIES OR UP TO 12 SMALLER ONES

- 3 cups all-purpose flour
- 1¼ teaspoons salt
- ½ cup (4 ounces) lard
- 4 tablespoons cold unsalted butter, cut into small cubes (½ inch or smaller)
- 1 large egg
- ⅓ cup cold water
- 2 teaspoons white vinegar

ZUCCHINI TACO PIE

This is, without apology, one of those "hide the veggies" dishes that's a staple in magazines for families with young children, the little critters who often thwart our best efforts to feed them a healthy diet. If you can relate, I'm almost certain you'll achieve acclaim and critical success with this dish. Dicing the zucchini and mixing it with ground beef and taco seasoning gives this savory pie filling kid credibility and broad appeal. And while I don't use taco seasoning mix all that much, it serves a useful purpose here. Serve with guacamole and chips, or a green salad and ranch dressing. If you're looking for a meatless harvest pie that's somewhat similar to this one, I recommend the Meatless Tostada Pot Pies on page 203.

1 Prepare the pie dough as for a double-crust pie, separating it into a larger and smaller disk. Refrigerate for at least 1½ to 2 hours before rolling.

2 On a sheet of lightly floured waxed paper, roll the larger portion of dough into a 13-inch circle. Invert the pastry over a 9- or 9½-inch deep-dish pie pan, center it, and peel off the paper. Gently tuck the pastry into the pan without stretching it, letting the edge of the pastry drape over the sides of the pan. Refrigerate while you prepare the filling.

3 Heat the olive oil in a large skillet. Add the onion and sauté for 5 minutes over medium heat. Stir in the zucchini and carrot; salt and pepper lightly. Cook the vegetables for 6 to 7 minutes, stirring often, until they're tender.

4 Heat a separate nonstick skillet. Add the beef and cook over medium heat, stirring often, until cooked through. Drain off most of the fat, then add the beef to the vegetables, along with the diced tomato, seasoning mix, and water. Bring to a simmer and cook, stirring, for a minute or so, until saucy and thick. Remove from the heat and let cool.

5 Preheat the oven to 375°F (190°C). Sprinkle the refrigerated pie shell with ½ cup of the cheese. Stir the remaining 1 cup cheese and sour cream into the filling. Transfer the filling to the pie shell and smooth the top with a spoon. Moisten the edge of the pie shell with a wet fingertip or pastry brush.

6 Roll the other half of the dough into a 10-inch circle. Drape it over the filling and press the edges of the pastry together to seal. Using a paring knife, trim the excess dough flush with the edge of the pan. Crimp the edge with a fork, and use the fork to poke the top pastry several times to make steam vents. Brush the top with the egg glaze.

7 Bake the pie for 45 to 50 minutes, until the top crust is golden brown. You may also see juice bubbling up through the fork holes. Transfer the pie to a rack and cool for at least 30 minutes before serving. Refrigerate leftovers. Reheat slices on a baking sheet, in a 300°F (150°C) oven, for about 15 minutes.

MAKES 6 TO 8 SERVINGS

Slab Pie Dough (page 148), prepared as for a double-crust pie

3 tablespoons olive oil

1 large onion, chopped

3½ cups finely diced zucchini

½ cup finely diced carrot

Salt and freshly ground black pepper

1 pound ground beef

1 cup seeded and finely diced tomato

1 (1-ounce) packet taco seasoning mix

¾ cup water

1½ cups grated cheddar or Monterey Jack cheese

2 tablespoons sour cream or ranch dressing

1 egg, lightly beaten, for glaze

Tomato Time

When was the last time you experienced the true deliciousness of a fresh tomato — at once sweet and acidic, kissed by warm rains and sunshine and the lingering aroma of damp soil? It was last summer, right? Or this one, if you're lucky.

Summertime is tomato time. These fruits don't travel well across miles or time, and their flavor has a direct correlation to their distance from your kitchen. Is it any wonder that tomatoes are always at the top of our list of favorite homegrown veggies?

It comes down to 6 to 8 weeks of authentic tomato flavor — 6 to 8 weeks of tomato and mozzarella salads, gazpacho, tomato sandwiches, homemade marinara sauce, baked stuffed tomatoes, and, of course, tomato pies and tarts. The trick is to get your fill while you can, because after that it's 10 months of soulless tomatoes from who-knows-where.

In theory I have no use for winter tomatoes from the supermarket. In practice I buy my share, but almost never the softball-size pink ones; they're beyond help. The smaller ones — the cherry and grape tomatoes, and even some with the vines attached — seem to fare better in flavor and texture. It helps to slice them in half and toss them with a pinch of sugar and salt and a splash of lemon juice. They still won't taste like the real deal, but they'll do until next summer.

CREAMY BUFFALO CHICKEN, TOMATO, AND CORN PIE

This is perhaps the most delicious thing you will ever put in your mouth, according to my wife, Bev, who after 15 years with me and the creation of numerous cookbooks is getting harder and harder to impress. So I take that as quite a compliment. One thing is for sure: this dinner pie isn't for the faint of palate. The combination of blue cheese, buffalo wing sauce, ranch seasoning, and garlic makes for quite a bold statement, tempered beautifully by the chicken and vegetables. Summer is clearly the best season for making this pie, but it's hearty and rich enough to serve in the dead of winter, too, using frozen corn kernels and the best long-distance tomatoes you can get your hands on.

1 Prepare the pie dough, and refrigerate it for at least 1½ to 2 hours before rolling.

2 On a sheet of lightly floured waxed paper, roll the dough into a 13-inch circle. Invert the pastry over a 9- or 9½-inch deep-dish pie pan, center it, and peel off the paper. Gently tuck the pastry into the pan without stretching it. Sculpt the overhanging dough into an upstanding ridge; flute the edges, if desired. Refrigerate for at least 1 hour, or place in the freezer for 30 minutes.

3 Preheat the oven to 400°F (200°C). Bring a small saucepan of salted water to a boil. Add the corn kernels and boil for 5 minutes. Remove from the heat and drain. Core the tomatoes and slice them thinly. (Don't seed them; you'll need the moisture for this pie.)

4 Combine the cream cheese, blue cheese, mayonnaise, onion, buffalo wing sauce, ranch seasoning, and garlic in a bowl. Stir well.

5 To assemble the pie, sprinkle all the cheddar over the bottom of the piecrust. Cover with half of the chicken, half of the corn, and half of the tomato slices, and salt and pepper the tomatoes lightly. Spread half of the creamy mixture over the tomatoes. Repeat the layering one more time — chicken, corn, and tomato slices — and finish with the remaining creamy mixture.

6 Bake the pie for 35 minutes. While the pie bakes, put the cracker crumbs in a small bowl. Add the butter and rub them together thoroughly.

7 After 35 minutes, reduce the heat to 375°F (190°C). Slide out the pie and spread the cracker crumbs evenly over the top. Bake for another 20 to 25 minutes, covering the pie with aluminum foil if the crumbs start to become too brown. When the pie is done, you should be able to see the creamy pie juices bubbling up here and there through the crumbs. Transfer the pie to a cooling rack and cool for 20 to 30 minutes before slicing. Refrigerate leftovers. Reheat leftover slices right in the pan, in a 300°F (150°C) oven, for about 15 minutes.

MAKES 8 SERVINGS

Good Basic Pie Dough (page 145)

2 cups corn kernels, fresh or frozen

2 medium-size ripe tomatoes

4 ounces cream cheese, well softened

1 cup crumbled blue cheese

⅔ cup mayonnaise

½ cup minced red onion

⅓ cup buffalo wing sauce

1 tablespoon ranch seasoning mix (the powdered kind, in a packet)

2 garlic cloves, minced

1 cup grated sharp cheddar cheese

2 cups finely chopped cooked chicken

Salt and freshly ground black pepper

1 cup fine plain cracker crumbs

2 tablespoons unsalted butter, softened

FRESH TOMATO PIE WITH GARDEN PESTO

You could spin the tomato pie idea a hundred different ways, but even then you'd be hard-pressed to improve on this rendition. It's influenced less by traditional Southern recipes for tomato pie than it is by good old pizza margherita; indeed, I often refer to it as "pizza in a pastry," a thick layer of tomatoes covered with a golden, melted-cheesy topping. We take the extra step of peeling the tomatoes, whose skins would otherwise become papery-chewy when cooked. I can't say I've never cheated and prepared this with questionable winter tomatoes, but it's hardly worth the effort. Save it for summer.

1 Prepare the pie dough, and refrigerate it for at least 1½ to 2 hours before rolling.

2 On a sheet of lightly floured waxed paper, roll the dough into a 13-inch circle. Invert the pastry over a 9- or 9½-inch deep-dish pie pan, center it, and peel off the paper. Gently tuck the pastry into the pan. Sculpt the overhanging dough into an upstanding ridge; flute the edges, if desired. Refrigerate for at least 1 hour, or place in the freezer for 30 minutes.

3 Preheat the oven to 375°F (190°C). Prick the bottom of the pie shell six or seven times with a fork. Tear off a sheet of aluminum foil about 16 inches long. Gently line the pie shell with the foil, pressing it into the creases so it fits like a glove. Add a thick layer of dried beans, banking them up the sides.

4 Bake the pie shell for 25 minutes. Slide it out and carefully remove the foil and beans. Repoke the holes if they've filled in. Slide the shell back in and bake for another 6 to 8 minutes. Transfer the pie shell to a cooling rack. (Once it is cooled, dab a little cream cheese or sour cream into the fork holes to plug them.)

5 Core the tomatoes and halve them crosswise. Gently squeeze out the pulp, and cut each half into bite-size chunks. Put 3 cups of the chunks into a colander placed over a large bowl. (Use any excess tomato in another dish.) Salt the tomatoes liberally, and set aside for about an hour to drain.

6 Melt the butter in a large skillet. Add the onions and cook over low heat until caramelized, stirring often, about 20 minutes.

7 Stir the mayonnaise in a large bowl until smooth. Add the cheddar, Parmesan, and black pepper. Mix gently, just to combine; the mixture will be dense and clumpy.

8 Preheat the oven to 375°F (190°C) when you're ready to assemble the pie. Sprinkle the bread crumbs evenly in the pie shell. Lift the tomatoes out of the colander, give them a gentle squeeze, and arrange the chunks evenly in the pie shell. Scatter the onions over the tomatoes, then dollop them with the pesto. Using your hands, distribute the cheese mixture in small clumps evenly over the tomatoes.

MAKES 8 SERVINGS

Good Basic Pie Dough (page 145)

4 large ripe tomatoes, peeled (see page 156)

Salt

3 tablespoons unsalted butter

2 large onions, halved and sliced

¾ cup mayonnaise

1½ cups grated sharp cheddar cheese

½ cup finely grated Parmesan cheese

⅛ teaspoon freshly ground black pepper

1½ tablespoons Italian-style bread crumbs

2–3 tablespoons pesto (page 98)

9 Bake the pie for 30 minutes, then reduce the heat to 350°F (180°C) and bake for another 20 to 25 minutes, until golden brown and bubbly. Transfer the pie to a rack and cool for at least 30 minutes before serving.

AN EASY WAY TO PEEL TOMATOES

Fill a large saucepan two-thirds full of water, and bring to a boil. Meanwhile, using a sharp serrated knife, cut a very shallow X on the bottom of the tomatoes. Using a strainer or tongs, lower the tomatoes into the boiling water. Count to 20, remove the tomatoes, and place them in a bowl or on a cutting board. After a minute or so, you'll notice that the skins have shriveled and loosened near the cuts. When the tomatoes are cool enough to handle, peel off and discard the skins before proceeding with your recipe. Note that some cooks place the tomatoes in a bowl of ice water as they come out of the boiling water, to help stop the cooking, but it's not necessary when preparing Fresh Tomato Pie (page 154).

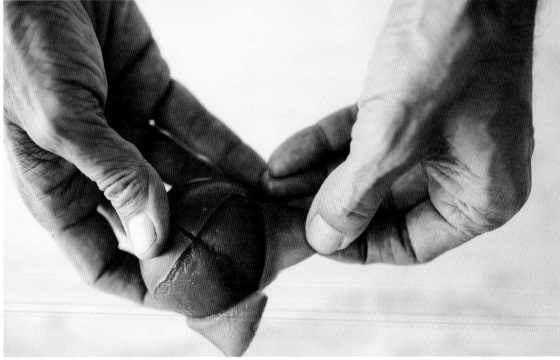

CHERRY TOMATO, BACON, AND BLUE CHEESE TART

This combination sounds like the start of a delicious salad or favorite sandwich, but it's actually the lineup for a spectacular summer tart, perfect for company or any other special occasion. Just add a fresh cucumber salad and corn on the cob. Notice that there's no egg to bind the ingredients. Rather, cheeses and cream meld together and form a bacon-infused sauce that both thickens the tart and blankets the tomatoes in flavor.

1 Prepare the pie dough, and refrigerate it for 1½ to 2 hours before rolling.

2 On a sheet of lightly floured waxed paper, roll the dough into a 12- to 12½-inch circle. Invert the pastry over a 9½-inch fluted tart pan, preferably one with a removable bottom. Center the dough, then peel off the paper. Carefully, so you don't cut the dough on the edge of the pan, tuck the pastry into the pan. Fold over any overhanging dough, and press it against the sides to beef them up. Refrigerate for at least 1 hour, or place in the freezer for 30 minutes.

3 Preheat the oven to 375°F (190°C). Prick the bottom of the pie shell six or seven times with a fork. Tear off a sheet of aluminum foil about 14 inches long. Gently line the tart shell with the foil, pressing it into the creases so it fits like a glove. Add a thick layer of dried beans, banking them up the sides. Place the pan on a rimmed baking sheet.

4 Bake the tart shell for 25 minutes. Slide it out and carefully remove the foil and beans. Repoke the holes if they've filled in. Slide the shell back in and bake for another 6 to 8 minutes. Transfer the baking sheet and shell to a cooling rack. (Once the shell is cooled, dab a little cream cheese or sour cream into the fork holes to plug them.)

5 Preheat the oven to 375°F (190°C). Line a large rimmed baking sheet with parchment paper or foil and oil it lightly. Mound the halved cherry tomatoes in the middle of the sheet, drizzle with the olive oil, and spread the tomatoes out in a single layer. Salt and pepper lightly. Roast for about 25 minutes, until soft and juicy. Transfer to a rack and cool.

6 Heat a medium skillet, preferably nonstick. Add the bacon and cook until crisp; remove the bacon to a plate. Add the onions to the skillet and sauté for 2 minutes, no longer. Remove the pan from the heat, leaving the onions in the pan.

7 Preheat the oven to 375°F (190°C) when you're ready to assemble and bake the tart. Sprinkle the Parmesan evenly in the tart shell. Cover the Parmesan with the tomatoes, spreading them around evenly. Crumble the bacon over the tomatoes, then scatter the onions. Crumble the blue cheese over everything, pressing the chunks down into the filling. Drizzle the cream evenly over the filling. Bake the tart on the rimmed sheet for about 45 minutes, until the tart is bubbly and golden brown. Transfer to a rack and cool to lukewarm before serving.

MAKES 8 SERVINGS

Oil for the parchment paper

Whole-Wheat Pie Dough (page 145)

1 generous pint ripe cherry tomatoes, halved

1½ tablespoons olive oil

Salt and freshly ground black pepper

4 bacon strips

1 large onion, chopped

2 tablespoons finely grated Parmesan cheese

5–6 ounces blue cheese

⅓ cup heavy cream

RICE AND SUMMER SQUASH PIE

Like a lot of folks these days, my wife and I eat our share of rice and other grains, so we're always on the lookout for clever ways to use up the leftovers. (Even next-day stir-fried rice loses its charm after a while.) One possibility you might not have considered is using these leftover grains, along with one or more veggies, to bulk up your dinner pies. Among my favorites in this category are the savory pies made with yellow summer squashes and zucchini. Either can be successfully used here in what is essentially a savory rice pudding in a crust. I especially like it with the whole-wheat crust.

1 Prepare the pie dough, and refrigerate it for at least 1½ to 2 hours before rolling.

2 On a sheet of lightly floured waxed paper, roll the dough into a 13-inch circle. Invert the pastry over a 9- or 9½-inch deep-dish pie pan, center it, and peel off the paper. Gently tuck the pastry into the pan without stretching it. Sculpt the overhanging dough into an upstanding ridge; flute the edges, if desired. Refrigerate for at least 1 hour, or place in the freezer for 30 minutes.

3 Preheat the oven to 375°F (190°C). Prick the bottom of the pie shell six or seven times with a fork. Tear off a sheet of aluminum foil about 16 inches long. Gently line the pie shell with the foil, pressing it into the creases so it fits like a glove. Add a thick layer of dried beans, banking them up the sides.

4 Bake the pie shell for 25 minutes. Slide it out and carefully remove the foil and beans. Repoke the holes if they've filled in. Slide the shell back in and bake for another 6 to 8 minutes. Transfer the pie shell to a cooling rack. (Once it's cooled, dab a little cream cheese or sour cream into the fork holes to plug them.)

5 Using the large holes on a box grater, grate enough of the squash to make about 3 cups. Scoop up the squash and squeeze it between your palms to express most of the liquid. Measure out 2½ cups of the squash; that's how much you'll need.

6 Melt the butter in a large skillet. Stir in the onion and sauté for 7 to 8 minutes, until clear. Then stir in the garlic and squash. Add a bit of salt and pepper. Cook, stirring, for 1 to 2 minutes, just long enough to wilt the squash. Remove from the heat.

7 Put the rice in a large bowl. Add the squash and toss gently to combine. When the mixture has cooled, add the cheddar, parsley, and dill, and toss gently to combine.

MAKES 8 SERVINGS

	Whole-Wheat Pie Dough (page 145) or Good Basic Pie Dough (page 145)
2 or 3	small summer squashes
3	tablespoons unsalted butter
1	large onion, chopped
2	garlic cloves, minced
	Salt and freshly ground black pepper
2	cups cooked rice, quinoa, or couscous
1½	cups grated sharp cheddar cheese or other melting cheese
2–3	tablespoons chopped fresh parsley
1	tablespoon chopped fresh dill
3	large eggs
1¼	cups half-and-half or milk
2	teaspoons Dijon mustard
⅓	cup grated Parmesan cheese

8 In a separate bowl, whisk the eggs until frothy, then whisk in the half-and-half, mustard, ½ teaspoon salt, and ¼ teaspoon black pepper. Pour this custard over the rice mixture and stir to combine. Pour the filling into the partially prebaked shell. Sprinkle the Parmesan over the top.

9 Bake the pie for about 45 minutes, until the top is golden brown. The custard should be set, with no sign of uncooked egg in the center. Transfer the pie to a cooling rack and cool for at least 30 minutes before serving. Refrigerate leftovers. Reheat leftovers on a baking sheet, loosely covered with foil, for 12 to 15 minutes in a 300°F (150°C) oven.

ABOUT THOSE DRIED BEANS

I've always used dried beans to weigh down my pie shells when I prebake them. The weight of the beans keeps the crust from puffing up while it bakes. I like to push or bank the beans high up the sides of the pan to keep the sides of the pastry from drooping.

The beans and the foil lining are removed from the shell late in the prebaking, after the shell has set and is able to hold its own shape. You don't even have to remove the pie shell from the oven when you do this. Just slide out the oven rack and gently lift out the foil with the beans in it. (The foil usually cools down quickly when you slide out the rack; you may not even need oven mitts to lift it.) Then slide the shell back in the oven for a few more minutes to complete the prebaking.

Don't throw away those beans after you use them — they can be used repeatedly for the same purpose (but not for eating, as they won't take up water after being baked). Let them cool completely, right in the foil, and transfer them to a jar. Seal the jar and store until next time. By the way, larger beans, such as dried kidney or black beans, are a better choice than small beans, such as lentils, in case one winds up in the shell; the big ones are easier to spot.

GREEN PEA AND PARMESAN CHEESE TARTLETS

When I was a kid, green peas were a form of torture inflicted once a week by my mother, who was so busy managing a dinner table for nine that she rarely noticed that mine wound up on the kitchen floor or upended onto my sister Joanne's plate (Joanne is the family's Patron Saint of Pea Haters). Eventually, the relationship between peas and me warmed, but only after I discovered that peas have more appeal when they're all dressed up. These little tarts are about as dressy as it gets: a pea purée flavored with Parmesan, onion, and garlic, tucked inside little baked shells. They're dusted with more Parmesan and warmed just before serving, the perfect little harvest appetizer. There's a bit of hand work and detail here, but it's well worth the effort.

1 Prepare the pie dough, and refrigerate it for at least 1½ to 2 hours before rolling.

2 Lightly butter a standard-size 12-cup muffin pan. Cut 12 strips of waxed paper, ¼ inch wide and 5 inches long, and lay one in and across each cup, leaving tabs of equal length on either side. You'll use these tabs later to loosen the shells.

3 When the pastry is ready, roll it ⅛ inch thick, about the same you would for a pie dough. Using a 3-inch round biscuit cutter, and working quickly so the dough doesn't warm too much, cut the dough into 12 rounds. (You may have to overlap and press the trimmings together and then cut a few more to get 12.) Tuck the rounds evenly into the shells, carefully pressing without stretching the dough. It helps to use something to press them with, like a spice jar, so they go in evenly. Poke each shell bottom twice with a fork. Freeze the pan for 20 to 30 minutes, until the shells are firm. Preheat the oven to 375°F (190°C).

4 Have ready 12 paper muffin-cup liners, and press one into each shell. Fill each one with enough dried beans to reach the top of the shell. Bake for 20 minutes. Lift out the liners and beans. If the shells don't appear to be fully baked, with a light golden hue, lower the heat to 300°F (150°C) and put them back in the oven without the beans for another 5 minutes. When they're done baking, transfer the pan to a cooling rack. Cool thoroughly, then gently lift up on the tabs to loosen the shells, but leave them in the pan for now.

5 Heat 2 tablespoons of the olive oil in a large skillet. Add the onion and sauté over moderate heat for 7 to 8 minutes. Stir in the garlic, cook another 30 seconds, and add the peas and ¼ cup of the stock. Salt lightly, and add pepper to taste. Cover the skillet and steam the peas for 5 minutes, stirring occasionally. If you're using fresh peas, they'll probably need more time and additional stock. When the peas are tender, remove from the heat, uncover, and cool for 15 minutes.

MAKES 12 TARTLETS

Butter for the muffin pan

Good Basic Pie Dough (page 145)

4–5 tablespoons light olive oil

¾ cup finely chopped onion

2 garlic cloves, minced

3 cups fresh or frozen peas

¼ cup chicken stock or water, plus more if needed

Salt and freshly ground black pepper

½ cup finely grated Parmesan cheese, plus a little more for sprinkling on top

1 tablespoon unsalted butter, softened

½ teaspoon lemon juice

6 Combine the peas, ½ cup Parmesan, butter, lemon juice, and 2 tablespoons olive oil in a food processor. Process to a fairly smooth purée, adding more salt and pepper as needed. If the purée needs a little moisture, add more water or stock 1 teaspoon at a time.

7 About 20 minutes before serving, preheat the oven to 325°F (170°C). Remove the shells from the pan, and spread enough pea purée in each one to reach the top of the shell. Arrange them on a baking sheet. Dust each one with grated Parmesan, and drizzle sparingly with olive oil. Warm in the oven for 12 to 15 minutes. Transfer to a serving plate and serve warm.

EGGPLANT, TOMATO, AND SAUSAGE PIE

I think eggplant is one of our most versatile but sadly underappreciated vegetables. Beyond eggplant Parmesan, it rarely grabs the headlines in our kitchens. But eggplant represents a world of opportunity for the harvest baker, and here's a good example. We begin with a sort of thick stew made with eggplant, Italian sausage, and tomatoes. That goes into our pie shell first, then it's topped off, moussaka-style, with a Parmesan-flavored white sauce. If it sounds like a bit of work, it is. But it yields the sort of oh-my, I-never-ate-anything-half-this-good dividends you just don't get every day. Serve with steamed broccoli or sautéed broccoli rabe.

1 Prepare the pie dough, and refrigerate it for at least 1½ to 2 hours before rolling.

2 On a sheet of lightly floured waxed paper, roll the dough into a 13-inch circle. Invert the pastry over a 9- or 9½-inch deep-dish pie pan, center it, and peel off the paper. Gently tuck the pastry into the pan without stretching it. Sculpt the overhanging dough into an upstanding ridge; flute the edges, if desired. Refrigerate for at least 1 hour, or place in the freezer for 30 minutes.

3 Heat 2 tablespoons of the olive oil in a large skillet. Add the onion and sauté for 5 minutes over medium heat. Break up the sausage meat and add it to the skillet. Cook for 2 to 3 minutes, stirring, then add the remaining 2 tablespoons oil, eggplant, garlic, salt, and pepper to taste. Stir in the basil and thyme.

4 Cover the skillet and cook over medium heat for 6 to 8 minutes, stirring occasionally, until all of the eggplant is soft. Push the eggplant and sausage to the edge of the pan with a wooden spoon, and add the tomatoes to the middle of the skillet. Cook for 2 minutes, stirring occasionally. Stir the vinegar into the tomatoes, then remove from the heat.

5 Preheat the oven to 375°F (190°C). For the Parmesan topping, melt the butter in a medium saucepan; whisk in the flour and paprika. Whisk over medium heat for 1 minute, then whisk in the milk and simmer for 1 to 2 minutes, until thickened. Salt and pepper the sauce to taste, and whisk in the Parmesan. Simmer gently for 30 seconds, then remove from the heat.

6 Sprinkle the cornmeal evenly in the cold pie shell. Spoon in the eggplant and sausage. Top with the tomatoes and smooth them with a spoon. Pour the Parmesan sauce evenly over the tomatoes and smooth it out, too. (You may need to reheat it gently, with a bit more milk, to make it thick and pourable.)

7 Bake the pie for 45 to 50 minutes, until the crust and topping are a rich golden brown. Transfer to a cooling rack and cool for at least 30 minutes before serving. Refrigerate leftovers. Reheat slices, loosely wrapped in foil, in a 300°F (150°C) oven for about 15 minutes.

MAKES 8 SERVINGS

Good Basic Pie Dough (page 145)

4 tablespoons light olive oil

1 large onion, chopped

½ pound uncooked Italian sausage meat (without casings)

5 cups peeled and cubed eggplant (1 medium-large)

2 garlic cloves, minced

½ teaspoon salt

Freshly ground black pepper

1 tablespoon chopped fresh basil

2 teaspoons chopped fresh thyme or oregano

1 large tomato, cored, seeded, and coarsely chopped

1½ teaspoons balsamic vinegar

1 tablespoon yellow cornmeal, for sprinkling in the shell

PARMESAN CHEESE TOPPING

2 tablespoons unsalted butter

2 tablespoons all-purpose flour

⅛ teaspoon smoked paprika or paprika

1¼ cups milk or half-and-half

Salt and freshly ground black pepper

½ cup grated Parmesan cheese

NOTE: The cornmeal in the shell helps absorb moisture that might otherwise saturate the bottom crust. For additional insurance you can sprinkle 1 cup grated melting cheese, such as mozzarella or cheddar, over the cornmeal.

COLLARD, QUINOA, AND SAUSAGE DINNER PIE WITH SESAME SEEDED CRUST

This delicious dinner is made with quinoa, but you could just as easily use leftover rice, bulgur, or couscous. The grain is combined with another favorite of mine, braised collard greens, and also turkey sausage. Eggs, cottage cheese, and cheddar cheese help bind the pie, but this is much less like an eggy quiche and more like a savory rice and veggie pudding. It's great just the way it is, but I sometimes sprinkle panko bread crumbs on top and dot it with butter about 10 minutes before it comes out of the oven to make the top nice and crispy. Seeding your crust is a neat touch; you'll want to try it on some of your other pies, too.

1 Prepare the pie dough, and refrigerate it for at least 1½ to 2 hours before rolling.

2 On a sheet of lightly floured waxed paper, roll the dough into a 12½-inch circle. Sprinkle evenly with the seeds, and roll over them with your pin to embed them and make a 13-inch circle. Invert the pastry over a 9- or 9½-inch deep-dish pie pan, center it, and peel off the paper. Gently tuck the pastry into the pan without stretching it. Sculpt the overhanging dough into an upstanding ridge; flute the edges, if desired. Refrigerate for at least 1 hour, or place in the freezer for 30 minutes.

3 Preheat the oven to 375°F (190°C). Prick the bottom of the pie shell six or seven times with a fork. Tear off a sheet of aluminum foil about 16 inches long. Gently line the pie shell with the foil, pressing it into the creases so it fits like a glove. Add a thick layer of dried beans, banking them up the sides.

4 Bake the pie shell for 25 minutes. Slide it out and carefully remove the foil and beans. Repoke the holes if they've filled in. Slide the shell back in and bake for another 6 to 8 minutes. Transfer the pie shell to a cooling rack. (Once it's cooled, dab a little cream cheese or sour cream into the fork holes to plug them.)

5 Heat the olive oil in a large skillet or sauté pan. Add the bacon and cook over moderate heat for 4 to 5 minutes, stirring occasionally, until the bacon renders a good deal of fat. Add the onion and sauté for 7 to 8 minutes. Stir in the collards and garlic, cook for 2 minutes, and add the stock, hot sauce, and Worcestershire sauce. Cover and braise the collards for about 15 minutes, stirring occasionally. Remove the lid and cook off the liquid until there's just a thin glaze left in the pan. Remove from the heat and stir in the quinoa. Cool. Preheat the oven to 375°F (190°C).

MAKES 8 SERVINGS

Good Basic Pie Dough (page 145)

1–1½ tablespoons sesame seeds

1½ tablespoons light olive oil

2 bacon strips, diced

1 large onion, chopped

8 cups destemeed, coarsely chopped collard greens (about 1¼ pounds)

2 garlic cloves, minced

1 cup chicken or beef stock

½ teaspoon hot sauce, or more to taste

½ teaspoon Worcestershire sauce

1½ cups cooked quinoa

3 large eggs

⅔ cup cottage cheese

½ pound fully cooked turkey sausage, in bite-size chunks

1 cup grated sharp cheddar cheese

6 Whisk the eggs in a large bowl. Whisk in the cottage cheese. Add the collard and quinoa mixture, turkey sausage, and cheese. Stir with a wooden spoon or large fork, until everything is combined but not compacted. Turn the filling into the shell.

7 Bake the pie for 45 to 55 minutes, until the filling is cooked through. It won't puff much, if at all, but it will feel springy when pressed in the center. Transfer to a rack and cool for at least 10 minutes before slicing. Refrigerate leftovers. Reheat slices in a 300°F (150°C) oven, directly on a baking sheet, loosely covered with foil, for about 12 minutes.

Collard Charm

I knew little about the charms of collards in my early years as a cook, but I've made up for it since moving south several years ago. Collards are now on my short list of favorite greens, and very near the top.

I'm hoping collards don't become the new kale, because I think they'd be put off by all the publicity, the fuss about being rich in vitamins, minerals, and fiber. Collards are proud of their humble roots. And they like to keep company with other salt-of-the-earth ingredients that bring out their best — an onion and a ham hock in the pot, a dash of hot sauce or vinegar on the plate.

Collards are available year-round in many supermarkets, but Southerners will tell you they're in their prime during the cooler months, especially after the first frost. If you run across them, treat yourself to a bunch. Look for firm leaves with a minimum of yellowing. Unless the leaves are on the small side, you'll want to cut out the stems — they take longer to cook than the leaves — and then coarsely chop the leaves. Agitate thoroughly in a large bowl of water, then drain. For a simple side dish, simmer the collards until tender in enough beef broth to barely cover, with a chunked onion, sliced bacon, and maybe a spoonful of barbecue sauce.

BRUSSELS SPROUTS TART AU GRATIN

Aside from a flurry of attention around the holidays, Brussels sprouts seem to fly below many a cook's radar. This creamy tart might help. We pack a pound of bacon-braised Brussels sprouts into a partially baked tart shell and drench them in a thick blanket of mustardy cheese sauce made with buttery French Comté. As the tart bakes, the sauce oozes down between the Brussels sprouts, creating a creamed vegetable tart that's rich and decadent enough to be a meal in itself and versatile enough to go with any cold-weather roast that's on the menu. *Heavenly* doesn't begin to do this tart justice.

1 Prepare the tart dough; then wrap it and refrigerate for at least 2 hours before rolling.

2 On a sheet of lightly floured waxed paper, roll the dough into a 12- to 12½-inch circle. Invert the pastry over a 9½- by 1-inch-high fluted tart pan, preferably one with a removable bottom. Center the dough, then peel off the paper. Carefully, so you don't cut the dough on the edge, tuck the pastry into the pan. Fold over any overhanging dough, and press it against the sides to beef them up. Refrigerate for at least 1 hour, or place in the freezer for 30 minutes.

3 Preheat the oven to 375°F (190°C). Prick the bottom of the pie shell six or seven times with a fork. Tear off a sheet of aluminum foil about 14 inches long. Gently line the tart shell with the foil, pressing it into the creases so it fits like a glove. Add a thick layer of dried beans, banking them up the sides.

4 Place the pan on a rimmed baking sheet. Bake the tart shell for 25 minutes. Slide it out and carefully remove the foil and beans. Repoke the holes if they've filled in. Slide the shell back in and bake for another 6 to 8 minutes. Transfer the shell to a cooling rack. (Once it's cooled, dab a little cream cheese or sour cream into the fork holes to plug them.)

5 Remove any tired outer leaves from the Brussels sprouts, and trim the root ends flush; quarter lengthwise. Cook the bacon in a large skillet or sauté pan until crisp. Transfer the bacon to a plate and set aside to cool. Spoon off all but about 3 tablespoons of the fat. Add the onion to the skillet and sauté for 7 to 8 minutes over medium heat. Stir in the Brussels sprouts and ¼ cup of the water. Add salt and pepper to taste. Cover and braise the Brussels sprouts for 5 to 7 minutes, until barely tender, adding more water if it evaporates. Uncover the pan for the last minute to cook off any excess liquid. Remove from the heat.

MAKES 8 SERVINGS

	Good Basic Pie Dough (page 145)
1	pound Brussels sprouts
4	bacon strips
1	large onion, chopped
¼–⅓	cup water
	Salt and freshly ground black pepper
3	tablespoons unsalted butter
2	tablespoons all-purpose flour
1½	cups half-and-half or milk
½	cup chicken stock
2	teaspoons Dijon mustard
2	cups grated Comté cheese

6 Preheat the oven to 375°F (190°C). Melt the butter in a medium saucepan. Add the flour and whisk over moderate heat for 1 minute. Whisk in the half-and-half about a third at a time, adding successive portions as it thickens. Whisk in the chicken stock. Bring to simmer, then remove from the heat. Whisk in the mustard and 1 cup of the cheese. Season the sauce with salt and pepper to taste.

7 Transfer the Brussels sprouts to the tart shell, making one even layer. Pour the cheese sauce evenly over the top. Using a fork, push the Brussels sprouts this way and that so the sauce settles in. Sprinkle the remaining 1 cup cheese over the top. Bake the tart on the rimmed sheet for 40 to 45 minutes, until the tart is bubbly and golden brown. Transfer the tart to a rack and cool for 15 minutes before serving. Refrigerate leftovers. Reheat leftover slices on a baking sheet for 15 minutes in a 350°F (180°C) oven.

CARROT AND LEEK PIE

I love big flavors and bold seasonings, but some of the most successful dishes happen when ingredients get to speak softly for themselves. That is the case with this one, one of the most popular garden pies I make. First we gently sauté the carrots and leeks in butter to help bring out their sweetness. The remaining ingredients mostly serve to bind everything together, not influence the flavor; we want the carrots and leeks to shine. The pie has a moist, compact texture, and each slice has a gorgeous profile, a mosaic of finely textured carrots and leeks. If you use vegetable stock instead of chicken stock, this pie will please vegetarians immensely. I'll usually serve it as the main dish with sautéed greens on the side.

1 Prepare the pie dough, and refrigerate it for at least 1½ to 2 hours before rolling.

2 On a sheet of lightly floured waxed paper, roll the dough into a 12- to 12½-inch circle. Invert the pastry over a standard (not deep dish) 9- or 9½-inch pie pan, center it, and peel off the paper. Gently tuck the pastry into the pan without stretching it. Sculpt the overhanging dough into an upstanding ridge; flute the edges, if desired. Refrigerate for at least 1 hour, or place in the freezer for 30 minutes.

3 Quarter the leeks lengthwise up to the root end, but don't cut through the end. Fan out the sections and rinse them under running water to wash out any sand and grit. Slice the leeks thinly. Melt 3 tablespoons of the butter in a large sauté pan. Stir in the leeks. Cook over moderate heat for 2 to 3 minutes, until wilted, stirring often. Stir in the carrots and cook for another couple of minutes. Add the stock, and salt and pepper the vegetables with a light hand. Cover the pan and cook the vegetables gently for 5 minutes, stirring occasionally. Remove from the heat and stir in the vinegar. Set aside to cool.

4 Preheat the oven to 375°F (190°C). Whisk the eggs and cottage cheese in a large bowl. Whisk in ½ teaspoon salt. Add the cooled vegetables, Havarti, 2 tablespoons of the bread crumbs, and parsley. Mix gently but thoroughly.

5 Sprinkle 1 tablespoon of the remaining bread crumbs over the pie shell. Turn the filling into the shell and smooth with a spoon. Sprinkle the remaining 2 tablespoons of bread crumbs evenly on top and dot with the remaining 2 tablespoons butter. Bake for 45 to 50 minutes, until the top has developed a rich golden-brown crust. Transfer to a rack and cool for 20 to 30 minutes before serving. Refrigerate leftovers. Reheat individual slices on a baking sheet or in the pan, loosely covered with foil, in a 300°F (150°C) oven for about 12 minutes.

MAKES 8 SERVINGS

Good Basic Pie Dough (page 145)

3 thick leeks, white and pale green parts only

5 tablespoons unsalted butter

1 pound carrots, peeled and grated

¼ cup chicken stock or vegetable stock

Salt and freshly ground black pepper

2 teaspoons red wine vinegar

2 large eggs

1 cup cottage cheese

1 cup grated Havarti cheese or Monterey Jack cheese

5 tablespoons Italian-style bread crumbs

2 tablespoons chopped fresh parsley or dill (or 1 tablespoon of each)

NEW POTATO, SPINACH, AND BLUE CHEESE SKILLET TART

It's hard to beat the rustic appeal of a pie or a tart baked in a cast-iron skillet. One of the things I love about skillet-baked tarts is how the bottom crust always seems to be so nicely done — extra-crisp and almost cracker-like. What we do here is line the skillet with pie dough, fill it with braised onions, new potatoes, and spinach, then enrich everything with cheeses and a bit of heavy cream. As you can imagine, it makes an irresistible one-skillet meal. If you don't have a cast-iron skillet, any other rugged ovenproof skillet should do. By the way, if you like this flavor combination, try the Potato, Bacon, and Blue Cheese Pizza (page 124).

1 Prepare the pie dough, and refrigerate it for at least 1½ to 2 hours before rolling.

2 On a sheet of lightly floured waxed paper, roll the dough into a 13- to 13½-inch circle. Invert the pastry over a 9½- or 10-inch cast-iron skillet, center it, and peel off the paper. Gently tuck the pastry into the pan, letting the edges rest against the sides of the pan. Refrigerate while you make the filling.

3 Preheat the oven to 375°F (190°C). Fry the bacon strips in another large skillet until crisp. Transfer to a plate. Leave 2 to 3 tablespoons of fat in the pan; add the onions and sauté for 10 minutes over medium heat, until soft and light golden. Add the potatoes, salt and pepper them to taste, and stir in 3 tablespoons of the chicken stock. Cover the pan and gently steam-cook the potatoes, adding more liquid if needed, until the potatoes are about halfway done. Stir in the spinach and garlic and continue to cook until all of the spinach is wilted, about 2 minutes. Remove the potatoes from the heat and cool briefly. They should be slightly underdone, and very little liquid should be left in the pan.

4 Stir the Parmesan into the skillet vegetables, then scrape the vegetables into the skillet pie shell. Crumble the blue cheese over the vegetables, drizzle on the cream, and sprinkle with the rosemary. Crumble the bacon over the top. Fold the edge of the pastry over the filling.

5 Bake the tart for 40 to 50 minutes, until it is golden brown and bubbly. Transfer to a cooling rack and cool for about 10 minutes before slicing and serving in large wedges. Wrap leftovers in foil and refrigerate. Reheat leftovers on a baking sheet in a 300°F (150°C) oven for 12 to 15 minutes.

MAKES 6 TO 8 SERVINGS

Good Basic Pie Dough (page 145)

4 bacon strips

1 large onion, halved and thinly sliced

1–1¼ pounds (about 8 to 10) small new potatoes, cut into bite-size chunks

Salt and freshly ground black pepper

3–6 tablespoons chicken stock or water

8 ounces (several large handfuls) baby spinach

2 garlic cloves, minced

½ cup finely grated Parmesan cheese

¾ cup crumbled blue cheese

½ cup heavy cream

1 tablespoon chopped fresh rosemary

DOUBLE-CRUST CABBAGE PIE

One of the things I love most about harvest baking is serving familiar produce in unfamiliar ways that surprise and delight people — dishes they want to go home and try for themselves. This cabbage pie is a great example. Cabbage, our featured vegetable, is slowly braised in chicken stock, tucked between a top and a bottom pastry, and baked to a glossy, golden finish. The ricotta cheese makes for a semidry filling, so be sure the cabbage is nicely saturated with the stock when it comes out of the skillet. If you have some leftovers in the fridge, chopped cooked chicken or sausage tastes great mixed in with the cabbage. Or go totally meatless and substitute vegetable stock for the chicken stock.

1 Prepare the dough as for a double-crust pie, and refrigerate for at least 1½ to 2 hours before rolling.

2 Melt the butter in a very large sauté pan or pot. Add the onion and sauté for 5 minutes over moderate heat. Add all of the cabbage, increase the heat slightly, and cook, stirring, for 5 minutes, until the cabbage starts to wilt. Stir in about ¼ cup of the chicken stock, and add a bit of salt and pepper; you'll add more as the cabbage cooks. Cover, reduce the heat, and braise the cabbage for 6 to 7 minutes, stirring occasionally.

3 Continue cooking and seasoning the cabbage, to taste, for 20 to 30 minutes, adding more stock as needed. By the time the cabbage comes off the heat, it should be very tender and have a slightly caramelized appearance. It should also be well moistened by the stock, but there shouldn't be excess moisture in the pan. Remove from the heat and transfer the cabbage to a large bowl. Cool thoroughly.

4 While the cabbage cools, roll out the pastry for the pie shell. On a sheet of lightly floured waxed paper, roll the larger half of the dough into a 13-inch circle. Invert the pastry over a 9- or 9½-inch deep-dish pie pan, center it, and peel off the paper. Gently tuck the pastry into the pan without stretching it; let the excess pastry hang over the sides of the pan. Refrigerate. Preheat the oven to 375°F (190°C).

5 When the cabbage has cooled, add the ricotta cheese. Set aside a small spoonful of beaten egg for the glaze; add the remaining beaten egg to the cabbage, along with 1 cup of the Gruyère, the Parmesan, and the parsley. Mix well, until everything is evenly combined.

MAKES 8 SERVINGS

Slab Pie Dough (page 148), prepared as for a double-crust pie

3 tablespoons unsalted butter

1 large onion, halved and thinly sliced

8 cups very thinly sliced green cabbage

⅔–1 cup chicken stock

Salt and freshly ground black pepper

1 cup ricotta cheese

2 large eggs, lightly beaten

1½ cups grated Gruyère or Jarlsberg cheese

⅓ cup grated Parmesan cheese

2–3 tablespoons chopped fresh parsley

6 On a sheet of lightly floured waxed paper, roll the other half of the dough into a 12-inch circle. Sprinkle the remaining ½ cup Gruyère over the pie shell. Turn the cabbage into the shell and smooth with a spoon. Moisten the edge of the pastry with a wet fingertip, and invert the top pastry over the filling. Press the pastry along the edges to seal. Using a paring knife, trim the pastry so it is flush with the edge of the pan. Crimp the edge all around with a fork. Brush the top pastry with the reserved egg, and poke several steam vents in the top with a fork.

7 Bake the pie for 45 to 50 minutes, until the top is a rich golden brown, turning the pie 180 degrees midway through baking. Transfer to a rack and cool for at least 15 minutes before slicing. Refrigerate leftovers. Reheat slices right in the pan, loosely covered with foil, in a 325°F (170°C) oven, for 12 to 15 minutes.

CURRIED SWEET POTATO AND SPINACH TART

I like sweet potatoes, but I'm always trying to find new ways to dress them up. Curry powder does the trick here. The bottom half of this tart is, essentially, a curried sweet potato gratin; the top, a thick layer of sautéed spinach. I love the contrasting colors and interplay of creamy potatoes and lean greens. Serve this with roasts, or cut larger slices and make it the centerpiece of your meal.

1 Prepare the pie dough; then wrap it and refrigerate for at least 2 hours before rolling.

2 On a sheet of lightly floured waxed paper, roll the dough into a 12- to 12½-inch circle. Invert the pastry over a 9½- by 1-inch-high fluted tart pan, preferably one with a removable bottom. Center the dough, then peel off the paper. Carefully, so you don't cut the dough on the edge of the pan, tuck the pastry into the pan. Fold over any overhanging dough, and press it against the sides to beef them up and increase their height. Refrigerate for at least 1 hour, or place in the freezer for 30 minutes.

3 Preheat the oven to 375°F (190°C). Prick the bottom of the pie shell six or seven times with a fork. Tear off a sheet of aluminum foil about 14 inches long. Gently line the tart shell with the foil, pressing it into the creases so it fits like a glove. Add a thick layer of dried beans, banking them up the sides. Place the shell on a rimmed baking sheet.

4 Bake the tart shell for 25 minutes. Slide it out and carefully remove the foil and beans. Repoke the holes if they've filled in. Slide the shell back in and bake for another 6 to 8 minutes. Transfer the shell and baking sheet to a cooling rack. (Once it's cooled, dab a little cream cheese or sour cream into the fork holes to plug them.)

5 Heat 2 tablespoons of the olive oil in a large skillet or sauté pan. Add the onion and sauté for 6 to 7 minutes over medium heat. Stir in the garlic, cook briefly, and add the spinach (in batches, if it can't all fit in the pan). Stir in the 2 tablespoons chicken or vegetable stock. Salt the greens lightly, and add pepper to taste. Cover the skillet and cook the greens until they're tender and wilted. Remove from the heat, uncover, and cool.

6 Heat the remaining 1½ tablespoons oil in a large skillet, preferably non-stick. Stir in the potatoes. Cook over moderate heat for 2 minutes, stirring once or twice. Add the curry powder and stir to coat the potatoes. Add the heavy cream, ¼ cup stock, brown sugar, and ⅛ to ¼ teaspoon salt. Bring to a simmer. Cook for 1 minute, then remove from the heat and let cool for 15 minutes. (The potatoes won't be cooked through, just heated.) Preheat the oven to 375°F (190°C).

MAKES 8 SERVINGS

Good Basic Pie Dough (page 145)

3½ tablespoons light olive oil

1 medium onion, chopped

2 garlic cloves, minced

1 pound baby spinach or mix of baby greens

¼ cup plus 2 tablespoons chicken or vegetable stock

Salt and freshly ground black pepper

1½ medium-large sweet potatoes, peeled and sliced ⅛ inch thick

1 tablespoon curry powder

¾ cup heavy cream

1½ teaspoons light brown sugar

1 cup grated sharp cheddar cheese

7 Sprinkle half of the cheese in the shell. Spoon the sweet potato slices and their sauce evenly into the shell, and top with the remaining cheese. Spoon the greens over the top; cover the tart loosely with foil. Bake the tart on the rimmed sheet for 30 minutes. Uncover the tart and continue to bake until the sauce bubbles thickly underneath, about 20 minutes more. Transfer the tart to a rack and cool for at least 10 minutes before serving. Refrigerate leftovers. Reheat slices in a 300°F (150°C) oven, directly on a baking sheet and loosely covered with foil, for about 12 minutes.

BALSAMIC ONION AND MUSHROOM TART WITH FRESH SAGE

I've been noticing more and more recipes for balsamic onion jam lately, not to mention more and more producers who are selling similar products online. I'm a fan of these concoctions, so it occurred to me that these flavors could be the basis of a terrific tart. I included mushrooms because I knew they'd be a good fit. And instead of taking the quiche route, I came up with a ricotta cheese and Parmesan topping that would complement the main ingredients but form a separate second layer on top.

1 Prepare the pie dough, and refrigerate it for at least 1½ to 2 hours before rolling.

2 On a sheet of lightly floured waxed paper, roll the dough into a 12- to 12½-inch circle. Invert the pastry over a 9½- by 1-inch-high fluted tart pan, preferably one with a removable bottom. Center the dough, then peel off the paper. Carefully, so you don't cut the dough on the edge of the pan, tuck the pastry into the pan. Fold over any overhanging dough, and press it against the sides to beef them up and increase their height. Refrigerate for at least 1 hour, or place in the freezer for 30 minutes.

3 Preheat the oven to 375°F (190°C). Prick the bottom of the shell six or seven times with a fork. Tear off a sheet of aluminum foil about 16 inches long. Gently line the pie shell with the foil, pressing it into the creases so it fits like a glove. Add a thick layer of dried beans, banking them up the sides. Place the shell on a rimmed baking sheet. Line the sheet with parchment paper if your tart pan has a removable bottom, just in case butter leaks out.

4 Bake the tart shell for 25 minutes. Slide it out and carefully remove the foil and beans. Repoke the holes if they've filled in. Slide the shell back in and bake for another 6 to 8 minutes. Transfer the shell, right on the sheet, to a cooling rack. (Once it is cooled, dab a little cream cheese or sour cream into the fork holes to plug them.)

5 Melt the butter in a large skillet or sauté pan. Add the onions and cook, stirring, for 6 to 7 minutes over medium heat. Stir in the mushrooms and cook for another 5 to 6 minutes, until they release their moisture and most of it evaporates. Stir in the balsamic vinegar, brown sugar, and salt and pepper to taste. Stir in the sage, then remove from the heat and set aside to cool.

MAKES 8 SERVINGS

Good Basic Pie Dough (page 145)

3 tablespoons unsalted butter

2 large onions, halved and thinly sliced

8 ounces white mushrooms, thinly sliced

3 tablespoons balsamic vinegar

2 teaspoons packed light brown sugar

Salt and freshly ground black pepper

2 tablespoons chopped fresh sage or 2 teaspoons dried

1 cup ricotta cheese

½ cup finely grated Parmesan cheese

2 large eggs

½ cup milk or half-and-half

6 Combine the ricotta cheese, Parmesan, eggs, and milk in a blender. Add a big pinch of salt and pepper. Purée the mixture until smooth.

7 Preheat the oven to 375°F (190°C). Distribute the onion mixture evenly in the shell. Pour on the ricotta mixture without mixing it into the onions, carefully smoothing the top with a spoon. Bake for 45 to 50 minutes. The top will probably crack a little and should appear somewhat dry. Transfer to a rack and cool for 20 to 30 minutes before serving. Refrigerate leftovers. Reheat leftovers on a baking sheet, loosely covered with foil, for 10 to 12 minutes in a 300°F (150°C) oven.

Asparagus: The Delicious, Delicate Spear

The best asparagus comes from my brother-in-law Dean's garden. I'm not sure what his secret is — whether it's his soil or some secret sauce he puts on it — but those fat, tasty spears really make this quiche and create a gorgeous green mosaic with every slice. (Dean tells me that his stash is for close family only. We send our regrets.)

According to Dean, an asparagus patch takes several years to start producing an abundant crop. He harvested a handful of spears the first year, and a few more the year after, but by his fourth or fifth year he had a plentiful supply for weeks on end. If you don't have a Dean in your life, you'll have to find a good local market for your asparagus. Spring is when you'll see the best price and quality. Choose spears at least ½ inch in diameter with tight buds at the tip and smooth skin. They should be at least two-thirds green. If the spears are withered or flabby, don't bother.

The best way to store asparagus is in water, in the refrigerator. Trim the ends off the spears when you get them home, and place them upright in about an inch of water so they stay fresh and retain their sweetness. Many cooks prefer to use just the tender top half or two-thirds of the spears, but if you trim the lower sections with a vegetable peeler or paring knife — carefully whittling up from the bottom of the spear toward the tip — you can remove the tough, fibrous skin and eat what's underneath.

ASPARAGUS AND CREAMY POTATO QUICHE

Potatoes are a great way to bulk up a quiche, especially when you're serving it for breakfast or brunch. But if I want to move the needle a little higher on the impress-o-meter, I'll add asparagus, too. The trick is to keep the spears a tad on the crisp side during the precooking, so they aren't soft when the quiche is done. Don't skimp on the mustard and dill — they tie all the flavors together. If you don't have a tart pan with 2-inch sides, use a deep-dish pie pan instead.

1 Prepare the pie dough. Refrigerate it for 1½ to 2 hours before rolling.

2 On a sheet of lightly floured waxed paper, roll the dough into a 13½-inch circle. Invert the pastry over a 9½-inch by 2-inch-deep removable-bottom tart pan, center it, and peel off the paper. Gently tuck the pastry into the pan without stretching it, taking care not to tear the pastry on the sharp edge of the pan. Fold over any overhanging dough, and press it against the sides to beef up the side walls. Refrigerate for at least 1 hour, or place in the freezer for 30 minutes.

3 Preheat the oven to 375°F (190°C). Prick the bottom of the pie shell six or seven times with a fork. Tear off a sheet of aluminum foil about 16 inches long. Gently line the tart shell with the foil, pressing it into the creases so it fits like a glove. Add a thick layer of dried beans, banking them up the sides.

4 Place the pan on a large rimmed baking sheet. Bake the tart shell for 25 minutes. Slide it out and carefully remove the foil and beans. Repoke the holes if they've filled in. Slide the shell back in and bake for another 6 to 8 minutes. Transfer the baking sheet and tart shell to a cooling rack. (Once it's cooled, dab a little cream cheese or sour cream in the fork holes to plug them.)

5 Melt the butter in a large skillet, preferably nonstick. Add the scallions and sauté gently for 2 minutes. Add the garlic and potatoes and sauté for 1 minute. Stir in the stock, cover the skillet, and gently braise the potatoes for 5 minutes. Add the asparagus; salt lightly, and add pepper to taste. Cover and cook for 3 to 4 minutes, until the asparagus and potatoes are just barely done. Remove the lid and cook off any liquid left in the pan. Transfer to a plate to cool.

6 Preheat the oven to 375°F (190°C). Whisk the crème fraîche and flour in a large bowl until smooth. Whisk in the half-and-half and the eggs, one at a time. Whisk in the mustard, dill, ½ teaspoon salt, and ¼ teaspoon black pepper.

7 Sprinkle ½ cup of the cheese in the tart shell. Add the skillet vegetables and spread them out evenly. Sprinkle 1 cup of the cheese over the vegetables. Whisk the custard one more time, then ladle it over the filling. Sprinkle the remaining 1 cup cheese on top. Bake the quiche on the rimmed sheet for about 45 to 50 minutes, until golden and puffy. Transfer the sheet to a cooling rack and cool for at least 30 minutes before slicing. Refrigerate leftovers. Reheat individual slices on a baking sheet, in a 300°F (150°C) oven, for 10 to 12 minutes.

MAKES 8 SERVINGS

Good Basic Pie Dough (page 145)

3 tablespoons unsalted butter

6 scallions (white and pale green parts), thinly sliced

1 garlic clove, minced

½ pound creamer potatoes or other small potatoes, quartered

¼ cup chicken stock or water

1 pound asparagus, top halves only, in 1-inch pieces

Salt and freshly ground black pepper

8 ounces (1 cup) crème fraîche, store-bought or homemade (page 284)

1½ tablespoons all-purpose flour

⅔ cup half-and-half

5 large eggs

1 tablespoon Dijon mustard

1 tablespoon chopped fresh dill

2 cups grated extra-sharp cheddar cheese or Gruyère cheese

BACON AND EGG BREAKFAST PIE

You see a lot of recipes for this sort of thing coming out of New Zealand but rarely this country — perplexing, given what a good idea it is. I won't pretend to be an expert, but the basic idea is a pastry shell, sometimes puff pastry, layered with stuff we like to eat for breakfast, topped with whole eggs and then more pastry or another kind of topping to protect the eggs from the direct heat of the oven. Using those broad strokes, I put a layer of spinach and quasi home fries in the shell first, crumbled bacon over that, added the eggs, then covered the eggs with thinly sliced tomatoes and cheese. The surprising twist, the part nobody ever expects, is the whole baked eggs that show up in the middle of the pie.

1 Prepare the pie dough, and refrigerate it for at least 1½ to 2 hours before rolling; the oat and cornmeal dough can be rolled sooner.

2 On a sheet of lightly floured waxed paper, roll the dough into a 13-inch circle. Invert the pastry over a 9- or 9½-inch deep-dish pie pan, center it, and peel off the paper. Gently tuck the pastry into the pan without stretching it. Sculpt the overhanging dough into an upstanding ridge; flute the edges, if desired. Refrigerate for at least 1 hour, or place in the freezer for 30 minutes.

3 Melt the butter in a very large skillet or sauté pan, preferably nonstick. Stir in the onion and cook for 5 minutes over medium heat, stirring often. Add the potatoes. Cook, stirring often, for 3 to 4 minutes. Add the water or stock, a little at a time, covering the pan to trap the moisture and steam the potatoes. When the potatoes are still slightly underdone, stir in the paprika and spinach. Add a pinch of salt and pepper. Cook for several more minutes, until all the spinach is wilted and any loose liquid has cooked off. Scrape the mixture onto a plate to cool.

4 Preheat the oven to 375°F (190°C). To assemble the dish, sprinkle about half of the cheese evenly in the shell. Spoon the potato and spinach mixture over the cheese as evenly as possible. Drizzle the cream over the vegetables. Using the back of a spoon, make six to eight shallow depressions in the vegetable layer to hold the eggs. Break the eggs, one at a time, into a small bowl — keeping the yolks intact — and slide them into the depressions. Salt and pepper the eggs lightly.

5 Cover the eggs with an overlapping layer of tomato slices. Lightly salt and pepper the tomato layer, and crumble the bacon on top. Bake for 30 minutes, then slide out the pie and sprinkle with the remaining cheese. Bake for another 20 minutes, until the cheese is golden brown. There are few traditional telltale signs that the pie is done; overall elapsed time is the best indicator. Transfer the pie to a cooling rack and cool for at least 10 minutes before serving. Refrigerate leftovers. Reheat them right in the pan, in a 300°F (150°C) oven, for 12 to 15 minutes.

MAKES 8 SERVINGS

Whole-Wheat Pie Dough (page 145), Good Basic Pie Dough (page 145), or Oat and Cornmeal Pie Dough (page 147)

2 tablespoons unsalted butter

½ medium onion, finely chopped

1¼ cups peeled, diced potatoes, ½-inch cubes

¼–⅓ cup water or chicken stock

½ teaspoon paprika

½ pound baby spinach (about 8 cups, packed)

Salt and freshly ground black pepper

2 cups grated sharp cheddar cheese or other melting cheese

2–3 tablespoons heavy cream

6–8 large eggs

1 medium-large ripe tomato, cored and very thinly sliced

8–10 pieces crisp cooked bacon

GREEN PEA AND TURKEY SAUSAGE QUICHE

Green peas certainly aren't the first thing you think of when it comes to making quiche, so I was thrilled to discover what a natural they are. The trick was coming up with the right flavor partners so the pea addition didn't come across as weird or contrived, then everything came together like, well, peas in a pod. I found the answer in relatively mild but meaty turkey sausage and tangy Swiss cheese, which — along with some Dijon mustard to spice things up — make for one fine quiche. I think you'll be pleasantly surprised.

1 Prepare the pie dough, and refrigerate it for at least 1½ to 2 hours before rolling.

2 On a sheet of lightly floured waxed paper, roll the dough into a 13-inch circle. Invert the pastry over a 9- or 9½-inch deep-dish pie pan, center it, and peel off the paper. Gently tuck the pastry into the pan without stretching it. Sculpt the overhanging dough into an upstanding ridge; flute the edges, if desired. Refrigerate for at least 1 hour, or place in the freezer for 30 minutes.

3 Preheat the oven to 375°F (190°C). Prick the bottom of the pie shell six or seven times with a fork. Tear off a sheet of aluminum foil about 16 inches long. Gently line the pie shell with the foil, pressing it into the creases so it fits like a glove. Add a thick layer of dried beans, banking them up the sides.

4 Bake the pie shell for 25 minutes. Slide it out and carefully remove the foil and beans. Repoke the holes if they've filled in. Slide the shell back in and bake for another 6 to 8 minutes. Transfer the pie shell to a cooling rack. (Once it's cooled, dab a little cream cheese or sour cream into the fork holes to plug them.)

5 Melt the butter in a large sauté pan. Stir in the onion and sauté for 6 to 7 minutes over medium heat, then add the peas. If the peas are fresh, add 3 to 4 tablespoons of water to the pan; if they're frozen, you won't need it. Salt lightly. Cover the pan and gently cook the peas over moderate heat for 4 to 5 minutes, stirring occasionally. Add the turkey sausage and garlic. Cook for several minutes more, until the peas are tender and the sausage is heated. Remove from the heat and set aside to cool.

6 Preheat the oven to 375°F (190°C). Whisk the eggs, half-and-half, sour cream, and mustard in a large bowl, until blended. Add the flour, ½ teaspoon salt, pepper, and parsley; whisk again, until evenly combined. Scatter half of the cheese in the pie shell, and top with the peas and sausage. Slowly pour the custard over the vegetables, and sprinkle on the rest of the cheese.

7 Bake for 40 to 50 minutes, until the quiche is golden brown and slightly puffy. The center of the quiche should be wobbly, not loose or soupy. Transfer the quiche to a rack and cool. Serve warm or at room temperature. Refrigerate leftovers. Reheat slices in a 300°F (150°C) oven on a baking sheet or right in the pan, loosely covered with foil, for 12 to 15 minutes.

MAKES 8 SERVINGS

Good Basic Pie Dough (page 145) or Whole-Wheat Pie Dough (page 145)

3 tablespoons unsalted butter

1 large onion, finely chopped

1½ cups fresh or frozen green peas

½ teaspoon salt, plus some for cooking the peas

½ pound fully cooked turkey sausage, cut into bite-size chunks

1 garlic clove, minced

4 large eggs

1 cup half-and-half or light cream

⅓ cup sour cream

1 tablespoon Dijon mustard

1 tablespoon all-purpose flour

¼ teaspoon freshly ground black pepper

1 tablespoon chopped fresh parsley or dill

1½–2 cups (6 to 8 ounces) grated Swiss cheese or Gruyère cheese (or substitute some feta for the Swiss)

CRÈME FRAÎCHE CORN QUICHE

Here's an impressive showcase for fresh summer corn that deserves a place on your summer recipe bucket list. Part Southern-style spoonbread, part savory corn pudding, it's got a soft, tangy French accent courtesy of the crème fraîche. To help bring out the sweet flavor of the corn, I haven't included any sautéed onions or other veggies, but feel free to do so if you like.

1 Prepare the pie dough, and refrigerate it for at least 1½ to 2 hours before rolling.

2 On a sheet of lightly floured waxed paper, roll the dough into a 13-inch circle. Invert the pastry over a 9- or 9½-inch deep-dish pie pan, center it, and peel off the paper. Gently tuck the pastry into the pan without stretching it. Sculpt the overhanging dough into an upstanding ridge; flute the edges, if desired. Refrigerate for at least 1 hour, or place in the freezer for 30 minutes.

3 Preheat the oven to 375°F (190°C). Prick the bottom of the pie shell six or seven times with a fork. Tear off a sheet of aluminum foil about 16 inches long. Gently line the pie shell with the foil, pressing it into the creases so it fits like a glove. Add a thick layer of dried beans, banking them up the sides.

4 Bake the pie shell for 25 minutes. Slide it out and carefully remove the foil and beans. Repoke the holes if they've filled in. Slide the shell back in and bake for another 6 to 8 minutes. Transfer the pie shell to a cooling rack. (Once it's cooled, dab a little cream cheese or sour cream into the fork holes to plug them.)

5 Preheat the oven to 375°F (190°C). Combine the milk and cornmeal in a small saucepan. Heat gently, whisking almost nonstop, for 5 to 8 minutes, until the milk thickens to the consistency of heavy cream. Pour the liquid into a bowl. Add the butter, mustard, salt, and pepper. Whisk until smooth.

6 Put the corn in a medium saucepan with enough water to cover; salt lightly. Bring to a boil and cook at a low boil for 5 minutes. Drain and cool briefly. Transfer the corn to a food processor and pulse repeatedly, until the corn is roughly chopped.

7 Combine the crème fraîche and flour in a large bowl. Whisk well. Whisk in the eggs, one at a time, followed by the thickened milk mixture and chopped corn. Stir in 2 cups of the cheese and the chives. Carefully pour or ladle the filling into the quiche shell. Sprinkle the remaining ½ cup cheese on top.

8 Bake the quiche on the center oven rack for 40 to 45 minutes, until it rises up noticeably and the top is golden brown. When you give the quiche a little nudge, it should jiggle as a whole and not seem soupy in the center. Transfer to a cooling rack. Slice and serve warm. Refrigerate leftovers. Reheat individual slices for 12 to 15 minutes on a baking sheet, loosely covered with foil, in a 300°F (150°C) oven.

MAKES 8 TO 10 SERVINGS

Good Basic Pie Dough (page 145)

- 1 cup milk
- 2 tablespoons cornmeal
- 2 tablespoons unsalted butter, in ¼-inch slices
- 1 tablespoon Dijon mustard
- ¾ teaspoon salt
- ¼ teaspoon freshly ground black pepper
- 2½ cups corn kernels, preferably freshly cut
- 1 cup (8 ounces) crème fraîche, store-bought or homemade (page 284)
- 1 tablespoon flour
- 4 large eggs
- 2½ cups grated extra-sharp cheddar cheese
- 2 tablespoons chopped chives

Fresh Corn: Summer Candy

I grew up in New Jersey, the Garden State, near enough to cornfields and farm stands to have known the flavor of just-picked corn from a very early age. It's a knowingness — pure, simple, and sweet — you can never quite forget, and against which no prepackaged stand-in will ever compare. When corn season finally arrives, I grill it with butter and seasonings; put fresh-cooked kernels in quesadillas, guacamole, and salsas; and generally behave like the proverbial kid in the candy store.

Not living near a source of just-picked corn is almost grounds for relocation. If a move isn't in the cards, at least obey a few guidelines for preserving and enjoying fresh corn at its peak.

- Buy your sweet corn as close to the farm as possible, the same day that it's picked, if you can. Then plan to serve it the same day.

- Choose corn with golden-to-brown silk. A little stickiness is fine, but if the silk is black or dry, the corn isn't freshly picked.

- Pull back the husks — which should be green and supple, not dry and yellow — and look at the kernels: you want them plump and tightly spaced, not shriveled or indented, another sign of age. Press hard enough to burst a few kernels; the liquid should be pleasantly creamy. (Stares from the vendor may be decidedly less pleasant.)

- When you get it home, don't let the corn sit around at room temperature; refrigerate it immediately — shucking it first, if you like — to keep it as sweet as possible.

ROASTED TOMATO, CORN, AND CHEDDAR CHEESE QUICHE

Let me say right off the bat that if you're looking for a "quick and easy" quiche, this is not the one. However, if your aim is to make a quiche that says summer like no other — and you don't mind roasting a few plum tomatoes — you've come to the right page. I find myself roasting bushels of plum tomatoes each year. Roasting concentrates their flavor and sweetness, rendering them perfect for all manner of harvest baking. In this rich and creamy quiche, we team them up with fresh corn, herbs, and sharp cheddar cheese to create a fabulous summer tart for alfresco dining.

1 Prepare the pie dough, and refrigerate it for at least 1½ to 2 hours before rolling.

2 On a sheet of lightly floured waxed paper, roll the dough into a 12- to 12½-inch circle. Invert the pastry over a 9½- by 1-inch-high fluted tart pan, preferably one with a removable bottom. Center the dough, then peel off the paper. Carefully, so you don't cut the dough on the edge of the pan, tuck the pastry into the pan. Fold over any overhanging dough, and press it against the sides to beef them up. Refrigerate for at least 1 hour, or place in the freezer for 30 minutes.

3 Preheat the oven to 375°F (190°C). Prick the bottom of the pie shell six or seven times with a fork. Tear off a sheet of aluminum foil about 14 inches long. Carefully line the tart shell with the foil, pressing it into the creases so it fits like a glove. Add a thick layer of dried beans, banking them up the sides.

4 Place the tart on a rimmed baking sheet. Bake the tart shell for 25 minutes. Slide it out and carefully remove the foil and beans. Repoke the holes if they've filled in. Slide the shell back in and bake for another 6 to 8 minutes. Transfer the shell to a cooling rack. (Once it's cooled, dab a little cream cheese or sour cream into the fork holes to plug them.)

5 Preheat the oven to 375°F (190°C). Put the corn kernels in a small saucepan with enough water to cover by 1 inch. Bring to a boil and boil for 5 to 7 minutes, until tender. Strain, then transfer the corn to a plate to cool.

6 Prepare the custard: Whisk the eggs in a large bowl until evenly blended. Whisk in the heavy cream, light cream, mustard, salt, paprika, and a pinch of pepper. Scatter the corn evenly in the tart shell. Cover with half of the cheese. Slowly pour or ladle the custard over the corn and cheese. Place the tomato halves, cut side up, on top, and cover with the remaining cheese. Sprinkle the herbs over the filling.

7 Place the pan on a rimmed baking sheet if you're using a removable bottom pan. Either way, bake the quiche for 40 to 45 minutes, until it's golden brown and puffy. Transfer to a rack and cool to lukewarm before serving.

MAKES 8 SERVINGS

Good Basic Pie Dough (page 145)

1½ cups fresh-cut corn kernels

3 large eggs

½ cup heavy cream

½ cup light cream

1 teaspoon Dijon mustard

½ teaspoon salt

⅛ teaspoon paprika

Freshly ground black pepper

1½ cups (6 ounces) grated sharp cheddar cheese

5 or 6 good-size roasted plum tomatoes (page 282)

2 tablespoons coarsely chopped fresh chives or parsley

BROCCOLI, ONION, AND CHEDDAR QUICHE

Broccoli and cheddar quiche has been around forever, and they're a classic team. Here's my favorite version. There are a couple of little tricks to ensuring that this gets the praise it deserves: Don't overcook the broccoli (see step 5); caramelize the onions so they're sweet and golden; and, my cardinal rule for almost any quiche custard, don't skimp on the Dijon mustard. Quiche just isn't the same without it. Finally, be sure to use plenty of good sharp or extra-sharp cheddar cheese.

1 Prepare the pie dough, and refrigerate it for at least 1½ to 2 hours before rolling.

2 On a sheet of lightly floured waxed paper, roll the dough into a 12- to 12½-inch circle. Invert the pastry over a 9½- by 1-inch-high fluted tart pan, preferably one with a removable bottom. Center the dough, then peel off the paper. Carefully tuck the pastry into the pan. Fold over any overhanging dough, and press it against the sides to beef them up and increase their height. Refrigerate for at least 1 hour, or place in the freezer for 30 minutes.

3 Preheat the oven to 375°F (190°C). Prick the bottom of the pie shell six or seven times with a fork. Tear off a sheet of aluminum foil about 14 inches long. Gently line the tart shell with the foil, pressing it into the creases so it fits like a glove. Add a thick layer of dried beans, banking them up the sides.

4 Place the shell on a rimmed baking sheet. Bake the tart shell for 25 minutes. Slide it out and carefully remove the foil and beans. Repoke the holes if they've filled in. Slide the shell back in and bake for another 6 to 8 minutes. Transfer the shell and baking sheet to a cooling rack. (Once it's cooled, dab a little cream cheese or sour cream into the fork holes to plug them.) Keep the oven set to 375°F (190°C).

5 Melt the butter in a large skillet. Stir in the onion and sauté over moderate heat for 12 to 15 minutes, stirring often, until it begins to caramelize. Stir in the garlic during the last minute or so. Add the broccoli, and salt and pepper everything lightly; then cover the skillet and remove from the heat. Uncover the broccoli every couple of minutes to check on it, and as soon as it shows the slightest bit of tenderness when pierced with a paring knife, leave the lid off.

6 Whisk the eggs in a large bowl until evenly blended. Whisk in the half-and-half, heavy cream, mustard, ¾ teaspoon salt, ¼ teaspoon pepper, and thyme. Spread the sautéed mixture evenly in the tart shell, and top with half of the cheese. Whisk the custard again, then slowly pour or ladle it over the filling. Distribute the remaining cheese over the top.

7 Bake the quiche on the rimmed sheet for 40 to 45 minutes, until slightly puffy and golden brown. Transfer the quiche to a cooling rack. Serve warm or at room temperature. Reheat leftovers on a baking sheet, loosely covered with foil, in a 300°F (150°C) oven for 10 to 12 minutes.

MAKES 8 SERVINGS

Good Basic Pie Dough (page 145)

3 tablespoons butter

1 large onion, halved and thinly sliced

2 garlic cloves, minced

3 cups broccoli florets

Salt and freshly ground black pepper

5 large eggs

¾ cup half-and-half or light cream

⅔ cup heavy cream

1 tablespoon Dijon mustard

¼ teaspoon dried thyme or ½ teaspoon fresh

1½–2 cups grated extra-sharp white cheddar cheese

SPAGHETTI SQUASH AND PARMESAN CHEESE QUICHE

Most of us eat spaghetti squash as a side dish tossed with a little butter and Parmesan. But it can also be a standout when used less traditionally — as, say, the featured ingredient in this beautiful and delicious quiche. After roasting the squash (see page 190), I sauté sliced mushrooms and an onion, mix in the squash to soak up all the wonderful mushroom flavor, and pile it into the shell with Parmesan cheese. Pour the custard on top, and into the oven it goes. Everyone will love it.

1 Prepare the dough, and refrigerate it for at least 1½ to 2 hours before rolling.

2 On a sheet of lightly floured waxed paper, roll the dough into a 12- to 12½-inch circle. Invert the pastry over a 9½- by 1-inch-high fluted tart pan, preferably one with a removable bottom. Center the dough, then peel off the paper. Carefully, so you don't cut the dough on the edge of the pan, tuck the pastry into the pan. Fold over any overhanging dough, and press it against the sides to beef them up and increase their height. Refrigerate for at least 1 hour, or place in the freezer for 30 minutes.

3 Preheat the oven to 375°F (190°C). Prick the bottom of the pie shell six or seven times with a fork. Tear off a sheet of aluminum foil about 14 inches long. Gently line the tart shell with the foil, pressing it into the creases so it fits like a glove. Add a thick layer of dried beans, banking them up the sides. Place the shell on a rimmed baking sheet.

4 Bake the tart shell for 25 minutes. Slide it out and carefully remove the foil and beans. Repoke the holes if they've filled in. Slide the shell back in and bake for another 6 to 8 minutes. Transfer the shell and baking sheet to a cooling rack. (Once it's cooled, dab a little cream cheese or sour cream into the fork holes to plug them.) Keep the oven set to 375°F (190°C).

5 Melt the butter in a large skillet. Add the onion and sauté for 5 minutes over medium heat. Stir in the mushrooms and garlic, cover, and gently cook the mushrooms over low heat for a couple of minutes. Stir in the spaghetti squash, tossing with two forks to mix it up. Remove from the heat and let cool briefly. Add the Parmesan to the squash and mix it in gently with two forks; add a bit of salt and pepper to taste.

6 Whisk the eggs in a large bowl until evenly blended. Whisk in the half-and-half, heavy cream, flour, mustard, and thyme. Spread the squash mixture evenly in the tart shell without compacting it. Slowly pour the custard over the filling, nudging the squash this way and that so the custard settles all around it. Sprinkle the grated cheddar over the top.

7 Bake the quiche on the rimmed sheet for approximately 45 minutes, until slightly puffy, wobbly, and golden brown. Transfer to a cooling rack. Serve warm or at room temperature. Reheat leftovers on a baking sheet, loosely covered with foil, in a 300°F (150°C) oven for 10 to 12 minutes.

MAKES 8 SERVINGS

Good Basic Pie Dough (page 145) or Oat and Cornmeal Pie Dough (page 147)

3 tablespoons unsalted butter

1 medium onion, chopped

1½ cups thinly sliced mushrooms

2 garlic cloves, minced

2½ cups baked spaghetti squash (page 190)

⅔ cup freshly grated Parmesan cheese

Salt and freshly ground black pepper

3 large eggs

1 cup half-and-half or milk

⅓ cup heavy cream

1 tablespoon all-purpose flour

2 teaspoons Dijon mustard

1 teaspoon chopped fresh thyme or ½ teaspoon dried

⅔ cup grated cheddar, fontina, or other mild melting cheese

How to Bake Spaghetti Squash

Baking spaghetti squash is mostly like baking any other winter squash.

- Rinse and dry your squash to remove sand and dirt.

- Using a chef's knife, halve the squash lengthwise, and scoop out the seeds.

- Place the squash cut side up on a rimmed baking sheet lined with foil or parchment. Brush the flesh with olive oil.

- Bake in a preheated 375°F (190°C) oven for 50 to 60 minutes, until tender when pierced with a paring knife. Transfer to a cooling rack.

- Cool briefly, then rake a large fork over the flesh to loosen the "spaghetti" and scoop it out.

To remove any excess liquid, transfer the squash to a strainer placed over a bowl and drain for 30 to 60 minutes. You may or may not get much liquid.

BOLOGNESE SLAB PIE WITH BROCCOLI RABE

Bolognese sauce is widely considered the meat sauce among meat sauces. And it's a great opportunity for the harvest cook, filled with onions, celery, carrots, garlic, tomatoes, and fresh herbs. Traditionally used for lasagna and tagliatelle, it also makes a first-rate filling for an Italian-style meat pie such as this one. To balance out the richness of the pie, we add a layer of sautéed broccoli rabe, whose slightly bitter flavor is a nice contrast. Bring it to the table in dramatic fashion, hot from the oven and right in the pan, and your guests will swoon.

1 Prepare the slab pie shell. Mix ¼ cup of Parmesan with the bread crumbs in a small bowl. Sprinkle the mixture evenly over the shell. Place in the freezer while you work on the rest of the dish.

2 Heat about half of the olive oil (2½ tablespoons) in a large pot. Add the onion, carrot, and celery. Cook the vegetables over moderate heat for 6 to 7 minutes, stirring often. Stir in the garlic. Add the beef and let it brown, breaking it up thoroughly with a wooden spoon as it cooks. When the meat is browned, remove the pan from the heat. Tilt the pan up, so the fat runs to one side, and spoon off about two-thirds of the fat; discard.

3 Put the pan back on the heat. Stir in the wine and bring to a low boil. Cook off about half of the wine, then add the tomatoes, tomato paste, basil, oregano, thyme, 1 teaspoon salt, and ½ teaspoon pepper. Heat for 5 to 10 minutes, until the mixture returns to a boil, then reduce the heat and simmer for 15 to 20 minutes, until thick but still saucy. Stir in the cream and continue to simmer for about 10 minutes. When the sauce is done, it will be good and thick, with some of the thick liquid puddling on top of the meat. Taste, and adjust the seasoning as needed; it will likely need a little more salt. Remove from the heat and stir in ⅓ cup of the Parmesan. Transfer to a shallow baking dish to cool.

4 Meanwhile, heat the remaining 2½ tablespoons olive oil in a large pot. Add the broccoli rabe; salt lightly, and add a few tablespoons of water. Cover the dish and cook the broccoli rabe over moderate heat, stirring often, for 10 to 15 minutes, until tender. Keep adding water, a few tablespoons at a time, as needed. When the greens are done and any excess liquid has cooked off, remove them from the heat.

5 Preheat the oven to 400°F (200°C). Spoon the meat sauce evenly into the slab pie shell. Distribute the broccoli rabe evenly over the sauce, pressing it gently into the sauce to help keep it moist. Sprinkle with ⅓ cup Parmesan, and drizzle with a bit of olive oil. Bake the pie for 30 minutes, then reduce the heat to 375°F (190°C) and bake for 20 minutes more, until the sauce is good and bubbly. Transfer the pie to a cooling rack. Sprinkle with the remaining ⅓ cup Parmesan. Cool briefly, then slice and serve.

MAKES 8 TO 10 SERVINGS

Slab Pie Dough (and Shell) (page 148)

1¼ cups finely grated Parmesan cheese

2 tablespoons Italian-style or plain bread crumbs

5 tablespoons olive oil, plus a little for drizzling

1 large onion, finely chopped

1 large carrot, finely diced

1 small celery stalk, finely chopped

3 garlic cloves, minced

1¾–2 pounds ground beef (chuck)

¾ cup dry red wine

3½ cups cored and diced tomatoes (preferably fresh)

1 tablespoon tomato paste

¼ cup chopped fresh basil or 1 tablespoon dried

1 tablespoon chopped fresh oregano or 1½ teaspoons dried

2 teaspoons fresh thyme or 1 teaspoon dried

Salt and freshly ground black pepper

¼ cup heavy cream

2 bunches broccoli rabe, coarsely chopped

SWISS CHARD GALETTE

Few things are as fetching or as fabulous to eat as a well-made savory galette. And while it may look fancy, a galette is actually easier to prepare than your average pie or tart since you don't have to roll the dough precisely, prebake the crust, flute the dough, or get it into the pan. Just cover the dough with your filling, fold over the edges, and bake. Here's an old favorite of mine made with sautéed onions, Swiss chard, and cheeses, which meld together and create a sort of heavenly chard gratin on crust. Make it the centerpiece of your meal, serve it as an appetizer, or cut smaller wedges to accompany a roast chicken.

1 Prepare the pie dough, and refrigerate it for at least 1½ to 2 hours before rolling.

2 Remove the stems from the Swiss chard and discard them. Coarsely chop the leaves, place them in a bowl of cool water, and agitate well to remove any sand or grit. Thoroughly drain the leaves in a colander.

3 Heat the olive oil in a large sauté pan or skillet. Stir in the onion; salt and pepper lightly. Cook the onion over moderate heat for 10 minutes, stirring often. Stir in the garlic and Swiss chard. Add a bit more salt and pepper and a few shakes of Worcestershire sauce. Cook the chard over medium heat for 5 to 8 minutes, until it is thoroughly wilted and tender and all of the excess moisture has cooked off. Remove from the heat and let cool.

4 Mix the ricotta and Parmesan in a small bowl.

5 Preheat the oven to 400°F (200°C). On a large sheet of parchment paper, roll the dough into one 14- by 11-inch oblong. Lift the paper and dough onto a large baking sheet. (If you don't have parchment, roll the dough onto a sheet of waxed paper and invert it onto your baking sheet. Peel off the paper and proceed.)

6 Dollop the cheese mixture here and there over the dough, leaving a 1½-inch border of uncovered dough all around. Use a spoon or fork to flatten out the dollops. Cover the cheese mixture with the cooled Swiss chard and onions, spreading it around evenly. Sprinkle with half of the Gruyère. Using the parchment, a spatula, or a dough scraper to help lift, fold the border of dough up around the edges of the filling. The dough will sort of self-pleat as you go. Brush the pastry border with the egg glaze, and sprinkle with poppy seeds.

7 Bake the galette on the middle oven rack for about 35 minutes. Slide it out of the oven, top with the remaining Gruyère, and continue to bake for about 10 minutes, until the crust is a rich golden brown. Transfer the sheet to a cooling rack and cool the galette for at least 10 minutes before serving. Refrigerate leftovers. Reheat slices on a baking sheet, loosely covered with foil, in a 300°F (150°C) oven for 10 to 12 minutes.

MAKES 6 TO 8 SERVINGS

　　 Good Basic Pie Dough (page 145)

2　 medium-size bunches Swiss chard

3　 tablespoons olive oil

1½　large onions, halved and thinly sliced

　　 Salt and freshly ground black pepper

2　 garlic cloves, minced

　　 Worcestershire sauce

½　 cup ricotta cheese

½　 cup grated Parmesan cheese

1½　cups grated Gruyère or Comté cheese

1　 egg beaten with 1 tablespoon water, for glaze

　　 Poppy seeds, for sprinkling

POTATO, ARUGULA, AND TOMATO GALETTE

The challenge of a potato galette is to add enough other good stuff to make it interesting. With that in mind, we lay down a base of creamy ricotta cheese enriched with chicken stock and Parmesan and provide a moist blanket of onion, tomatoes, and arugula on top. Potatoes never had it so good. Serve something refreshing and lean on the side, such as carrots and cucumbers with vinaigrette.

1 Prepare the pie dough, and refrigerate it for at least 1½ to 2 hours before rolling.

2 Peel the potatoes and slice them a little less than ¼ inch thick. Place in a large saucepan with plenty of salted water to cover. Bring to a boil, then lower the heat and cook at a low boil until the slices are almost tender, about 4 to 5 minutes. Drain the potatoes and rinse under cold running water. Spread the potatoes out on a large baking sheet lined with paper towels. Pat dry and set aside to cool.

3 Heat the oil in a large skillet over moderate heat. Add the bacon and cook for several minutes, until it renders some fat. Stir in the onion and cook for 4 to 5 minutes. Add the tomato and cook for several more minutes, stirring. Then stir in the arugula and ¼ cup of the chicken stock. Season generously with salt and pepper. Cover the skillet and cook gently for several minutes, stirring occasionally, until the arugula has wilted. Remove from the heat and stir in the rosemary. It's good if there's a little liquid sitting in the pan because this mixture goes over the potatoes and the moisture will flavor the spuds.

4 Combine the ricotta, Parmesan, and remaining ¼ cup chicken stock in a bowl; whisk to smooth. Add salt and pepper to taste.

5 Preheat the oven to 400°F (200°C). On a large sheet of parchment paper, roll the dough into one 14- by 11-inch oblong. Lift the paper and dough onto a large baking sheet. (If you don't have parchment, roll the dough onto a sheet of waxed paper, invert it onto your baking sheet, and peel off the paper.

6 Leaving a 1½- to 2-inch border of dough all around, spread the pastry with half of the ricotta mixture, smoothing it with a spoon. Arrange the potatoes over the ricotta in tight, overlapping rows; you want a thick layer of potatoes, but don't be surprised if you don't need all the slices. Salt and pepper the potatoes well. Dollop the remaining ricotta mixture here and there over the potatoes. Spoon the arugula and tomato mixture on top. Using the parchment, a spatula, or a dough scraper to help lift, fold the border of dough up around the edges of the filling.

7 Bake the galette for about 45 minutes. If you're adding the mozzarella, sprinkle it on for the last 5 minutes of baking. When done, the pastry border will be golden brown; you may or may not see a little liquid bubbling up from the ricotta mixture. Transfer the sheet to a cooling rack and cool for 10 to 15 minutes before serving. Refrigerate leftovers. Reheat slices on a baking sheet, loosely covered with foil, in a 300°F (150°C) oven for 10 to 12 minutes.

MAKES 6 TO 8 SERVINGS

Good Basic Pie Dough (page 145)

4 medium-size red potatoes

1 tablespoon light olive oil

3 bacon strips, thinly sliced crosswise

½ large onion, finely chopped

1 large tomato, cored and diced

¼ pound arugula (several large handfuls) or baby spinach

½ cup chicken stock

Salt and freshly ground black pepper

1–2 teaspoons fresh rosemary or ½ teaspoon dried

1 cup ricotta cheese

⅓ cup finely grated Parmesan cheese

1 cup grated mozzarella or other melting cheese (optional)

TOMATO SLAB PIE

A slab pie, be it savory or sweet, refers to any pie that's baked in a jelly roll pan instead of a round pan. There are advantages to this architectural arrangement, perhaps the most important being that for roughly the same amount of effort, you end up with an attractive dish that serves 12 to 15 people instead of the usual 8 to 10. So slab pies are a natural for large summer gatherings. This all-tomato version, finished with a dusting of snipped chives and garlic, is as good as you'll encounter. The tomatoes are enhanced by a generous coat of Dijon mustard on the crust, while the cream and cheese turn the tomatoes into something like a tomato gratin.

1 Prepare the slab pie shell; refrigerate. You may also freeze it if you want to make it several days ahead. (Cover it with plastic wrap, and overwrap with foil before freezing.)

2 Preheat the oven to 400°F (200°C) when you're ready to start assembling the pie. Put one rack in the bottom of your oven, and position another in the middle. Using your finger, push most of the seeds out of each tomato half, but not all of them; you want the tomatoes to be a little juicy. Cut the tomatoes into ⅛-inch-thick slices.

3 Spoon the mustard into the pie shell. Using the back of the spoon, smear it over the entire bottom. Scatter half of the cheddar evenly over the shell.

4 Make two or three lengthwise rows of tomato slices in the shell. If your tomatoes are quite large, you'll only have room for two rows. Overlap them by quite a bit, so they form a thick tomato layer. Dice some of the extra slices, and fill in any gaps between or outside the rows with these smaller chunks.

5 Drizzle the heavy cream here and there over the tomatoes. Salt and pepper them liberally. Mix the Parmesan with the remaining cheddar in a small bowl, and scatter the cheese over the top of the pie. Sprinkle on the chives and minced garlic.

6 Bake the pie on the lower rack for 20 minutes. Then reduce the heat to 375°F (190°C), move the pie to the middle rack, and bake for another 25 to 30 minutes, until quite bubbly and a deep golden brown. Transfer the pan to a cooling rack and cool for at least 20 to 30 minutes before slicing. If at any point in the baking you notice that the crust is puffing up a bit in a certain area, take a long skewer and poke through the filling and pastry. The bubble will immediately collapse. Refrigerate leftovers. Reheat, loosely covered with foil, in a 300°F (150°C) oven for 10 to 15 minutes.

MAKES 12 TO 15 SERVINGS

Slab Pie Dough (and Shell)
(page 148)

4 large tomatoes, cored and halved

3 tablespoons Dijon mustard

2½ cups grated extra-sharp cheddar cheese

⅓ cup heavy cream

Salt and freshly ground black pepper

⅓ cup grated Parmesan cheese

2–3 tablespoons chopped chives

2 garlic cloves, minced

BISCUIT-CRUSTED CHICKEN POT PIE

Somewhere inside me is an irresponsible little boy who would be happy to eat nothing but chicken pot pies day in and day out. I grew up on the frozen variety (I'll still eat a couple of them each year for nostalgia's sake), but I've long since become an ardent fan of the homemade pot pie, of which there are two types: pastry topped and biscuit topped. This is the latter, crowded with chicken, broccoli, carrots, and peas, heavily cloaked in a creamy sauce — and it is outrageously good. The recipe is written around individual servings, but you could also bake it in a 9-inch deep-dish pie pan (see note). Keep the biscuit topping on the thin side, so you end up with the right proportion of biscuit to filling (about twice as much filling). If you don't need all the dough, cut it into biscuits anyway, freeze them unbaked, and bake within a week or so. No need to thaw them out first; they'll just take about 5 minutes longer to bake.

1 Prepare the flour/butter biscuit mixture, but don't add the buttermilk just yet. Keep the flour/butter mixture in the fridge while you prepare the filling.

2 Combine the chicken stock, peas, and carrots in a large saucepan. Bring to a simmer, and simmer for about 3 minutes, just until the carrots lose their crunch. Stir in the broccoli, chicken, cream, sage, and thyme. Add salt — taking into account the saltiness of your stock — and pepper to taste. Bring the mixture back to a simmer.

3 Combine the flour and softened butter in a small bowl, smearing them together with a spoon. As the filling simmers, add this thickener about 1 tablespoon at a time, stirring it in thoroughly before adding the next tablespoon. Your liquid should thicken up nicely by the time you've added most of the thickener. If you think it needs to be thicker, add the final tablespoon, and continue to simmer for 2 to 3 minutes. Remove the filling from the heat. Taste again, and see if it needs more salt or seasoning.

4 Preheat the oven to 400°F (200°C). Select six individual deep pie dishes — about 1¼ cups capacity is ideal — butter them well, and place them on a parchment-lined baking sheet. Divide the filling evenly among them.

5 Finish mixing up the biscuits, and allow the dough to rest for several minutes. How much dough you use for each pie will depend on the diameter of the dish. You may have to adjust as you go. For starters, pinch off a piece of dough about the size of a large golf ball. With your hands well floured, shape it into a ball, then flatten it into a disk about ⅓ inch thick. Place the disk on top of one filled portion. Repeat for the remaining dishes. Bake the pot pies on the sheet for 22 to 25 minutes, until the filling is bubbly and the biscuits are crusty and golden brown. Transfer the dishes to a rack and cool for about 10 minutes before serving.

MAKES 6 SERVINGS

Butter for the pie pans

Cornmeal Buttermilk Biscuits (page 42); see step 1

3 cups flavorful chicken stock

1½ cups fresh or frozen peas

1½ cups sliced carrots

3 cups broccoli florets

2½ cups cooked chicken, in bite-size pieces

¾ cup heavy cream

2 teaspoons chopped fresh sage or 1 teaspoon dried

1 teaspoon fresh thyme or ½ teaspoon dried

Salt and freshly ground black pepper

5 tablespoons all-purpose flour

4 tablespoons unsalted butter, softened

NOTE: To make one full-size pie instead of individual ones, transfer the filling to a buttered, deep-dish pie pan or casserole dish no more than 9 inches in diameter. Place the dough on a well-floured surface and roll it about ⅓ inch thick. Trim the dough to fit the pan and drape it over the filling. Bake as above. (Scraps can be cut into biscuits to bake now or freeze and bake later.)

CURRIED VEGETABLE POT PIES

You don't need beef or chicken or any other meat, for that matter, to make a really satisfying pot pie. A medley of root vegetables gives this crusted curry pie heartiness to spare. If you're inclined to improvise, however, go ahead and add those leftover vegetables in the fridge — a serving of corn, green beans, or peas — or replace the diced sweet potato with winter squash or parsnips. This here is a regular veggie party, so if you want to serve something on the side, consider a crisp salad or maybe cool applesauce to balance the spiciness of the curry.

1 Prepare the pie dough, but instead of forming one large disk, divide it into five or six pieces, depending on the number of servings you need. The smaller number will allow you to make the top crust slightly thicker (there is no bottom crust). Shape the pieces into balls, then flatten them into disks about ½ inch thick. Place the disks on a plate, and refrigerate for 1½ to 2 hours before rolling.

2 Heat the oil in a large pot. Stir in the onion and cook over medium heat for 8 to 10 minutes, stirring often. Add the garlic, ginger, curry powder, coriander, and black pepper. Cook for 1 minute, stirring, then stir in the stock. Add the carrots, potatoes, sweet potatoes, chickpeas, and ½ teaspoon salt. Bring to a boil. Lower the heat, cover the pot, and simmer for 10 to 12 minutes, until the vegetables are almost tender. Stir in the tomato and spinach. Continue to simmer for several minutes, until the spinach is wilted.

3 Stir 1 cup of the coconut milk and the brown sugar into the curry. (Don't worry if it looks curdled; the cornstarch thickener will smooth things out.) In a small bowl, stir the remaining 3 tablespoons coconut milk with the cornstarch until smooth. Stir this slurry into the vegetables. Return the mixture to a very low boil and cook for 2 minutes, stirring. Remove from the heat. Sample the curry and see if it needs any additional salt or pepper. Set aside to partially cool.

4 Preheat the oven to 375°F (190°C). Have ready the number of individual pot pie bakers that you need. These could be individual pie pans, large ramekins, or mini casseroles with a capacity of 1¼ to 1½ cups. Butter them and place them on a parchment-lined baking sheet. Divide the curry mixture among them, leaving about ½ inch between the filling and the top of the dishes.

5 Working with one piece of dough at a time, roll it just large enough to cover the filling of one pie, and drape the pastry over the filling. Repeat for the remaining pies. Lightly brush the pastry with the egg glaze. Bake the pot pies, on the sheet, for about 45 minutes, until the filling is bubbly and the pastry is golden brown. Transfer the dishes to a rack and cool for at least 10 minutes before serving.

MAKES 5 OR 6 POT PIES

Butter for the pie pans or ramekins

Oat and Cornmeal Pie Dough (page 147) or Good Basic Pie Dough (page 145)

3 tablespoons vegetable oil or other neutral oil

1 large onion, chopped

3 garlic cloves, minced

1 tablespoon minced fresh ginger

2½ tablespoons curry powder

½ teaspoon ground coriander

¼ teaspoon freshly ground black pepper

2½ cups chicken or vegetable stock

2 cups thinly sliced carrots

1½ cups peeled and diced red-skinned potatoes

1 cup peeled and diced sweet potato

1 (15-ounce) can chickpeas, rinsed

½ teaspoon salt

1 cup diced tomato

2 or 3 large handfuls baby spinach (5 to 6 ounces)

1 cup plus 3 tablespoons coconut milk

1 tablespoon brown sugar

1 tablespoon cornstarch

1 egg beaten with 1 teaspoon water, for glaze

SHEPHERD'S PIE WITH COLLARDS AND BEEF

I love driving the country roads of my adopted South, taking in the scenery and jumping at every opportunity to stop and chat with anyone who has a load of watermelons, corn, or collards to sell from the back of a pickup. Among the many things I love to do with collards is use them in this saucy, Southern-style shepherd's pie in place of the traditional peas and carrots. The beef filling has a touch of barbecue sauce and smoked paprika, to give it some real country flavor. To mix it up we've replaced the mashed potato topping with a three-roots mash made with spuds, rutabaga, and parsnips. (You could stick with straight potatoes if you like, but this hybrid mash has a sweet, earthy flavor that's indescribably good.) For the crust I like the Oat and Cornmeal Pie Dough, but feel free to choose another. Don't be alarmed by the number of ingredients here. This is not complicated, and you can make the filling a day ahead.

1 Prepare the pie dough, dividing it into four equal pieces. Shape each one into a ½-inch-thick disk. Wrap individually in plastic, and refrigerate for 45 minutes to an hour before rolling.

2 Make the filling: Heat the oil in a large pot. Stir in the onion and celery. Cook for 5 minutes over medium heat, then add the ground beef. Brown the meat, breaking it up with a wooden spoon. When the meat has browned, take the pot off the heat, tilt the pan, and spoon off (and discard) about two-thirds of the fat.

3 Put the pot back on the heat, and stir in the smoked paprika, cumin, and garlic. Cook for 30 seconds, stirring, then add the collards, beef stock, ¼ teaspoon salt, and a grinding of black pepper. Bring to a simmer, stirring occasionally; cover the pot and simmer the filling for 15 minutes. Remove the lid and stir in the tomato paste, barbecue sauce, brown sugar, and Worcestershire sauce.

4 Continue to cook at a low boil, uncovered, for another 10 minutes. Shake 1½ tablespoons of the flour over the filling. Cook, stirring often, until the mixture takes on a saucy, stew-like consistency; this won't take more than a few minutes. Add a little more of the remaining flour if the liquid looks too thin. Taste, adjusting the seasoning as needed. Remove from the heat and transfer the filling to a shallow baking dish to cool. Cover and refrigerate until needed.

MAKES 4 SERVINGS

Oat and Cornmeal Pie Dough (page 147)

2 tablespoons vegetable oil or light olive oil

1 medium onion, finely chopped

1 celery stalk, finely chopped

1 pound ground beef (chuck)

½ teaspoon smoked paprika

¼ teaspoon ground cumin

2 garlic cloves, minced

5 cups well-chopped collard greens (stems removed)

2½ cups beef stock

Salt and freshly ground black pepper

1 tablespoon tomato paste

1 tablespoon barbecue sauce

1 teaspoon light brown sugar

Worcestershire sauce

1½–2 tablespoons all-purpose flour

5 Make the topping: Combine the potatoes, rutabaga, and parsnips in a large saucepan. Add plenty of water to cover; salt well. Bring the vegetables to a low boil and cook for about 15 minutes, until all the vegetables are tender (the rutabaga will probably take the longest). Drain in a colander (save the liquid for soup), then transfer the vegetables back to the saucepan. In a separate small saucepan, warm ⅓ cup heavy cream (or other liquid) with the butter until the butter melts. Using a potato masher, mash the vegetables well, gradually adding the cream mixture, along with salt and pepper to taste. Add a little more warm cream, as needed. Cover the pan to keep it warm.

6 Preheat the oven to 400°F (200°C). Adjust your oven rack so it is one position below center. Put a large baking sheet on the rack to preheat. Have ready four individual pie dishes of approximately 1¼ cups capacity. Working with one piece of dough at a time, roll it into a 7- to 8-inch circle. Line one of the dishes with it, pinching the overhang into an upstanding ridge, or at least as much of a ridge as the overhang allows. (The ridge will help contain the filling.) Repeat for the other pieces of dough. Place in the freezer for 15 minutes.

7 Divide the filling evenly among the pie shells. Spoon a big mound of mashed veggies on top of the filling, smoothing it with a spoon. Put the dishes on the baking sheet, and bake for 40 to 45 minutes. When the pies are done, you may see the filling bubbling up around the edge, and the edge of the pastry will be a light golden brown. Transfer the pies to a rack and cool for 10 to 15 minutes before serving.

MASHED ROOTS TOPPING

2 cups peeled and chunked potatoes

2 cups peeled and chunked rutabaga

1 cup peeled and sliced parsnips

Salt

⅓–½ cup heavy cream, light cream, or chicken stock

4 tablespoons unsalted butter

Freshly ground black pepper

SPICED EGGPLANT AND LENTIL TURNOVERS

Eggplant is an exquisite soaker-upper of flavors, but it's easy to get stuck in a rut with eggplant Parmesan and ratatouille. These little hand pies offer a fresh take, filled with a well-seasoned mixture of eggplant, French lentils, feta cheese, and fresh tomato. They have a spicy and exotic Mediterranean disposition. We make them large-appetizer size, and you should end up with 12 for your gathering, provided you don't start eating the eggplant right from the pan, as you'll be tempted to do. Vegetarians should note that while the filling here is meatless, the dough contains lard. To skip the lard, use the Slab Pie Dough on page 148.

1 Prepare the turnover dough as instructed. Divide the dough into equal quarters, and divide each quarter into three equal pieces. Shape each piece into a ball, and flatten into disks almost ½ inch thick. Place the disks on a plate, cover with plastic wrap, and refrigerate for 1½ to 2 hours before rolling.

2 Pick over the lentils and remove any detritus; place them in a mesh sieve and rinse well. Transfer to a large saucepan. Add the bay leaf and enough water to cover by an inch or so. Do not salt; it can prevent the lentils from softening. Bring to a boil. Reduce the heat and cook at a low boil for 30 to 35 minutes, until the lentils are just tender, replenishing the water if it becomes too low. Transfer the lentils to a sieve. Drain but don't rinse, then put them back in the saucepan; remove the bay leaf. Stir in a few pinches of salt.

3 Heat ¼ cup of the olive oil in a large pot. Stir in the onion and eggplant. Add a large pinch of salt. Cook over medium heat, partially covered, for 7 to 8 minutes, stirring occasionally. Add another tablespoon or two of olive oil, and stir in the garlic, cumin, smoked paprika, coriander, caraway seed, and cayenne. Add ¼ cup water or stock and the tomato paste, in small dollops. Mix well, then stir in 2½ cups of the cooked lentils. Taste, adding salt, pepper, the fresh parsley, and several squeezes of lemon juice, as desired. The mixture should be thick and moist but not runny. You may need to add more water, by the tablespoon, to moisten. Remove from the heat and let cool.

4 Preheat the oven to 375°F (190°C). Line two large baking sheets with parchment paper. If you don't have parchment, you can put these directly on the sheets. Working with one piece of dough at a time, roll it into an oblong about 6 inches long and 5 inches wide. Draw an imaginary line (the short way) across the center of the dough, and place about 2 tablespoons of the eggplant mixture just to one side of that line; leave a border of pastry at least ¾ inch wide all around. Pile a mounded tablespoon each of the crumbled feta cheese and diced tomato on top of the eggplant. Moisten the edge of the pastry with a damp pastry brush, and fold the uncovered half of the dough over the filling. Line up the edges of the pastry, and press to seal.

RECIPE CONTINUED ON NEXT PAGE

MAKES 12 TURNOVERS

Turnover Dough (page 150)

1 cup dried French green lentils

1 bay leaf

Salt

¼–⅓ cup olive oil

½ large onion, finely chopped

1 large eggplant, peeled and diced in ½-inch pieces (about 5 cups)

2 garlic cloves, minced

1 teaspoon ground cumin

½ teaspoon smoked paprika

½ teaspoon ground coriander

½ teaspoon caraway seed (preferably crushed)

⅛ teaspoon ground cayenne pepper, or to taste

¼ cup water or stock, plus more as needed

1 tablespoon tomato paste

Freshly ground black pepper

¼ cup finely chopped fresh parsley

Lemon juice (a few squeezes)

1¼ cups crumbled feta cheese

1¼ cups finely diced fresh tomato

1 egg beaten with 1 teaspoon water, for glaze

5 Using a pastry wheel or paring knife, trim the dough to make a nicely rounded edge. Crimp the edge with a fork and place the turnover on one of the baking sheets. Repeat for all of the pieces of dough. Brush each turnover sparingly with the egg glaze (see the box below), and poke the top once or twice with the tip of a paring knife or the tines of a fork to make steam vents.

6 Bake the turnovers for about 40 minutes, until golden brown. If you have room, you can bake them on separate oven racks and switch them about midway through. Or you can refrigerate one batch, right on the sheet, while the first one bakes. Transfer the baked turnovers to a rack and cool for about 10 minutes before serving.

NOTE: If you'd like to make these ahead, they freeze beautifully. Prepare as directed, but do not apply the glaze. Place close together on small baking sheets. Freeze. In a couple of hours, once they're frozen, transfer them to freezer bags and freeze for up to 2 months. To bake, place them on your baking sheet, apply the glaze, and bake as directed. They'll take 45 to 50 minutes to heat through.

GLAZE WITH A LIGHT TOUCH

Anytime you apply an egg wash or a glaze to your doughs, bread, or pastry, do it with a light touch. If you paint it on thickly, the glaze invariably runs off your item and then onto or into your pan, where it burns and causes sticking problems. So it's best to barely dampen your pastry brush and brush it on very lightly. Start at the top, and work your way toward the edges. By the way, don't throw out any unused glaze. Store it in a jar for a day or two, at most, in case you need it. Mix it with a fork before reusing.

MEATLESS TOSTADA POT PIES

I'm not alone in my love of tostadas, so I'm inclined to believe that a tostada-style pot pie will find an appreciative audience. The usual platform — a crispy fried tortilla — is gone, replaced by a flaky pie shell stuffed with seasoned corn, tomatoes, black beans, and fresh herbs. A bit of cream transforms the filling into a sort of saucy cowboy stew, while the cheddar cheese and ranch dressing melt together on top and cover the pie in a golden-brown blanket. Piled high with garnishes, it makes for one sassy Tex-Mex dish with a twist.

1 Prepare the pie dough as directed, but divide it into four equal pieces. Shape each piece into a ball, and flatten them into ½-inch-thick disks. Wrap individually in plastic wrap and refrigerate for at least 1½ hours before rolling.

2 Heat the oil in a large skillet. Stir in the onion and carrot. Cook over moderate heat for about 7 minutes, stirring often. Add the garlic, chili powder, and cumin, and cook another 30 seconds, stirring nonstop. Stir in the stock and tomato paste, until smooth. Stir in the black beans, corn, and tomatoes; add salt and pepper to taste. Stir in the parsley. Remove from the heat.

3 When you're almost ready to bake these, roll one piece of dough into a 6- to 6½-inch circle, and line an individual (approximately 1-cup capacity) pie pan with it. The top edge of the pastry will probably just reach the top edge of the pan. Repeat for the remaining pieces of dough. Refrigerate the pie shells for 20 minutes.

4 Preheat the oven to 375°F (190°C). Place a baking sheet that's large enough to hold all four pies on the middle rack.

5 Divide the filling evenly among the pie shells. If the pies aren't too full and you want to give the edge a slightly different look, take the edge of the pastry and sort of drape it back over the filling, creating a rounded-off perimeter. Pour exactly 2 tablespoons cream into each pie, and divide the cheese evenly over the tops. Smear 2 tablespoons ranch dressing over each one.

6 Transfer the pies to the preheated baking sheet. Bake for 35 to 40 minutes, until the tops are a rich golden brown and the pies are bubbling. Transfer the pies to a cooling rack and cool for at least 10 minutes before serving, passing the garnishes at the table, starting with a bed of shredded lettuce.

MAKES 4 POT PIES

Good Basic Pie Dough (page 145)

3 tablespoons vegetable oil or light vegetable oil

1 medium onion, chopped

1 large carrot, finely diced

3 garlic cloves, minced

1 teaspoon chili powder

1 teaspoon ground cumin

⅓ cup vegetable stock or water

2 teaspoons tomato paste

1 cup canned black beans, rinsed

1 cup fresh-cut or frozen-and-thawed corn kernels

1 cup quartered cherry tomatoes or seeded and diced fresh tomato

Salt and freshly ground black pepper

2 tablespoons chopped fresh parsley or cilantro

½ cup heavy cream

1½ cups grated extra-sharp cheddar cheese

½ cup ranch dressing

Optional garnishes: shredded iceberg lettuce, avocado chunks, sour cream, and diced tomato

SPICED BEEF POT PIE WITH WINTER VEGGIES

This pot pie, a spicy beef stew with a pastry crust, is a bonanza for anyone with garden-to-table aspirations — there are sweet and baking potatoes, carrots, tomatoes, celery, onions, and herbs. But the thing that really sets it apart from others like it is the blend of seasonings, including curry, cumin, smoked paprika, and fennel seeds. It's a bold and robust combination that smells wonderful and telegraphs a dish that's oh-so-tantalizing, familiar yet exotic, and the perfect midwinter cure for cabin fever.

1 Prepare the pie dough, and refrigerate it for at least 1½ to 2 hours before rolling.

2 Heat 2 tablespoons of the olive oil in a large pot. Add the meat and brown for about 4 minutes, stirring occasionally. (Do this in two batches if you think it will be crowded; the meat needs some room to brown properly.) Transfer the meat to a bowl.

3 Add the remaining 2 tablespoons olive oil to the pot, and stir in the onion, celery, and carrots; salt and pepper lightly. Cook for 5 minutes over moderate heat, partially covered, stirring several times. Stir in the sweet potato, potato, garlic, curry powder, paprika, cumin, fennel seed, and allspice. Cook, stirring, for 2 minutes. Add the browned beef, wine, beef broth, rosemary, and bay leaf. Add ¼ teaspoon salt; you'll probably need more as it simmers, depending on the saltiness of the broth. Add plenty of pepper. Bring to a low boil, then reduce the heat, cover, and simmer for 10 minutes.

4 After 10 minutes, taste the broth and see how it's doing. Add more salt and pepper as needed. Simmer, covered, for 10 minutes. Taste again, and simmer a few minutes more.

5 Transfer a half ladleful of the stew liquid to a small bowl. Add the flour, and whisk well to smooth. Stir this slurry back into the stew. Simmer gently for several minutes, until the stew develops some body. Taste again, and correct the seasoning as needed. Stir the diced tomatoes into the stew. Simmer for 5 minutes more, then remove from the heat and let cool. You can assemble the dish when the stew is lukewarm or transfer the stew to a shallow casserole and refrigerate overnight before using. (I prefer the latter, if there's time; stews always taste better the next day. Either way, do be sure to completely cool it.)

MAKES 6 TO 8 SERVINGS

	Butter for the pie pan or casserole
	Good Basic Pie Dough (page 145)
4	tablespoons olive oil
1–1¼	pounds beef stew meat
1	large onion, chopped
1	celery stalk, chopped
2	carrots, thickly sliced
	Salt and freshly ground black pepper
1	medium sweet potato, peeled and diced
1	small baking potato, peeled and diced
4	garlic cloves, minced
1½	teaspoons curry powder
½	teaspoon smoked paprika
½	teaspoon ground cumin
½	teaspoon crushed fennel seed
¼	teaspoon ground allspice
¾	cup dry red wine
2½	cups beef broth
1	teaspoon chopped fresh rosemary
1	bay leaf
2½	tablespoons all-purpose flour
⅓	cup diced canned tomatoes or fresh tomatoes, or a spoonful of tomato paste
1	egg beaten with 1 teaspoon water, for glaze

6 When you're ready to bake, preheat the oven to 375°F (190°C). Butter a 9½-inch deep-dish pie pan or a medium shallow casserole dish with the same approximate capacity. (You don't want to use a deep casserole dish, because if the pastry sits too low in the dish, it won't turn golden brown the way it should.) Spoon the filling into the dish, to within ¼ inch of the top edge. Roll the pastry slightly larger and to the same shape as the pan; drape it over the filling, tucking the pastry down next to the filling. Using a toothpick or the tip of a paring knife, poke several holes in the top so steam can escape. Brush sparingly with the egg glaze.

7 Line a large baking sheet with parchment paper or aluminum foil. Place the pie on the sheet and bake for 45 to 50 minutes, until the filling is bubbly hot and the crust is golden brown. Transfer the pie to a rack and cool for at least 10 minutes before serving.

RATATOUILLE COBBLER

By now, just about everyone has heard of ratatouille, the classic French dish of stewed summer vegetables, which — when I googled it — was preceded in the search results by the animated movie of the same name. I'm not sure what to make of that, but I am sure that this cobbler twist on the original will be met with critical acclaim. The stewed veggies are topped with Parmesan cheese biscuits, which are simply the Cornmeal Buttermilk Biscuits (page 42) with a couple of minor alterations. The whole thing is baked until the biscuit topping is golden brown. All you need is a salad to go with it.

1 Heat the olive oil in a large heavy pot. Add the onion and cook over medium heat for 3 to 4 minutes. Add the eggplant, zucchini, and bell pepper. Continue to cook for 8 to 10 minutes, stirring often. Be sure to scrape along the bottom of the pan with your wooden spoon; eggplant is prone to sticking. Stir in the garlic and cook for another minute or two.

2 Stir the diced tomatoes into the vegetables. Gradually add salt and pepper to taste as the dish simmers; it tends to need a fair amount of both. Reduce the heat slightly, cover the casserole, and simmer for about 10 minutes.

3 Stir in the pesto and tomato paste. Simmer the dish, uncovered, for a few more minutes, gradually adding a little water, up to ⅓ cup, to make the ratatouille a little saucy. This sauciness will help cook the biscuits from below as it simmers in the oven. Remove from the heat and add a teaspoon or two of balsamic vinegar, to taste, if the stew needs a little bit of acidity.

4 Preheat the oven to 400°F (200°C). Brush a little olive oil in a medium-size baking dish, and spread the ratatouille in it. It should come no higher than about halfway up the sides. Put the casserole in the oven; it's fine if the oven is still preheating. Start making the biscuits as soon as it goes in the oven.

5 Prepare the biscuits as directed, but make the following changes: Replace the ½ cup cornmeal with ⅓ cup finely grated Parmesan cheese plus 1 tablespoon cornmeal. (You will not be able to sift the Parmesan cheese, so just mix the dry ingredients together in a bowl.) In addition, increase the buttermilk to a total of 1 cup. The extra liquid will make the dough a little softer, like a drop biscuit. Leave the dough in the bowl; don't shape it or cut it into biscuits.

6 When the ratatouille starts to bubble, dollop big spoonfuls of the dough here and there over the surface. It's fine if there are gaps between the dollops, but try to have good coverage over the entire surface. Bake the ratatouille for 25 to 30 minutes, until the biscuit topping is a very rich golden brown. You can also check a biscuit by pulling it apart with a fork to see if it looks done underneath. But check one in the middle, since those take longer to cook through. Transfer the dish to a cooling rack and cool for about 10 minutes before serving.

MAKES 6 SERVINGS

- ⅓ cup olive oil, plus a little to coat the baking dish
- 1 large onion, chopped
- 1 large eggplant, peeled and cubed
- 3 small zucchini (1 to 1¼ pounds), cubed
- 1 large red or green bell pepper, cut into ¼-inch strips
- 3 garlic cloves, minced
- 3 cups cored and diced tomatoes (don't seed them)

  Salt and freshly ground black pepper
- 2 tablespoons pesto or ¼ cup chopped fresh basil
- 1 tablespoon tomato paste
- 1–2 teaspoons balsamic vinegar (optional)

  Cornmeal Buttermilk Biscuits dough (page 42), modified as in step 5
- ⅓ cup finely grated Parmesan cheese

NOTE: You may have noticed with ratatouille recipes that many cooks have their own little ways of doing things. Julia Child liked to peel her tomatoes. Others leave the skins on the eggplant. The version here is fairly straightforward, to keep it streamlined. But if you have any special ratatouille tricks or embellishments, feel free to incorporate them. Just keep the dish on the saucy side, so the biscuits have something to simmer in.

CABBAGE AND SAUSAGE SHORTBREAD

You don't often encounter the word *shortbread* with either *cabbage* or *sausage* directly in front of it, but here are all three together. This is part tart (by virtue of a simple, press-in shortbread crust) and part gratin, the cabbage and sausage blanketed by a simple sauce made with chicken stock and cream. It's also unabashedly rich, a special dish for a special occasion. This would be a cinch to make meatless by replacing the sausage with carrots or finely diced potatoes, among other vegetable possibilities. Simply cook them right along with the cabbage, and use vegetable stock instead of chicken. Make this your main dish, accompanied by dinner rolls and fried apple rings, or serve it as a side dish with roast meats.

1 Butter a 9- by 9-inch cake pan or similar-size shallow casserole dish.

2 Combine the flour, Parmesan, sugar, salt, and thyme in a food processor. Pulse several times to mix. Scatter the butter over the dry ingredients, and pulse the machine repeatedly until you have what looks like very fine crumbs. Sprinkle the water over the mixture. Give the machine long pulses until the mixture begins to form loose clumps; it should not gather in a ball around the blade. Transfer the mixture to your pan. Spread the crumbs around, and press them evenly into the bottom of the pan and about ¼ inch up the sides. Refrigerate for 1 hour, or freeze for 30 minutes. Preheat the oven to 350°F (180°C).

3 When the shortbread has chilled, bake it for 15 minutes. Transfer the pan to a rack and cool thoroughly.

4 Make the filling: Melt the butter in a large skillet or pot. Stir in the onion and cabbage; season with salt and pepper. Cook the cabbage over medium heat, partially covered, for about 20 minutes, stirring often, until the cabbage is quite tender. If the pan becomes dry at any point, stir in 2 to 3 tablespoons water. Season as needed. Stir in the sausage, cook for another minute or so, and remove from the heat. Uncover and set aside to cool.

5 Bring the chicken stock to a simmer in a small saucepan. In a small bowl, stir the cream and cornstarch until smooth. Stir the cornstarch mixture into the stock, and bring to a low boil. Cook gently for 1 minute, stirring, and remove from the heat. This sauce should have a consistency like buttermilk.

6 Set the oven to 350°F (180°C). Spread the sautéed cabbage mixture evenly over the shortbread crust. Pour the sauce evenly over the cabbage; use a fork to move the cabbage a little, so the sauce can settle in. Top with the cheddar. Bake the dish for 35 to 40 minutes, until bubbly and golden. Transfer to a rack, cool briefly, and serve.

MAKES UP TO 9 SERVINGS

CRUST

	Butter for the pan
1¼	cups all-purpose flour
¼–⅓	cup finely grated Parmesan cheese
1½	teaspoons sugar
½	teaspoon salt
1	teaspoon fresh thyme or ½ teaspoon dried
½	cup (1 stick) cold unsalted butter, cut into ½-inch cubes
1½	tablespoons cold water

FILLING

2½	tablespoons unsalted butter
½	large onion, chopped
5	cups chopped cabbage
	Salt and freshly ground black pepper
2	links (about 6 ounces) smoked sausage, diced
1	cup chicken stock
¼	cup heavy cream
1	tablespoon cornstarch
1	cup grated sharp cheddar cheese or other melting cheese

VEGETABLE AND BEEF HAND PIES

I love all sorts of turnovers, sweet and savory, but I really get excited about hearty hand pies like these. This recipe takes advantage of the harvest for onion, cabbage, and roots and draws inspiration from Cornish and Upper Peninsula pasty recipes. Braising the cabbage in beef broth adds much-needed moisture, which hand-size meat pies often lack. (Some cooks like to serve them with gravy, and ketchup is not unheard of as an accompaniment. I'm partial to Heinz chili sauce.) Worcestershire sauce, mustard, thyme, and garlic provide plenty of seasoning, and the cheddar adds a comforting richness. Serve with a big salad. If you have a way to reheat them, these hand pies are a boon for brown baggers.

1 Prepare the turnover dough, and refrigerate it for 1½ to 2 hours before handling it.

2 Melt the butter in a medium-large skillet. Add the cabbage and sauté over moderate heat for 5 minutes, stirring often. After 5 minutes, start adding the ½ cup of beef stock to the cabbage, a few tablespoons at a time. Keep adding more as it cooks off and soaks into the cabbage; this will only take a few minutes. Remove the cabbage from the heat when there's just a glaze of stock left in the pan. Transfer the cabbage to a large bowl, scraping out the pan well with a rubber spatula.

3 Add the rutabaga, carrot, and onion to the bowl with the cabbage. Add the ground chuck, breaking it into pieces. Using your hands, mix the ingredients lightly.

4 Blend the mustard, Worcestershire sauce, and garlic together in a small bowl. Pour it over the filling ingredients. Add ¾ teaspoon salt, plenty of black pepper, the thyme, and about 2 tablespoons beef stock. Mix well by hand. Add the cheese, and mix again thoroughly. Squeeze the filling a few times, so it starts clumping together a little; clumpy filling will mound nicely during assembly and make for a neater-looking pie. Refrigerate until you're ready to assemble the pies.

5 Preheat the oven to 375°F (190°C). Line a large baking sheet with parchment paper or lightly buttered aluminum foil.

MAKES 5 OR 6 HAND PIES

Turnover Dough (page 150)

2 tablespoons unsalted butter

3 cups finely chopped cabbage

½ cup beef broth, plus a little extra to moisten the ingredients

1 cup finely diced (¼ inch) rutabaga

1 cup finely diced carrot

½ medium onion, finely chopped

½ pound ground beef (chuck)

2 teaspoons Dijon mustard

1½ teaspoons Worcestershire sauce

2 garlic cloves, minced

Salt and freshly ground black pepper

2 teaspoons fresh thyme or 1 teaspoon dried

1 cup grated sharp or extra-sharp cheddar cheese

1 egg beaten with 1 teaspoon water, for glaze

6 To assemble the pies, divide the dough into five or six equal pieces, depending on the number of servings you need and how full you like your hand pies. (Obviously, fewer pies equals more filling in each.) Working with one piece of dough at a time, roll the dough into an oblong about 10 inches long and 7 inches wide, or slightly smaller if you have six pieces. Draw an imaginary line (the short way) across the center of the dough. Place a large mound of the filling — about ¾ cup, give or take — just to one side of that line, leaving a nearly 1-inch-wide border of uncovered dough all around. Brush the border lightly with a damp pastry brush, and fold the uncovered half of dough over the filling. Line up the edges, and press them together to seal.

7 Using a pastry wheel or paring knife, trim the edge neatly, removing the excess dough, and use a fork to crimp the edge. Place the hand pie on the baking sheet. Repeat for the other pies.

8 Poke the top of each pie with a fork once or twice to make steam vents. Brush each one sparingly with a bit of the egg glaze. Bake for 50 to 55 minutes, rotating the baking sheet 180 degrees midway through the baking. When done, the turnovers will be a rich golden brown. Transfer to a cooling rack and cool for at least 10 minutes before serving. Refrigerate leftovers. Reheat leftovers on a baking sheet, covered with foil, in a 300°F (150°C) oven for about 12 minutes.

SAVORY ASPARAGUS, HAM, AND BRIE PUDDING

You may know this casserole made with leftover pieces of bread as a "strata," but no matter what you call it, this is casual home cooking at its best. I bake a lot of harvest yeast breads, and there's no better way to repurpose the odds and ends than by turning them into pillowy-soft savory pudding with melty cheese, fresh asparagus, and ham. (Slightly dry bread is actually better than fresh because it absorbs more liquid.) Broccoli and spinach are good stand-ins, if asparagus is not in season. Serve it for brunch, lunch, or dinner, and be sure to let it sit for at least a couple of hours, even overnight, before baking so the custard has plenty of time to saturate the bread. The best version of this that I've made was with leftover chunks of Pepperoni and Veggie Pull-Apart Pizza (page 113).

1 Butter a medium-size shallow casserole dish. Spread the cubed bread out in the casserole dish while you're doing your prep, to help dry it out.

2 Peel the lower third of each asparagus spear with a vegetable peeler or a paring knife. Cut off the tender tips, and slice the remainder of the spears into 1-inch sections. (If you'd rather not use the lower sections, you'll need about a pound of asparagus.)

3 Melt the butter in a large skillet. Add the onion and cook over medium heat for 6 to 7 minutes, stirring often. Add the asparagus tips and chopped spears along with the garlic and continue to cook for 3 to 4 minutes, until the asparagus is not quite tender. Remove from the heat.

4 Whisk the eggs in a large bowl until frothy. Add the half-and-half, mustard, thyme, salt, and pepper. Whisk well.

5 Spoon the cooked vegetables evenly over the bread, then distribute the Brie, cheddar, and ham over that. Whisk the custard briefly, and pour it slowly over everything. Using a large spoon, gently press on the solids so they're submerged by the custard. Cover the dish loosely with foil and refrigerate for at least 2 hours; overnight is fine.

6 When you're ready to bake the pudding, preheat the oven to 350°F (180°C). Remove the foil from the dish and bake for 45 to 55 minutes. When the pudding is done, it will have puffed nicely and the surface will be golden brown. To check the center, carefully — so you don't leave a big crater — dig into it with a spoon or butter knife and see how it looks. It should not be soupy or look like there's a lot of uncooked custard. Transfer the pudding to a cooling rack and cool briefly before serving.

MAKES ABOUT 8 SERVINGS

Butter for the casserole dish

6 cups leftover cubed yeast bread (not sweet bread)

½ pound fresh asparagus

3 tablespoons unsalted butter

½ large onion, finely chopped

2 garlic cloves, minced

5 large eggs

2 cups half-and-half

1 tablespoon Dijon mustard

1 teaspoon fresh thyme or ¼ to ½ teaspoon dried thyme

¾ teaspoon salt

¼–½ teaspoon freshly ground black pepper

6–8 ounces Brie cheese, cut into small chunks (leave the rind on)

1 cup grated sharp cheddar or fontina cheese

1 cup diced cooked ham or smoked sausage

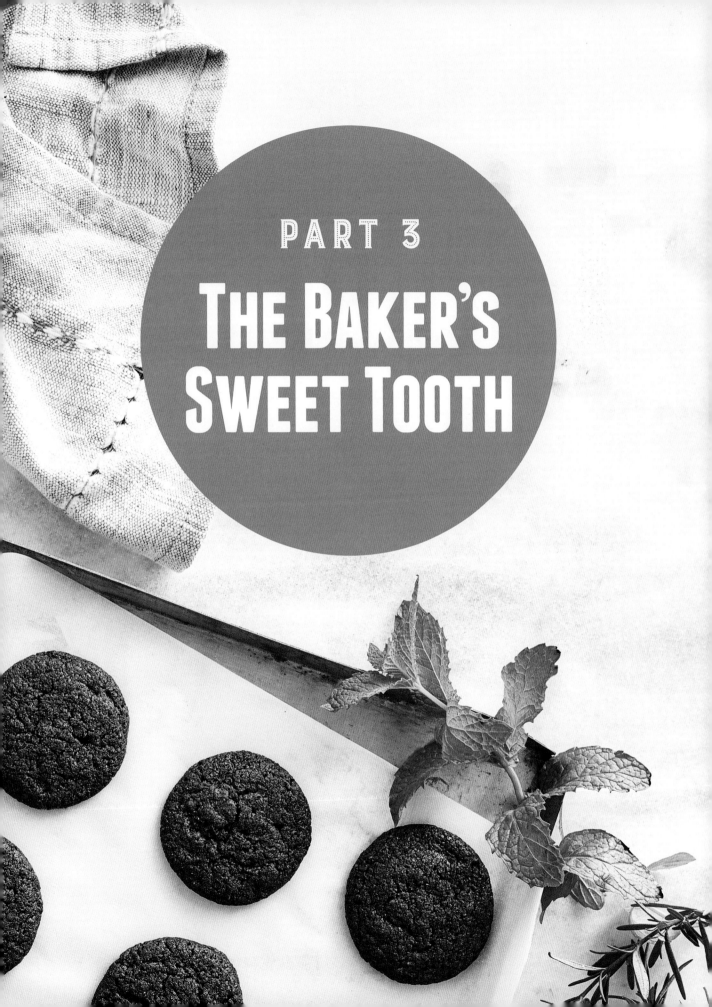

PART 3

The Baker's Sweet Tooth

6

COOKIES AND BARS
A Handful of Harvest Goodness

It's hard for anyone with a sweet tooth to keep his hand out of the cookie jar; trust me on this. But it's harder still when your favorites incorporate a delicious and surprising harvest twist. Juicy summer berries, tangy rhubarb, a spoonful of chopped fresh herbs — these are just a few of the trademark touches you'll discover in the following recipes, a short-but-sweet collection that's extra-long on garden goodness.

ROSEMARY LEMON SHORTBREAD COOKIES

Sometimes less is more in the harvest baker's kitchen, as with these delicate shortbread cookies flavored with a hint of rosemary. They're buttery, just sweet enough, and one of the most tender shortbread cookies you'll ever eat, thanks in part to the addition of confectioners' sugar. A short stack of these, tucked in a cellophane bag and tied off with ribbon, makes the perfect gift for all the herb lovers on your holiday gift list.

MAKES 36 COOKIES

- ½ cup granulated sugar, plus 6 to 8 tablespoons for coating
- 2 tablespoons chopped fresh rosemary
- 1 teaspoon freshly grated lemon zest
- ¾ teaspoon salt
- 1 egg yolk
- 2 cups all-purpose flour
- ¼ cup confectioners' sugar
- 1 cup (2 sticks) cold unsalted butter, cut into ½-inch pieces

1 Combine the granulated sugar, rosemary, lemon zest, and salt in the bowl of a food processor. Pulse five or six times. Add the yolk; pulse again several times. Add the flour and confectioners' sugar; pulse again to mix.

2 Remove the lid and scatter the butter pieces over the dry ingredients. Pulse the machine repeatedly, until the dough forms large clumps that start gathering together. Stop the machine before the dough clumps too much or balls up around the blade.

3 Turn the dough out onto a very lightly floured work surface and divide it in half. Gently squeeze and knead the dough several times to even out the consistency. Dust a long piece of waxed paper with 3 to 4 tablespoons of granulated sugar. Using your palms, roll one half of the dough on the granulated sugar and into a 1¾- to 2-inch-thick log. Repeat for the other half of the dough. Slip the logs into gallon food storage bags and refrigerate for at least 6 hours, or overnight.

4 Preheat the oven to 350°F (180°C) when you're ready to bake the cookies. Line a large baking sheet with parchment if you have it. (It's better not to use a dark baking sheet, if you have the choice, because it might cause the cookies to overbrown.) Unwrap the dough and place it on a cutting board. Using a serrated knife, cut the dough into rounds ⅓ inch thick. Place the rounds on the sheet about 1 inch apart. When the sheet is full, put any unused dough back in the fridge.

5 Bake the cookies for 15 to 17 minutes, until the edges are golden and the surface is starting to brown. Transfer to a rack and cool for a minute or two on the sheet; then take them off the sheet and let them finish cooling directly on the rack.

6 When the sheet has cooled, slice and bake the remaining cookies. You can also load up a second sheet while the first one bakes. However, don't put the cold cut cookies on a warm sheet, or the cookies will start to melt before they bake.

Herbs and Desserts

For most of us cooks, adding herbs to savory dishes is second nature. But fresh herbs have a solid place in the realm of desserts, too. The trick to pairing herbs and sweets is a delicate hand: your herbs should never steal the show. A dusting of Mint Sugar (page 286) or a few slivers of cinnamon basil on fresh sliced peaches is all you need to make an impact.

Most berry pies love a small spoonful of chopped mint or lemon thyme (or use a sprig of either as a garnish). A bit of chopped sage can add interest to apple cakes, or try adding a little dried, crumbled sage or rosemary to your pie crust; a spoonful of cornmeal in the crust makes it even more delicious.

Herb-infused whipped cream is an elegant addition to fresh berries or shortcake. Heat 1 cup heavy cream in a saucepan until the surface shimmers. Remove from the heat and add a teaspoon of fresh lavender buds or ¼ cup loosely packed and torn basil or mint leaves. Cover and let steep for 30 to 60 minutes, then strain through a fine-mesh sieve. Refrigerate the cream for 6 to 8 hours, and beat as usual to make whipped cream, adding sugar to taste.

CHOCOLATE SANDWICH COOKIES WITH SWEET HERB MASCARPONE

I'm not one to throw tea and garden parties, but if I did — and wanted to put an exclamation point on my fondness for herbs — this is what I'd serve. First we bake up a batch of crisp chocolate wafers, fine cookies in their own right (I have often used them to make homemade ice cream sandwiches). Then we mix up some mascarpone cheese with a little sugar and a spoonful of herbs; I offer two versions, one made with lavender and the other with a combination of fresh mint and rosemary. If you're not sold on the pairing of chocolate and herbs, I think you'll be pleasantly surprised. Use restraint, even if you're madly in love with the herbs in question; as with cologne, a whisper is better than a shout.

1 Using an electric mixer — handheld is fine — cream the butter in a mixing bowl. Gradually add the granulated sugar and then the brown sugar, beating on medium-high speed for 1 minute after each addition. Add the egg and vanilla and beat for another minute or two, until smooth and creamy.

2 Sift the flour, cocoa powder, baking soda, and salt into another bowl. Using a wooden spoon, stir the dry ingredients into the creamed mixture, about half of it at a time, until evenly mixed. Cover the dough with plastic wrap and refrigerate for at least 3 hours; longer, or overnight, is fine.

3 When you're ready to bake, preheat the oven to 350°F (180°C). Butter one or two large cookie sheets, or line them with parchment (see note). Using a spoon, scoop up the dough and shape it into 1-inch balls. Place them on the sheet, evenly spaced, leaving plenty of room between them because they'll spread. You'll probably get 12 on a sheet. Refrigerate the unused dough while the first batch bakes.

4 Bake the cookies for 17 to 18 minutes. They'll spread and rise slightly, and the surface will be covered with tiny holes. Transfer the sheet to a cooling rack and cool the cookies on the sheet for 5 minutes; they'll settle and flatten out almost right away. Using a thin spatula, transfer the cookies directly to the rack and cool thoroughly. Prepare and bake the remaining dough as above. Use a fresh baking sheet, or allow the first sheet to cool thoroughly before using it.

5 To make the filling, put the granulated sugar and lavender in a mortar and pulverize the mixture well by hand (or use an electric spice or coffee grinder to do it). Put the mascarpone cheese in a small bowl, and stir in the herb sugar. Refrigerate for at least an hour or two to firm up before using.

MAKES ABOUT 1 DOZEN SANDWICH COOKIES

COOKIES

Butter for the cookie sheet

¾ cup (1½ sticks) unsalted butter, softened

½ cup granulated sugar

½ cup packed light brown sugar

1 large egg, at room temperature

1 teaspoon vanilla extract

1 cup plus 2 tablespoons all-purpose flour

⅓ cup unsweetened cocoa powder

½ teaspoon baking soda

½ teaspoon salt

FILLING

2 tablespoons granulated sugar

1¼ teaspoons dried lavender, or 2 teaspoons chopped fresh mint plus ¼ teaspoon finely chopped fresh rosemary, or 2 tablespoons Mint Sugar (page 286) plus ¼ teaspoon finely chopped fresh rosemary

8 ounces cold mascarpone cheese

6 To assemble the cookies, spread a spoonful of the herb mascarpone over the bottom of one of the cookies. Top with another cookie to make a sandwich. Arrange on a tray or plate and serve. Refrigerate if you're not serving them within 15 minutes.

NOTE: Parchment paper works great here because it helps control the spreading of the cookies and promotes a slightly thicker cookie with nicely rounded edges. When the cookies are baked directly on a sheet, the bottom edges of the cookies look like they melted right into the baking sheet. This is a minor consideration, about which I and perhaps only two other people on the planet will care. But I still thought it worth mentioning in case both of you are reading this.

FRESH MINT BROWNIES

There are a lot of ways to make mint brownies with mint oil and extracts, but being something of a purist, I like this fresh mint version the best. These use a full cup of mint leaves, which might sound like a lot if you don't actually grow it and have firsthand knowledge of just how prolific mint can be. The leaves are finely ground with the sugar in a food processor, so there's nothing leafy or weird about the brownies' texture. They're just plain brownie delicious, with a soft underlying note of mint. Moist, soft, and thick, they are perfect for bagged lunches, hikes, or an any-time-of-day energy boost. They freeze beautifully, too.

1 Line an 8- by 8-inch cake or brownie pan with foil, and butter the foil. Or butter the pan and line it with a single sheet of parchment paper, letting it extend a little above the pan on two sides. (There's no need to line the other two sides that aren't covered.)

2 Cut the butter into large chunks, and place them in the top of a double boiler or a heatproof bowl placed over, but not in, barely simmering water. Add the chocolate as the butter starts to melt. When all of the chocolate has melted, remove the insert or bowl and whisk until smooth. Cool for 15 minutes. Preheat the oven to 350°F (180°C).

3 While the chocolate is cooling, combine the sugar and mint leaves in the bowl of a food processor. Pulse the machine repeatedly until the mint is very finely chopped.

4 Combine the flour, cocoa powder, cornstarch, and salt in a bowl. Whisk to combine.

5 Whisk the mint sugar into the partially cooled chocolate. Add the eggs, one at a time, whisking well after each addition. Whisk in the vanilla and lemon zest. Using a wooden spoon, mix the dry ingredients into the chocolate mixture in two installments, stirring just until thoroughly combined. Turn the batter into the prepared pan and smooth with a spoon.

6 Bake the brownies for 35 to 40 minutes. When done, the brownies will puff slightly and the top may develop cracks. A toothpick inserted in the center may have a few damp chocolate crumbs attached, but you don't want a lot of underbaked batter. Transfer to a rack and cool in the pan. Cut with a sharp knife, rinsing and drying the blade frequently to get nice clean cuts.

MAKES 16 BROWNIES

   Butter for the pan

½ cup (1 stick) unsalted butter

8 ounces bittersweet chocolate, coarsely chopped

1½ cups sugar

1 cup loosely packed mint leaves (as fresh as possible)

½ cup all-purpose flour

2 tablespoons unsweetened cocoa powder

2 tablespoons cornstarch

½ teaspoon salt

4 large eggs, at room temperature

1½ teaspoons vanilla extract

½ teaspoon freshly grated lemon zest

BROWN SUGAR RHUBARB TART SQUARES

If you're a Southerner, these squares will probably remind you of chess pie, and if you happen to be Canadian, you'll notice the resemblance to butter tarts, your beloved dessert with a sweet, semisolid filling. Whatever they remind you of, the addition of fresh rhubarb is a delicious novelty seldom associated with either. I think you'll thoroughly enjoy them. The tartness comes from both the fresh rhubarb and the vinegar; both help balance out the sweetness of the brown sugar. All of this wonderfulness goes atop a buttery almond shortbread crust that's delicious in its own right and brings out the best in the filling. Cut these bars into small squares, and serve them up for a special occasion, perhaps to celebrate the arrival of spring.

1 Butter a 9- by 9-inch cake pan, preferably nonstick. Cut four 9- by 1½-inch strips of parchment paper, and use them to line the sides of the pan. Use foil if you don't have parchment. Butter the strips.

2 Combine the almonds, granulated sugar, and ¼ teaspoon salt in a food processor. Using long pulses, process the nuts until they're finely ground. Add 1 cup of the flour and pulse to mix. Remove the lid and scatter the butter over the dry ingredients. Pulse repeatedly, until the mixture is still crumbly but starting to clump together. Transfer the mixture to the pan and spread it around evenly. Press it firmly into the bottom and about ¼ inch up the sides. Place the pan in the freezer for 15 minutes. Preheat the oven to 350°F (180°C).

3 Bake the crust for 15 minutes. Transfer to a rack and cool.

4 Spread the rhubarb out on a large, lightly buttered baking sheet. Bake for 12 minutes; this will soften and shrink the rhubarb slightly. Place the sheet on a rack and cool the rhubarb thoroughly. (Reserve any leftover rhubarb for another use.)

5 Combine the brown sugar, the remaining 1½ tablespoons flour, and a pinch of salt in a large bowl. Add the eggs and whisk thoroughly. Whisk in the melted butter, vinegar, and vanilla. Stir in the rhubarb. Pour the filling over the crust and spread it evenly. Bake for 35 to 40 minutes, until the filling is no longer wobbly; give the pan a nudge to check. The top should be nicely browned and crusty. If necessary, move the pan higher in the oven for the last 10 minutes so it's closer to the heat at the top of the oven. When done, transfer the pan to a rack. Cool thoroughly in the pan, and refrigerate until serving. Cut into small bars and serve.

MAKES 25 BARS

Butter for the pan and baking sheet

½ cup whole almonds

¼ cup granulated sugar

¼ teaspoon salt, plus a pinch for the brown sugar mixture

1 cup plus 1½ tablespoons all-purpose flour

½ cup (1 stick) cold unsalted butter, cut into ½-inch cubes

2 cups diced rhubarb, in ½-inch pieces (3 large stalks)

1⅓ cups packed light brown sugar

2 large eggs

5 tablespoons unsalted butter, melted and partially cooled

4 teaspoons white vinegar

1 teaspoon vanilla extract

BLUEBERRY OATMEAL CRUMB BARS

Everyone loves maple syrup with blueberry pancakes. Here maple and blueberry come together again in this maple-sweetened blueberry filling sandwiched between oatmeal and brown sugar crumb layers. I like to slice and freeze whatever bars we don't eat in the first day or two, wrapping them individually so they're ready to go when we are. (The bars aren't too thick, so they won't take long to thaw.) Freeze plenty of blueberries in the summer so you can make these all winter long. Store-bought frozen berries will work fine, too.

1 Butter a 9- by 9-inch cake pan. Combine the flour, oats, brown sugar, walnuts, and salt in a food processor. Pulse the machine repeatedly, until the oats and walnuts are finely ground. Remove the lid and scatter the butter over the dry ingredients. Pulse again until the mixture forms coarse, buttery crumbs. Spread a little more than half of the crumbs in the buttered pan and press them in evenly, pushing them about ¼ inch up the sides. Refrigerate the pan. Transfer the remaining crumbs to a mixing bowl and refrigerate them also.

2 Combine the blueberries, maple syrup, and granulated sugar in a large saucepan over moderate heat. If the berries are fresh, use a wooden spoon to break some of them up so they begin to juice (frozen ones should juice easily on their own). While the berries heat, combine the lemon juice, fruit juice, and cornstarch in a small bowl, smoothing it out with a finger to dissolve the cornstarch. When the berries start to boil, stir in the cornstarch liquid. Cook the berries at a low boil, stirring nonstop, for 45 seconds, until thickened. Remove from the heat, transfer to a pie plate or other shallow container, and cool to room temperature.

3 When you're ready to bake, preheat the oven to 350°F (180°C). Pour the blueberry filling over the unbaked crust and even it out with a spoon. Spread the remaining crumb mixture evenly over the fruit. Bake for about 40 minutes, until the fruit starts to bubble around the edges. Transfer to a rack and cool to room temperature before serving, preferably with vanilla ice cream. Refrigerate leftovers right in the pan.

MAKES 12 TO 16 SERVINGS

Butter for the cake pan

1¼ cups all-purpose flour

1 cup old-fashioned rolled oats

⅔ cup packed light brown sugar

¼ cup coarsely chopped walnuts

Scant ½ teaspoon salt

½ cup (1 stick) plus 2 tablespoons unsalted butter (cool but not hard-cold), cut into ½-inch pieces

Vanilla ice cream, for serving (optional)

FILLING

3 cups fresh or frozen blueberries

⅓ cup pure maple syrup

2 tablespoons granulated sugar

1 tablespoon lemon juice

1 tablespoon grape, apple, or cranberry juice, or water

4 teaspoons cornstarch

STRAWBERRY-FILLED SHORTBREAD BARS

If you want to give your fresh summer strawberries the royal treatment, this is your recipe. These are elegant and irresistible, a cut or two above your everyday fruit bars made with store-bought preserves. I think you'll appreciate the clever method of grating the chilled dough with a box grater. This helps give you a nice even bottom crust because you can spread the gratings around with ease. And it creates a textured, peaks-and-valleys top crust that will remind you of crumb cake.

1 Combine the flour, baking powder, and salt in a medium bowl. Whisk well to combine.

2 Using an electric mixer — preferably a stand mixer fitted with a flat beater — cream the butter on high speed until smooth and light, about 2 minutes. Gradually add the granulated sugar and beat another couple of minutes. Add the yolks and vanilla and beat again briefly.

3 With the mixer on low speed — or with a wooden spoon if you don't have a stand mixer — add the dry ingredients to the creamed mixture in four installments, mixing until just combined. When all the dry ingredients are incorporated, turn the dough out onto a floured surface and knead four or five times to smooth out the dough. Divide the dough in half, shape into large balls, and wrap them separately in plastic wrap. Refrigerate for at least 2 hours; overnight is fine.

4 When you're ready to proceed, have a 9- by 9-inch cake pan ready; don't use a smaller size. Put a sheet of waxed paper or parchment on your counter. Unwrap one piece of dough, and using the large holes of a box grater, grate the dough onto the paper, stopping several times to slide the gratings into your pan and spread them around evenly. When you're done grating, you should have a more or less level pile of evenly distributed gratings; make sure to get the dough into the corners. Gently pat it down without compacting it completely. Place the pan in the fridge while you make the filling.

5 Combine the strawberries, granulated sugar, and water in a medium saucepan. Gradually bring to a boil, stirring occasionally. Boil for 7 to 10 minutes, until the mixture has a medium-thick consistency. Spoon some of the liquid (not the fruit) onto a serving spoon and blow on it; it should not seem runny. Stir the lemon juice into the strawberry mixture. Transfer the mixture to a shallow casserole dish, spread it out, and refrigerate to cool.

MAKES 25 BARS

- 2½ cups all-purpose flour
- 1 teaspoon baking powder
- ½ teaspoon salt
- 1¼ cups (2½ sticks) unsalted butter, at room temperature
- 1¼ cups granulated sugar
- 2 egg yolks
- ½ teaspoon vanilla extract

  Confectioners' sugar, for dusting

FILLING

- 1 pound ripe strawberries, hulled and coarsely chunked
- ½ cup granulated sugar
- ¼ cup water
- 2 teaspoons lemon juice

6 Preheat the oven to 350°F (180°C). Adjust one of the oven racks so it is one position higher than the lowest setting. Spread the cooled strawberry filling as evenly as possible over the dough in the pan, taking care to get it in the corners. Grate the other half of the dough, stopping several times to spread the gratings evenly over the fruit, but *do not press down* this time. Bake on the lower rack for 30 minutes. Then move the pan up to the middle rack and bake until the top is golden brown, another 10 to 12 minutes.

7 Transfer the pan to a rack and cool for 5 minutes. Put some confectioners' sugar in a small sieve and dust the top of the shortbread with it. Cool completely and dust again until the top is well coated. Cut into bars and serve. Leftovers can be refrigerated and then brought to room temperature again before serving.

PUMPKIN: FRESH VS. CANNED

I'd like to report that in the fresh versus canned pumpkin debate I always come down on the side of fresh, but — alas — that's not the case. Even I, who've carved out a career teaching people how to cook from scratch, reach for canned pumpkin on a regular basis.

A lot of it boils down to supply: where on earth are you supposed to find a pie pumpkin, or any pumpkin for that matter, in the middle of July when you have an urge to make a pumpkin pound cake? The season is extremely short, and when they're done, they're done.

Another problem is that pumpkin purée, homemade or canned, is pretty blah on its own. It doesn't begin to resemble what we think of as "pumpkin flavor" until you add sugar, spice, salt, and enrichments like cream, at which point whatever subtle difference in flavor your fresh pumpkin might have had has been hopelessly obscured. It's not like you're comparing a ripe strawberry from a nearby farm to one that you bought at the supermarket in February.

Which is not to say that I'm not an ardent fan of making and baking with your own fresh pumpkin purée. As with any sort of from-scratch cooking, the process can be very satisfying. So you *should* make your own, compare it to canned purée, and draw your own conclusions.

OATMEAL CHOCOLATE CHIP PUMPKIN COOKIES

This is a soft cookie, not unlike a traditional chewy oatmeal cookie but even softer because of the pumpkin. There's a lot going on here — chocolate chips, nuts, coconut — so the pumpkin plays more of a supporting role, adding an autumn hue, some pumpkin flavor, and a novelty factor that both kids and adults find irresistible. These cookies go down easy, especially when chased with a cold glass of milk or apple cider. Don't be surprised if they turn into one of your fall regulars.

1 Combine the flour, oats, salt, baking soda, baking powder, cinnamon, and ginger in a large bowl. Mix well. Combine the butter, shortening, brown sugar, and granulated sugar in another large bowl. Using an electric mixer — handheld is fine — beat for 2 minutes, until smooth and creamy. Add the eggs, one at a time, beating well after each addition. Beat in the pumpkin and vanilla on low speed until evenly blended.

2 Add half of the dry ingredients to the pumpkin mixture and mix well. Stir in the remaining dry ingredients. Add the chocolate chips, nuts, and coconut. Mix again until everything is well combined. Cover and refrigerate the dough for 2 or more hours.

3 Preheat the oven to 350°F (180°C). Line two large cookie sheets with parchment paper if you have it. Otherwise, butter the sheets lightly.

4 Using about 3 tablespoons of dough for each cookie, shape the dough into rounds and place them on the first sheet, about 2½ inches apart. Flatten into ½-inch-thick disks. Bake on the middle oven rack for 15 to 17 minutes. When done, the cookies will have developed a light skin on the surface and will not feel squishy when you gently push on them. Transfer to a rack to cool on the sheet for 5 minutes, then transfer the cookies directly to the rack. Repeat for the remaining dough, using the second baking sheet (or wait for the first one to cool). Cool the cookies thoroughly, then transfer to a large, airtight storage container. Store at room temperature for a few days. Any cookies that you don't plan to eat within that time should be refrigerated or frozen.

MAKES ABOUT 30 COOKIES

- 2⅓ cups all-purpose flour
- 2 cups old-fashioned rolled oats
- ¾ teaspoon salt
- ¾ teaspoon baking soda
- ½ teaspoon baking powder
- ½ teaspoon ground cinnamon
- ¼ teaspoon ground ginger
- ¾ cup (1½ sticks) unsalted butter, softened
- ¼ cup vegetable shortening
- 1 cup packed light brown sugar
- ¾ cup granulated sugar
- 2 large eggs, at room temperature
- ¾ cup pumpkin purée, canned or fresh
- 1 teaspoon vanilla extract
- 1½ cups semisweet chocolate chips
- 1 cup chopped walnuts or pecans
- ½ cup flaked sweetened coconut

PECAN PUMPKIN SPICE COOKIES

If you've ever used pumpkin purée in cookies, you've probably noticed that it makes for a very cake-like cookie — which is fine if that's your intention, but what I wanted was a pumpkin cookie with a bit of chew to it, like a chewy oatmeal cookie, only a little less so. That quest led me here, where a combination of cream cheese, brown sugar, ground pecans, and whole-wheat pastry flour creates a tender, spicy cookie with just the right amount of chewiness. Please note that the modest amount of pumpkin purée results in a cookie with a subtle pumpkin taste. But there's just enough of it to catch your notice, and to make these a seasonal cookie you'll look forward to every fall.

MAKES ABOUT 30 COOKIES

- 1¼ cups pecan halves
- ⅓ cup packed light brown sugar
- 1½ cups whole-wheat pastry flour
- 1½ teaspoons ground cinnamon
- ¼ teaspoon ground ginger
- ¼ teaspoon ground allspice
- ½ teaspoon salt
- 8 ounces cream cheese, softened
- ½ cup (1 stick) unsalted butter, softened
- 1½ cups granulated sugar
- ½ cup pumpkin purée, canned or fresh (see page 226)
- ½ teaspoon vanilla extract

1 Preheat the oven to 350°F (180°C). Spread the pecans on a baking sheet. Toast the pecans for about 8 minutes, until they turn a shade darker and you can just start to smell them. Remove from the oven and immediately tilt the pecans off the sheet and onto your work counter or another baking sheet. Cool thoroughly.

2 When the pecans are completely cool, put them in a food processor along with the brown sugar. Using long pulses, process the nuts to a fine, gritty meal.

3 Combine the whole-wheat flour, 1 teaspoon cinnamon, ginger, allspice, and salt in a large bowl. Add the pecan meal. Mix well by hand, breaking up any little clumps that you come across.

4 Using an electric mixer — preferably a stand mixer fitted with the flat beater — cream the cream cheese and butter on medium speed. Gradually beat in 1 cup granulated sugar. Add the pumpkin and vanilla and beat on low speed until thoroughly combined. Add the dry ingredients on low speed in three installments, beating until evenly mixed. (If you're using a hand mixer, stir in the dry ingredients with a wooden spoon.) Cover the dough with plastic wrap, pressing one sheet directly over the dough and using another to cover the bowl. Refrigerate for at least 3 hours; overnight is fine.

5 When you're ready to bake, preheat the oven to 350°F (180°C). Line a large baking sheet with parchment paper or lightly buttered aluminum foil. In a small bowl, mix the remaining ½ cup granulated sugar and ½ teaspoon cinnamon. Use your hands to shape the dough into 1¼-inch balls. Roll each one in the cinnamon sugar and place them on the sheet about 2½ inches apart. Using the flat bottom of a glass, gently press down on the balls to flatten them slightly. Sprinkle the cookies with a little more cinnamon sugar and flatten again so they are a little less than ½ inch thick. (This dough is sticky, and this two-step flattening method keeps it from sticking to the glass.)

6 Bake the cookies one sheet at a time for 18 to 20 minutes. When they're done, you'll notice a very slight amount of browning, and the surface will have gone from smooth to crackly. Transfer the sheet to a rack and cool on the sheet for 5 to 8 minutes. Using a thin spatula, transfer the cookies to a cooling rack and continue to cool. For subsequent batches, use a second sheet and shape the cookies while the first batch is baking. If you're using the same sheet, let it cool down before adding a new batch of cookies.

PECAN-CRUSTED PUMPKIN CHEESECAKE BARS

This is pretty much a pumpkin cheesecake with a thinner profile. Baking it in bars means no fiddling with springform pans and water baths. But it's not so much the shape of these that you'll find memorable, it's the flavor — a pecan-studded crust, with a rich, spiced pumpkin filling and sweetened sour cream top. Nothing says autumn quite like these. If you're looking to dress up a plated presentation, drizzle a little caramel sauce over the bars.

1 Preheat the oven to 350°F (180°C). Lightly butter a 9- by 9-inch cake pan. Combine the pecans and brown sugar in a food processor; process until finely chopped. Transfer to a mixing bowl and add the graham cracker crumbs and salt. Mix briefly, then stir in the melted butter. Mix thoroughly — hands work best — adding a few drops of water if needed, so the mixture barely holds together when you squeeze it in your palm. Press the crumbs evenly into the bottom of the pan and just slightly up the sides. Bake on the middle oven rack for 8 minutes. Transfer to a rack and cool thoroughly. Set the oven to 325°F (170°C).

2 Using an electric mixer (handheld is fine), cream the cream cheese and brown sugar in a mixing bowl. Add the eggs, one a time, beating on medium speed after each addition. Mix the flour and spices in a small bowl; add to the cream cheese mixture and beat again. Beat in the pumpkin and cream on medium-low speed, just until everything is evenly blended.

3 Pour the filling over the crust, tilting the pan so it covers the crust evenly. Bake on the middle oven rack for 45 to 50 minutes. When done, the outer edges of the filling will have a drier look than the center and may be slightly puffed, but barely so. This isn't a filling that rises dramatically, if at all. Transfer to a rack and cool thoroughly.

4 Combine the sour cream, granulated sugar, and vanilla in a small saucepan. Heat very gently, stirring nonstop until it reaches a pourable consistency. Pour over the pumpkin filling, immediately tilting the pan to spread out the sour cream. Cool thoroughly, then cover the pan with foil; refrigerate for at least 3 to 4 hours before serving. These are very creamy bars, best eaten with a knife and fork.

MAKES 12 TO 16 SERVINGS

Butter for the cake pan

⅔ cup pecan halves

⅓ cup packed light brown sugar

1¼ cups graham cracker crumbs

¼ teaspoon salt

4 tablespoons unsalted butter, melted

FILLING

8 ounces cream cheese, softened

1 cup packed light brown sugar

2 large eggs, at room temperature

1 tablespoon all-purpose flour

½ teaspoon ground cinnamon

½ teaspoon ground ginger

½ teaspoon ground nutmeg

1 cup pumpkin purée, canned or fresh (see page 226)

⅓ cup heavy cream

SOUR CREAM TOPPING

1⅓ cups sour cream

⅓ cup granulated sugar

¼ teaspoon vanilla extract

7

CAKES
Pound, Coffee, Upside Down, and More

Every baker needs a handful of go-to, knock-your-socks-off cakes in her arsenal — to celebrate a special occasion, for gift giving, or to trot out when company is coming for a day or weekend. Any of these will do nicely. I almost never get the urge to create fancy decorated layer cakes; that's not my style, so you won't find those here. Rather, these are cakes that impress without pretense, valued more for their great taste, moist texture, and keepability than their decorative flourishes. The fact that they just happen to be some of the best harvest cakes you'll ever encounter is, well, the icing on the cake.

BACK BUMPER BLUEBERRY CREAM CHEESE POUND CAKE

It's hard to play favorites when it comes to harvest berry cakes, but this tender, creamy pound cake makes the job much easier. The alliterative name comes from the fact that it was a staple of ours for years at tailgating events, especially navy football games when we lived in Annapolis. I think it's still my most requested cake recipe. By all means, don't wait for your next tailgate party to try it, though. It's just right for picnics, potlucks, bag lunches, or breakfast on the run. Note that I partially freeze the blueberries (step 1) so they don't burst and leave streaks in the batter when you fold them in.

1 Butter a 9- by 5-inch loaf pan, and line the bottom and two long sides with a single piece of parchment. Let it extend an inch or so above the pan on each side so you have something to grab when you remove the cake. Spread the blueberries out on a large plate or small rimmed baking sheet, and put them in the freezer for about an hour to firm up.

2 Adjust the oven rack so it is one position below the middle. Preheat the oven to 350°F (180°C).

3 Sift the flour, baking powder, salt, and nutmeg into a large bowl. Using an electric mixer — preferably a stand mixer fitted with a flat beater — cream the butter and cream cheese in a large bowl until smooth and creamy. Gradually beat in the granulated sugar, stopping the machine to scrape down the sides as needed. Add the eggs, one at a time, beating well after each addition. Add the vanilla and lemon extract and mix in on low speed.

4 Add the dry mixture to the creamed ingredients, about a third at a time, beating on low speed until evenly mixed; scrape down the sides as needed. When all of the dry mixture has been added and the batter is smooth and creamy, add the blueberries. Using a wooden spoon or rubber spatula, fold them in gently but thoroughly. Scrape the batter into the prepared pan and smooth the top with a spoon.

5 Bake the cake for 30 minutes, then reduce the heat to 325°F (170°C) and bake for another 45 to 60 minutes. When done, the cake will have risen nicely and the exterior will be a rich golden color. A tester inserted deep into the center of the cake should come out clean.

6 Transfer the cake to a cooling rack and cool in the pan for 20 to 30 minutes. Slide the cake out of the pan and place it on the rack. Cool completely, then drizzle with a generous coating of Confectioners' Sugar Glaze. Slice and serve. I usually cover this with plastic wrap, overwrap it in aluminum foil, and store it in the refrigerator. Slice the cake while it's cold, but serve it at room temperature for best flavor. The cake also freezes beautifully for longer storage. Just slice, freeze, and remove pieces from the freezer as you need them.

MAKES 10 TO 12 SERVINGS

Butter for the pan

1½ cups fresh blueberries

1¾ cups all-purpose flour

1 teaspoon baking powder

¾ teaspoon salt

¼ teaspoon ground nutmeg

½ cup (1 stick) unsalted butter, softened

6 ounces cream cheese, softened

1¾ cups granulated sugar

4 large eggs, at room temperature

2 teaspoons vanilla extract

1 teaspoon lemon extract or finely grated zest of 1 lemon

Confectioners' Sugar Glaze (page 289)

BLUEBERRY GINGERBREAD

Blueberries and molasses have deep roots in New England, so I consider this to be a quintessential Yankee dessert. It has just the right balance among sweeteners — the brown sugar, molasses, and maple syrup — and the perfect amount of spice. I've played around with other diced fruits in this gingerbread, pears being one of my favorites. But it's always the plump, sweet blueberries that take me back to my New Hampshire years and remind me of those sweet, waning summer days I loved so much. Whipped cream or Vanilla Custard Sauce (page 290) is the topping of choice, but a dusting of confectioners' sugar is a welcome garnish, too.

1 Preheat the oven to 350°F (180°C). Butter a 9- by 9-inch cake pan.

2 Combine the butter, brown sugar, and egg in a large bowl. Using an electric mixer (handheld works fine), beat the mixture on medium-high speed for 1 to 2 minutes, until smooth and creamy. Add the molasses, maple syrup, and vanilla. Beat again until smooth.

3 Combine the all-purpose flour, whole-wheat flour, baking soda, salt, ginger, cinnamon, and cloves in another bowl. Whisk well to mix. Stir the dry ingredients into the creamed mixture in two stages, adding a little of the hot water if the batter starts to be too thick. Gradually add the rest of the hot water in several stages, stirring with a wooden spoon until smooth. Add the blueberries and fold them in until the batter is evenly mixed. Scrape the batter into the pan and smooth with a spoon.

4 Bake the gingerbread for about 50 minutes, until it is well risen and a tester inserted into the center of the cake comes out clean. Transfer to a rack and cool the cake in the pan for at least 30 minutes before serving.

MAKES 9 TO 12 SERVINGS

Butter for the pan

½   cup (1 stick) unsalted butter, softened

¾   cup packed light brown sugar

1   large egg, at room temperature

½   cup molasses

¼   cup pure maple syrup

½   teaspoon vanilla extract

1¼   cups all-purpose flour

1¼   cups whole-wheat pastry flour

1½   teaspoons baking soda

½   teaspoon salt

1½   teaspoons ground ginger

1   teaspoon ground cinnamon

½   teaspoon ground cloves

1   cup plus 2 tablespoons hot water

1¼   cups fresh or frozen blueberries

RICOTTA POUND CAKE WITH PEARS, WALNUTS, AND SAGE

If you've never made a cake with ricotta cheese before, this one is going to be a revelation. Like cream cheese, ricotta is one of those magical baking ingredients that turns your average cake (and muffins, too — see the blackberry muffins on page 31) into a fabulously moist treat, adding considerably to its shelf life. Many fruits can be used here, such as blueberries and raspberries in the summer. But because I like to make this in the fall, and especially around the holidays, my favorite additions are pears, walnuts, and a whisper of sage. This needs no adornment at all, but a light dusting of confectioners' sugar never hurts.

1 Butter a 9- by 5-inch loaf pan. Either dust the pan with flour, or line the bottom and two long sides with parchment paper, allowing a little overhang on each side so you have something to grab when you slide out the cake. Preheat the oven to 350°F (180°C).

2 Sift the flour, baking powder, and salt into a mixing bowl. Using an electric mixer — preferably a stand mixer fitted with a flat beater — cream the butter and ricotta cheese in a large bowl on medium-high speed for 1 minute. Gradually add the sugar, about ½ cup at a time, beating well after each addition. Add the eggs, one at a time, beating well after each addition. Beat in the vanilla and lemon extracts on low speed.

3 With the mixer on medium-low speed, add the dry ingredients in three installments, beating well after each addition. Switching to a wooden spoon or rubber spatula, add the pears, walnuts, and sage, and fold them in thoroughly, until the batter is evenly mixed. Transfer the batter to the prepared pan. Smooth the top with a spoon.

4 Place the cake on the middle oven rack and immediately lower the heat to 325°F (170°C). Bake for 75 to 90 minutes. When done, the cake will be a rich golden brown on top. A tester inserted deep into the middle of the cake will come out clean.

5 Transfer the pan to a cooling rack and cool for 1 hour. After an hour, run a thin spatula down the sides, between the paper and the pan, and slide the cake out of the pan and place it back on the rack. Cool the cake thoroughly before slicing. The cake will keep fine at room temperature for a couple of days, but if you'll have it around longer, store it in the fridge, wrapped in plastic and overwrapped in foil. It also freezes beautifully.

MAKES 10 OR MORE SERVINGS

Butter for the pan

1¾ cups all-purpose flour

2 teaspoons baking powder

½ teaspoon salt

¾ cup (1½ sticks) unsalted butter, softened

1 cup ricotta cheese, at room temperature

1½ cups sugar

3 large eggs, at room temperature

1 teaspoon vanilla extract

½ teaspoon lemon extract or 1½ teaspoons freshly grated lemon zest

1 cup peeled and finely diced ripe pears

½ cup chopped walnuts

¾ teaspoon dried sage or 1½ teaspoons chopped fresh

Glorious Peaches

I am blessed with good local peaches here in the Carolinas, but I wasn't always so lucky. When I lived in New Hampshire, where good peaches were difficult to find, I would have my sister ship me big boxes of them from down south. That arrangement worked well until, unbeknownst to me, she sent a box while I was on an extended vacation. By the time I picked them up, the parcel had taken on a rather dubious aroma, and the postmaster, who had relegated the curious parcel to a distant corner, handed it over with a look that made it perfectly clear that he didn't approve of whatever questionable activity I was engaged in.

I have better luck finding good peaches at local farm stands than chain supermarkets, which, sadly, often bypass local suppliers and ship them in from across the country. Take a few moments to size up your peaches before dropping them in your shopping cart. A nice bit of heft in proportion to size is a good sign because it means they are full of juice. A peachy fragrance is a good sign, but color is even more important. Look for skins with rich, vibrant tones. The flesh should not feel hard but rather yield under gentle finger pressure.

Of course, there's no better test than a taste test. If sample slices aren't available, just ask. The vendor might be happy to oblige. Unless I'm making a pie or another dish that requires all ripe fruit, I try to buy my peaches in various stages of ripeness so I can eat them throughout the week.

ALMOND AND FRESH PEACH COFFEE CAKE

This is not a fancy coffee cake — no streusel topping or tube pan required — but it has to be one of the most scrumptious cakes I've ever tasted. The secret to this taste-bud bliss is an arranged marriage between the toasted almond meal and fresh peaches, a match made in heaven. The peaches are diced and distributed over half the batter before the second half is added; a sprinkling of brown sugar and some dots of butter leave a thin but brittle-crusty finish on top. This deserves to be at or near the top of your summer peach recipe bucket list.

1 Preheat the oven to 350°F (180°C). Butter an 8- by 8-inch cake pan and dust it with flour. Spread the almonds on a baking sheet and roast them for 8 to 10 minutes. They're done when they've turned a shade or two darker and you can just start to smell their toastedness. Immediately slide them off the sheet and onto your counter or another sheet. Cool thoroughly.

2 When the almonds have cooled, transfer them to a food processor and process to a fairly fine meal; don't overdo it, or you'll get almond butter. Transfer to a bowl and mix in the flour, baking powder, and salt.

3 Preheat the oven to 375°F (190°C). Using an electric mixer — preferably a stand mixer — combine the ½ cup softened butter, ricotta cheese, and granulated sugar in a mixing bowl. Beat well on medium-high speed for 1 minute, until smooth and evenly mixed. Beat in the eggs one at a time, beating well after each addition. Add the vanilla, almond extract, and orange zest, and beat on low speed. Add the dry ingredients about half at a time, beating on low speed after each addition.

4 Spoon half of the batter into the prepared pan, smoothing it out evenly and into the corners. Scatter the diced peaches evenly over the batter. If the peaches are very juicy, don't include the juice; save it for the top. Dollop the remaining batter over the peaches and spread it evenly with a spoon. Sprinkle the brown sugar over the top. Dot with the 1½ tablespoons cold butter, dropping bits of it here and there. If you have any leftover peach juice, you can drizzle that over the top now.

5 Bake the coffee cake for 35 to 40 minutes. When done, the top will be crusty and golden and a toothpick inserted into the middle will come out clean. Transfer to a cooling rack. Slice and serve slightly warm or at room temperature.

MAKES 9 SERVINGS

Butter and flour for the cake pan

¾ cup whole almonds, blanched or skins on

1 cup all-purpose flour

1½ teaspoons baking powder

½ teaspoon salt

½ cup (1 stick) unsalted butter, softened, plus 1½ tablespoons cold butter

1 cup ricotta cheese, at room temperature

1 cup plus 2 tablespoons granulated sugar

2 large eggs, at room temperature

1 teaspoon vanilla extract

½ teaspoon almond extract

Finely grated zest of 1 orange

1¼ cups peeled and diced fresh peaches

2 tablespoons packed light brown sugar

PEACH PECAN SHORTCAKE

A fresh, juicy peach is a glorious thing, and I know of no better way to show off some good peaches than teaming them up with whipped cream and these rich pecan shortcakes. Bake the shortcake biscuits as close as possible to serving time, preferably within an hour or two. And don't even think about trying this with canned or out-of-season fruit.

1 Preheat the oven to 400°F (200°C). Line a large baking sheet with parchment paper, or butter the sheet very lightly.

2 Combine the flour, ⅓ cup sugar, baking powder, baking soda, and salt in a large bowl. Whisk well, or mix by hand, to combine. Add the butter, toss it with the dry mixture, and cut it into the dry ingredients with a pastry blender until the butter is broken into fine bits and the mixture resembles a coarse meal with some split pea–size pieces of fat. Mix in the chopped pecans. Refrigerate.

3 Whisk the egg in a mixing bowl until frothy, then whisk in the heavy cream and sour cream. Set aside 1½ tablespoons of the mixture in a small bowl for brushing on the shortcakes. Whisk the vanilla into the remaining larger portion. Remove the dry ingredients from the refrigerator, make a well in the center, and pour in the liquid. Stir well, until a firm dough forms. Turn the dough out onto a lightly floured work surface.

4 To form the shortcakes by hand, divide the dough into seven or eight equal pieces and shape them into balls. Place the balls on the baking sheet, evenly spaced; there's no need to flatten them because they'll settle a bit. If you prefer a more uniform look, pat the dough out on a lightly floured surface to a thickness of about ¾ inch, cut the dough into rounds with a biscuit cutter, and place them on the sheet. Either way, brush the top of each one with a little of the reserved cream mixture. Sprinkle lightly with sugar. Bake the shortcakes for 18 to 22 minutes, until they're a rich golden brown. Transfer them directly to a rack and cool.

5 When you're ready to serve, put the peach slices in a bowl and add 1 to 2 tablespoons sugar, depending on how sweet they are. Sprinkle on the lemon juice. Stir gently, then set aside for 5 minutes. Split the shortcakes, and put the bottoms on dessert plates. Top each one with plenty of peach slices and whipped cream. Top with the other half of the shortcake and serve.

MAKES 7 TO 8 SERVINGS

- 2 cups all-purpose flour
- ⅓ cup sugar, plus 1 to 2 tablespoons for the peaches if needed (and a little for sprinkling)
- 2 teaspoons baking powder
- ½ teaspoon baking soda
- ½ teaspoon salt
- 6 tablespoons cold unsalted butter, cut into ½-inch cubes
- ½ cup finely chopped pecans
- 1 large egg
- ½ cup heavy cream
- ⅓ cup sour cream or buttermilk
- ½ teaspoon vanilla extract
- 4 large ripe peaches, peeled and sliced
- 1 teaspoon lemon juice

  Whipped cream, for garnish

BLACKBERRY UPSIDE-DOWN CAKE

I've never met an upside-down cake I didn't like, though I have liked some more than others — this one, for instance. Blackberries might seem like unlikely suspects for an upside-down cake, but no, they're perfect. Layered in the bottom of the pan with brown sugar and butter, they bake into something like a thick glaze of blackberry preserves; you'll love the way it clings to the cake like deep purple jewels when you turn the cake out of the pan. The buttery cake itself is not overly thick; the fruit layer shouldn't seem like an afterthought. Topped with clouds of sweetened whipped cream, this is one summer dessert you'll want to make again and again.

1 Preheat the oven to 375°F (190°C). Pour the melted butter into a 9- by 9-inch cake pan, tilting the pan to spread it around. Dab a paper towel in the butter and use it to coat the sides, too. Scatter the brown sugar evenly over the butter, and spread the blackberries over the brown sugar.

2 Using an electric mixer (handheld is fine), beat the softened butter on medium-high speed. Gradually add the granulated sugar. Add the eggs, one at a time, beating well after each addition. Beat in about half of the buttermilk and the vanilla.

3 Sift the flour, baking powder, baking soda, salt, and cardamom into a mixing bowl. Add half of the dry ingredients to the creamed mixture, beating it in on low speed until smooth. Beat in the remaining buttermilk until smooth, followed by the remaining dry ingredients. Spoon the batter over the berries and smooth it out with a spoon.

4 Bake the cake for 20 minutes, then reduce the heat to 350°F (180°C) and bake 15 to 20 minutes more, until the cake is golden brown and a tester inserted into the center comes out clean (clean of cake crumbs — it's okay to see berry juice). Transfer the cake to a cooling rack.

5 Cool the cake for 5 to 10 minutes, then run a spatula around the outside of the cake to loosen it. Place a large flat plate or platter over the entire top of the pan — or use a small baking sheet — and carefully invert the cake onto it. (Gloves and oven mitts are a good idea, to guard against hot drips.) The cake will probably drop right out, but you may have to jiggle or tap the pan to help it along. Remove the cake pan. Cool the cake for about 15 minutes before serving.

MAKE 9 TO 12 SERVINGS

- 4 tablespoons unsalted butter, melted
- ½ cup packed light brown sugar
- 2½–3 cups fresh blackberries
- ½ cup (1 stick) unsalted butter, softened
- ¾ cup granulated sugar
- 2 large eggs, at room temperature
- ¾ cup buttermilk
- 1 teaspoon vanilla extract
- 1½ cups all-purpose flour
- 1½ teaspoons baking powder
- ½ teaspoon baking soda
- ½ teaspoon salt
- ¼ teaspoon ground cardamom or cinnamon

Maple Syrup

Wind your way through New England and points north in late winter or spring, when subfreezing nights give way to warming days, and you're liable to see great plumes of steam billowing up from wooden structures tucked in the trees. Slow down — it's sugaring season, and with a little bit of luck you'll be invited to watch the uniquely North American ritual of maple sap being boiled down to make maple syrup.

It takes about 40 gallons of sap to produce a gallon of maple syrup. Not long ago, all of it was collected by hand; today, for the most part, networks of tubing deliver sap to the sugarhouse, where the boiling takes place in large pans called evaporators. It's a small concession to modern times that in no way diminishes the magic of real maple syrup.

The earth may be buried under several feet of snow and frozen solid. But this is farming in the truest sense of the word: the harvest and processing of a great natural resource, skillfully transformed into maple syrup by dedicated men and women, many of whose families have been at it for generations. Check out my *Maple Syrup Cookbook* for more than 100 recipes that use maple syrup for breakfast, lunch, and dinner.

APPLE PECAN POUND CAKE WITH MAPLE SYRUP GLAZE

I love pound cakes made with cream cheese — it creates a rich, moist, creamy interior that can't be beat. The apples play a key role in this delicious pound cake. Unlike most fresh berries (or soft fruit), they won't burst and streak the batter, so you're guaranteed to end up with a nicely uniform, off-white crumb. Also, the apple pieces slowly release moisture into the cake, so it stays moist for days. This would be fabulous even without the maple glaze, so you could skip it, but I never do. Note that this cake requires a very large one-piece tube pan; a 14-cup capacity is the minimum size. The pan should be no more than two-thirds full of batter. If yours isn't quite large enough, bake the extra batter in small loaf pans or large ramekins.

1 Adjust your oven rack so it is one setting below the middle. Preheat the oven to 350°F (180°C). Butter a (preferably nonstick) 10-inch one-piece Bundt pan with a 14- to 18-cup capacity.

2 Using an electric mixer — preferably a stand mixer fitted with a flat beater — cream the butter and cream cheese on medium-high speed until soft and fluffy, about 2 minutes. Gradually add the sugar, beating well after each addition. Beat in the eggs, one at a time, beating well after each one. Add the vanilla and lemon extracts and beat them in on low speed.

3 Sift the flour, salt, baking powder, and cinnamon into a large bowl. Add these dry ingredients to the creamed mixture, about a third at a time, beating on medium-low speed after each addition until evenly mixed. Scrape down the sides of the bowl as needed. Switch to a wooden spoon or rubber spatula; add the apple, pecans, and raisins, and fold them into the batter until it's evenly mixed.

4 Bake the cake for 60 to 70 minutes. When done, the cake will have risen and the top should be golden brown. (Don't worry if there are cracks in the top; that's typical.) A tester inserted deep into the cake should come out clean. Transfer the cake to a rack and cool in the pan. When cool, invert the cake out of the pan (see De-panning a Tube Cake, at right) and onto a serving platter.

5 When you're ready, prepare the Maple Syrup Glaze, and immediately pour it over the cake, covering it as thoroughly as possible. The glaze will harden as it cools. The cake will keep for 3 days at room temperature. For longer storage cut it into several large sections and overwrap with plastic wrap. Slip these into plastic freezer bags and refrigerate for 1 week or freeze for up to 2 months.

MAKES 16 OR MORE SERVINGS

1½ cups (3 sticks) unsalted butter, softened, plus some for the pan

8 ounces cream cheese, softened

2⅔ cups sugar

6 large eggs, at room temperature

2 teaspoons vanilla extract

1 teaspoon lemon extract or finely grated zest of 1 lemon

3 cups all-purpose flour

1½ teaspoons salt

1 teaspoon baking powder

1 teaspoon ground cinnamon

1 large apple, peeled and finely diced

¾ cup coarsely chopped pecans

½ cup raisins

Maple Syrup Glaze (page 289)

De-panning a Tube Cake

Big pound cakes and other cakes baked in a one-piece tube pan can be tricky to remove from the pan. Here are a few tips for doing it successfully.

• First, cool your cake in the pan. It's okay if there's a touch of warmth still in the cake, but thorough cooling lets the cake settle and shrink a little, making it easier to remove. Warm cakes are much less stable and are prone to coming apart.

• If your cake pan has straight sides, carefully run a knife down and around the edge between the cake and pan to loosen it; this may not be necessary if you're using a newer nonstick pan. Go easy; you don't want to hack up your pretty cake (though if you do, there's always the glaze to cover it up). You can do this with a Bundt pan, too, but the curved sides make it a little more difficult.

• If your cake has risen up close to the top of the pan, you can simply place a platter on top and invert your cake onto the platter; it should drop right out. However, if your cake sits down in the pan by much more than half an inch, you could damage the cake when it drops out. You need to support the cake when you de-pan it, so here's my suggestion: Cut out a sturdy cardboard template that you can slip right onto the cake. It will look like a flat doughnut, with a hole in the middle to slide over the tube. Slip the cardboard template over the cake. Supporting the template with one of your hands (it helps to have big hands — borrow a pair if necessary), turn the pan over and slide the cake out of the pan.

• At this point, if you've used a straight-sided tube pan, the cake is upside down, so you will need to invert it again, directly onto your serving platter. If you've baked your cake in a Bundt pan, there's no need to re-invert it: the cake will be right-side up when you turn it out of the pan. (You'll need to gently slide it off the cardboard template if you used one.) Wipe the cardboard template with a barely damp sponge and save the template for next time.

SWEET POTATO POUND CAKE WITH MAPLE SYRUP GLAZE

Tender, sweet potato–moist, and faintly spiced, this pound cake is pretty enough to grace your most elegant cake plate and down-home enough to serve at a wood-cutting party or tailgate event. There's a bit of autumn (the sweet potatoes) and a bit of springtime (the maple syrup) in every bite. And don't forget that maple syrup is a harvested food, so it's right in tune with your harvest baking. Turning on the oven just to bake the potatoes is a bit of a pain, so plan ahead and put them in the oven earlier in the week at a time when you're already using it.

1 Preheat the oven to 350°F (180°C). Adjust your oven rack so it's one position below the middle. Butter a 12- to 14-cup one-piece tube pan and dust it with flour.

2 Sift the flour, baking powder, salt, baking soda, cinnamon, ginger, cloves, and nutmeg into a large bowl. Combine the granulated sugar, brown sugar, butter, and oil in a separate large bowl. Using an electric mixer — a stand mixer, if you have one — beat on medium-high speed until combined. Add the eggs, one at a time, beating well after each addition. Add the vanilla and sweet potato purée. Continue to beat until evenly blended.

3 Beat half of the dry ingredients into the liquid on low speed, until thoroughly mixed. Beat in the buttermilk on low speed. Add the remaining dry ingredients and blend them in on low speed, until the batter is evenly mixed. Stir in the pecans.

4 Turn the batter into the prepared pan and smooth with a spoon. Bake for 50 to 60 minutes, until a tester inserted deep into the cake comes out clean. Transfer the cake to a rack and cool in the pan for a good hour, until the cake is barely warm. Invert the cake out of the pan (see De-panning a Tube Cake, page 243) and onto a serving platter.

5 Spoon the Maple Syrup Glaze over the cake and allow to cool.

MAKES 16 SERVINGS

Butter for the pan

3 cups all-purpose flour

2 teaspoons baking powder

¾ teaspoon salt

½ teaspoon baking soda

¾ teaspoon ground cinnamon

½ teaspoon ground ginger

¼ teaspoon ground cloves

¼ teaspoon ground nutmeg

1 cup granulated sugar

1 cup packed light brown sugar

½ cup (1 stick) unsalted butter, softened

½ cup light olive oil or vegetable oil

4 large eggs, at room temperature

1½ teaspoons vanilla extract

1½ cup sweet potato purée (page 246)

½ cup buttermilk

1½ cups chopped pecans

Maple Syrup Glaze (page 289)

How to Make Sweet Potato Purée

Bake 'em? Wrap in foil? Microwave? Boil? Everyone seems to have his or her own favorite method for turning sweet potatoes into a smooth purée that's suitable for baking. Personally, I think baking the potatoes — as opposed to boiling them — concentrates the flavor and natural sugars, rather than washing them away.

1. Preheat your oven to 400°F (200°C). Line a large baking sheet with aluminum foil. I like a rimmed sheet so nothing flies off the edge at an inopportune moment. Have your oven rack positioned in the middle.

2. Scrub your sweet potatoes under running water, and leave the skins on. Poke each one two or three times with a paring knife, about ½ inch deep. Space the potatoes out on the baking sheet.

3. Bake the potatoes until a knife glides easily all the way through them. This will take anywhere from 45 minutes for small potatoes to an hour or more for large ones. Transfer the sheet to a cooling rack. Cool the potatoes thoroughly, and don't cut them open while they cool; you want to trap the heat, just in case the very centers are a tad underdone.

4. Cut open the potatoes, scoop out the flesh, and transfer to a food processor. Process, using long pulses, until the purée is smooth, scraping down the sides occasionally. Don't overdo it, unless you want a sweet potato smoothie.

For every pound of sweet potatoes, you should get about 1¼ cups of purée. Always bake an extra one or two if you're in doubt; no use cutting it close when you can freeze leftover purée in small freezer containers and use it later in soups, stews, pancakes, muffins, and other baked goods.

HONEY PARSNIP CAKE WITH MAPLE CREAM CHEESE FROSTING

Parsnip cake might not be the easiest sell if you have kids or other picky eaters on board, so perhaps you should keep some of the details about this cake to yourself until they've polished off their second piece. (Honesty is one thing, but full disclosure is quite another, right?) Just tell them it's sort of like a carrot cake; that should do the trick.

1 Preheat the oven to 325°F (170°C). Butter a 13- by 9-inch cake pan and dust it with flour, knocking out the excess.

2 Combine the walnuts or pecans in a food processor with the granulated sugar. Pulse the machine repeatedly until the nuts are finely ground.

3 Transfer the nut mixture to a large bowl. Add the flour, baking powder, baking soda, salt, cinnamon, ginger, and allspice. Mix well by hand, breaking up any clumps.

4 Combine the eggs, oil, buttermilk, honey, vanilla, and orange zest in a separate large bowl. Using an electric mixer (handheld is fine), beat on medium-high speed for 1 minute. Make a well in the dry mixture and add the liquid. Using a wooden spoon, or a mixer on low speed, mix the batter until evenly combined. Add the grated parsnips and fold them in with a rubber spatula until the batter is evenly mixed.

5 Turn the batter into the prepared pan and smooth with a spoon. Bake for 35 to 40 minutes, until the cake feels springy when pressed lightly and a toothpick inserted in the middle comes out clean. The honey will turn the surface of the cake a dark amber shade. Transfer the pan to a rack and cool the cake thoroughly.

6 To make the frosting, combine the cream cheese and butter in a large bowl. Using an electric mixer, beat on medium-high speed for about 2 minutes, until smooth. Beat in the vanilla. Add the confectioners' sugar, 1 cup at a time, beating on low speed until smooth. Add the maple syrup and lemon juice and beat for 30 seconds, until smooth and creamy. Spread a generous coating of the frosting over the cake. If you don't need all of it, you can always refrigerate the leftovers and use it on muffins or cupcakes.

MAKES 15 OR MORE SERVINGS

Butter and flour for the cake pan

1 cup walnut or pecan halves

1 cup granulated sugar

2 cups all-purpose flour

2 teaspoons baking powder

1 teaspoon baking soda

¾ teaspoon salt

1 teaspoon ground cinnamon

1 teaspoon ground ginger

½ teaspoon ground allspice

4 large eggs, at room temperature

1 cup vegetable oil or other neutral oil

¾ cup buttermilk

½ cup honey, warmed slightly

1 teaspoon vanilla extract

2 teaspoons grated orange zest

2 cups peeled and grated parsnips (2 to 3 large ones)

FROSTING

1 pound cream cheese, softened

4 tablespoons unsalted butter, softened

1 teaspoon vanilla extract

2 cups confectioners' sugar

3 tablespoons pure maple syrup or honey

2–3 teaspoons lemon juice

CHOCOLATE BEET CAKE

Tell folks that you can make a scrumptious chocolate cake using finely ground beets, and they often think you're pulling their leg. You may be wondering if the beets are detectable; they're not, in case you're hoping to keep this novelty a secret. They do, however, make for a moister-than-usual crumb, a moistness that's even more apparent after the cake's been well wrapped and allowed to sit overnight. If you're taking this to a potluck party or other event, consider dressing it up with the Chocolate Glaze on page 288. For around-the-house eating, it's optional.

1 Trim the stems and greens off the beets and scrub them well. Place them in a large saucepan with enough water to cover them. Bring to a boil. Reduce the heat, cover partially, and cook at a low boil for 30 to 45 minutes, until the beets are tender all the way through when pierced with a paring knife. Remove with a slotted spoon and set them aside on a plate to cool. When they're thoroughly cooled, slip off the skins (try rubbing them off with dry paper towels) and cut the beets into large chunks. Place in a food processor with the granulated sugar. Process the beets until they're very finely ground, but not quite puréed.

2 Put the butter in a heavy saucepan over very low heat. As it begins to melt, add the chocolate chips, swirling the pan to coat the chips. When the butter has melted, remove the saucepan from the heat and set aside for 5 to 10 minutes, until the chocolate is melted. Whisk until smooth, then set aside to cool.

3 Butter a 9- by 9-inch cake pan. Dust the pan with flour, knocking out the excess. Preheat the oven to 350°F (180°C).

4 Sift the flour, cocoa powder, baking powder, and salt into a mixing bowl.

5 Combine the eggs and brown sugar in another large bowl. Using an electric mixer (handheld is fine), beat on medium-high speed for 2 to 3 minutes, until light and foamy. Add the vanilla and beat on low speed. Gradually beat in the cooled chocolate on medium-low speed. Add the beets and blend them in on low speed.

6 Add the dry ingredients to the chocolate mixture in three installments, beating on low speed after each addition. Switch to a wooden spoon or rubber spatula for the last installment, incorporating it thoroughly. Pour the batter into the prepared pan, spreading it evenly.

7 Bake on the middle oven rack for 40 to 50 minutes, until the cake is risen and crusted over slightly (the cake will settle as it cools). A toothpick inserted into the center of the cake should come out clean. Transfer the pan to a cooling rack and cool thoroughly. Slice and serve at room temperature, with or without any type of glaze or frosting. (If you do use the Chocolate Glaze, pour it on after the cake has cooled.)

MAKES 12 TO 16 SERVINGS

Butter for the pan

2 medium beets (about ½ pound)

¼ cup granulated sugar

1 cup (2 sticks) unsalted butter

1 cup semisweet chocolate chips

1 cup plus 2 tablespoons all-purpose flour

¼ cup unsweetened cocoa powder

1½ teaspoons baking powder

¼ teaspoon salt

3 large eggs, at room temperature

1 cup packed light brown sugar

1 teaspoon vanilla extract

Chocolate Glaze (page 288), optional

SPICED BEET CAKE WITH CITRUS GLAZE

This is on my short list of favorite harvest cakes of all time, and pretty high up on that list, too. It's not one of those "quick and easy" cakes — you've got to cook and purée the beets, plump the raisins, zest fruit, and make the glaze, among other steps. But once you've tasted it you'll think the work is a small price to pay for such deliciousness. Moist, compact, and spicy, it has qualities that will remind you of carrot cake. However, thanks to the honey and beets, it's denser and moister, almost like a really good homemade fruitcake. In fact, this would be the perfect festive spice cake to serve at a holiday gathering.

1 Trim the stems and greens off the beets (see note below). Scrub the beets and put them in a pot with enough water to cover them by at least 1½ inches. Bring to a boil. Reduce the heat, cover partially, and cook at a low boil for 30 to 45 minutes, until the beets feel tender to the core when pierced with a paring knife. Drain. Transfer the beets to a plate and cool thoroughly. When cool enough to handle, peel them (try rubbing the skins off with dry paper towels) and dice them. Measure out 2 cups of diced beets. (Reserve any extra beets for another use.)

2 Put the raisins in a small bowl and add hot water to cover. Set aside. Butter a 12- to 14-cup tube pan or Bundt pan and dust it with flour. Set aside. Preheat the oven to 350°F (180°C).

3 Sift the flour, baking powder, baking soda, salt, cinnamon, nutmeg, and ginger into a large bowl. Combine the sugar and the 2 cups diced beets in a food processor. Process for 20 to 30 seconds to make a smooth purée, stopping the machine once or twice to scrape down the sides.

4 Using an electric mixer (handheld works fine), beat the honey, oil, and butter in a large bowl. Add the eggs, vanilla, lemon zest, and orange zest and beat on high speed for 1 minute. Blend the beet purée into the liquid on low speed.

5 Add half of the dry ingredients to the liquid and mix on low speed until evenly combined. Blend in the buttermilk and then the remaining dry ingredients. When the batter is evenly mixed, stir in the walnuts by hand. Drain the raisins in a colander, shake off the excess moisture, and stir those into the batter. Scrape the batter into the prepared pan. Bake for 50 to 60 minutes, until a tester inserted into the center of the cake comes out clean. Cool the cake in the pan, on a rack, until the cake is barely warm, 1 to 1½ hours. Invert the cake onto a serving platter (see De-panning a Tube Cake, page 243). Cool thoroughly, then drizzle liberally with the glaze. Refrigerate leftovers. This cake also freezes well.

NOTE: If they're in good shape, don't discard the beet greens; they're a great source of flavor and nutrition. For an easy side dish, rinse and coarsely chop the leaves. Sauté an onion in olive oil, add the greens and a little chicken stock, and cover and braise until tender.

MAKES 16 SERVINGS

Butter and flour for the pan

5 medium beets (about 1¼ pounds)

1½ cups dark or golden raisins

2⅔ cups all-purpose flour

1½ teaspoons baking powder

1 teaspoon baking soda

¾ teaspoon salt

1 teaspoon ground cinnamon

½ teaspoon ground nutmeg

¼ teaspoon ground ginger

1½ cups sugar

¾ cup honey

½ cup light olive oil or vegetable oil

½ cup (1 stick) very soft unsalted butter

4 large eggs, at room temperature

2 teaspoons vanilla extract

Finely grated zest of 1 lemon

Finely grated zest of 1 orange

½ cup buttermilk

1 cup chopped walnuts

Citrus Glaze (page 289)

CHOCOLATE SOUR CREAM ZUCCHINI CAKE WITH CHOCOLATE GLAZE

This is one heck of a cake on so many levels. For starters, nobody is ever going to guess there's zucchini in here, because it virtually disappears in the baking — there's not even a hint of vegetable flavor or nubbiness that you might expect from grated zucchini. What you will notice is what a moist cake this is, maybe the moistest chocolate cake you've ever had. I like to bake it in my 9- by 9- by 2-inch cake pan because it makes for a very tall, generously proportioned cake, but you could also use a 13- by 9-inch pan if you want the extra servings. (The baking time will be about 45 minutes in the larger pan.) To top it off, I use my favorite simple chocolate glaze. Unless you need a fancy decorated cake, this one is just about perfect for any occasion.

1 Put the grated zucchini in a colander placed over a large bowl. Salt it lightly, tossing gently to mix. Set aside for 30 minutes to drain.

2 Preheat the oven to 325°F (170°C). Butter a 9- by 9-inch cake pan.

3 Sift the flour, cocoa powder, baking soda, baking powder, and ¾ teaspoon salt into a bowl.

4 Combine the sugar, butter, oil, eggs, and vanilla in another large bowl. Using an electric mixer (handheld is fine), beat the ingredients on medium-high speed for 2 minutes, until well blended. Add one-third of the dry mixture to the liquid and blend it in on low speed. Beat in half of the sour cream, followed by another third of the dry mixture, the rest of the sour cream, and the remaining dry mixture. The batter will start to get heavier late in the mixing, and you may want to do the last bit of mixing with a wooden spoon or rubber spatula.

5 Lift the zucchini out of the colander and give it a gentle squeeze, but don't squeeze out all the moisture. Add the zucchini to the batter and fold it in with a rubber spatula until evenly mixed. Scrape the batter into the pan and smooth with a spoon.

6 Bake the cake on the middle oven rack for 60 to 70 minutes, until a tester inserted into the center of the cake comes out clean. Transfer the cake to a cooling rack and cool thoroughly.

7 When the cake has cooled, prepare the glaze, rewarming it if it has firmed up. When it has thickened slightly but is still thin enough to pour easily, slowly pour it over the cake, tilting the cake to spread it around. Cool for at least 10 minutes before slicing and serving.

MAKES 16 SERVINGS

Butter for the pan

3 cups grated zucchini (about 2 smallish ones)

¾ teaspoon salt, plus more for salting the zucchini

2½ cups all-purpose flour

⅔ cup unsweetened cocoa powder

1 teaspoon baking soda

½ teaspoon baking powder

1⅔ cups sugar

½ cup (1 stick) unsalted butter, softened

½ cup vegetable oil or light olive oil

2 large eggs, at room temperature

1¼ teaspoons vanilla extract

½ cup sour cream, at room temperature

Chocolate Glaze (page 288)

GINGERED CARROT CAKE WITH CREAM CHEESE MASCARPONE FROSTING

It's a common misconception that carrot cake was invented by the granola generation — of which I was a card-carrying member — when hippies started moving to the country and growing their own food. While carrots did become one of the most popular food trends of the 1970s, carrot cake has been around since medieval times, when it resembled more of a pudding. As with a lot of bakers, this was one of the first cakes I made. I've been experimenting and refining the formula for years, so I'm not joking when I say this is one tried-and-true recipe: attractive, perfectly moist, pleasantly sweet, and with just the right amount of extras in the way of pecans, dates, and pineapple.

1 Preheat the oven to 350°F (180°C). Butter a 13- by 9-inch cake pan and dust it with flour.

2 Combine the eggs, oil, brown sugar, granulated sugar, buttermilk, zest, and vanilla in a large bowl. Using an electric mixer (handheld is fine), beat on medium-high speed for 2 minutes.

3 Sift the flour, baking soda, baking powder, salt, ginger, and cinnamon into another large bowl. Make a well in the center and add the liquid ingredients. Stir with a wooden spoon, just until mixed. Add the carrots, dates, pecans, crystallized ginger, and drained pineapple. Stir again until the batter is evenly combined. Scrape the batter into the prepared pan and smooth it out with a spoon.

4 Bake the cake for 35 to 40 minutes, until a toothpick inserted into the center comes out clean. When you press gently on the middle of the cake, it should feel firm and springy. Transfer the cake to a rack and cool.

5 To make the frosting, combine the cream cheese, butter, and confectioners' sugar in a large bowl. Using an electric mixer, beat on medium-high speed until soft and creamy, 1 to 2 minutes. Add the vanilla and mascarpone cheese and beat on medium speed just until evenly combined. Don't overbeat the mascarpone, or it may become grainy. Leave the frosting at room temperature, and when the cake is thoroughly cool, smooth it on. Refrigerate the cake if not serving within an hour. To store, cover the pan with aluminum foil and refrigerate. Let slices stand at room temperature for about 30 minutes before serving. You can also freeze slices in plastic storage containers and bring them to room temperature before serving.

NOTE: The frosting gets an upgrade with rich mascarpone cheese, but it's expensive. If you'd rather skip it, increase the cream cheese to 16 ounces and omit the mascarpone.

MAKES UP TO 15 SERVINGS

Butter and flour for the pan

4 large eggs, at room temperature

1¼ cups light olive oil or vegetable oil

⅔ cup packed dark brown sugar

⅔ cup granulated sugar

⅔ cup buttermilk

Finely grated zest of 1 lemon or orange

2 teaspoons vanilla extract

2¼ cups all-purpose flour

1½ teaspoons baking soda

1 teaspoon baking powder

¾ teaspoon salt

1 teaspoon ground ginger

1 teaspoon ground cinnamon

2 cups grated carrots (use the large holes of a box grater)

1 cup chopped dates or raisins

1 cup finely chopped pecans

2 tablespoons minced crystallized ginger

1 (8-ounce) can crushed pineapple, drained (½ cup)

FROSTING

12 ounces cream cheese, at room temperature

½ cup (1 stick) unsalted butter, at room temperature

2 cups confectioners' sugar

1 teaspoon vanilla extract

8 ounces mascarpone cheese, at room temperature

MORAVIAN SUGAR CAKE

When the Moravians came to this country from Europe in the early 1700s to establish religious missions, they brought with them a love of sweet yeast cakes enriched with dairy products, the most well known of these being Moravian sugar cake. Given its history and credibility as a harvest cake (there's a cup of mashed potato in there), we'll overlook the fact that Moravian sugar cake is essentially a sponge for copious amounts of butter and sugar and simply enjoy it for the delicious cake that it is. You'll love the delightful contrast between the sugar-crunchy top and the soft interior. But the real treat is the way the butter oozes down into depressions in the dough and saturates the cake from within.

1 Peel and dice the potato. Transfer to a large saucepan and add enough water to cover it. Bring to a boil and boil for 10 to 12 minutes, until tender. Drain the potato and set it aside to cool. Put the potato through a ricer and set aside 1 cup's worth in a large bowl. (Reserve the rest for another use, such as thickening soups or sauces or adding to another yeast dough.)

2 Pour the lukewarm water into a small bowl and sprinkle on the yeast. Stir with a fork and set aside for 5 minutes to dissolve.

3 Mix the dissolved yeast into the mashed potatoes along with the granulated sugar, milk, egg, melted butter, and salt. Add 2 cups of the flour to the liquid, 1 cup at a time, stirring well after each addition. Add the flour in smaller quantities, no more than ¼ cup at a time, stirring well after each addition. Even if you're accustomed to making yeast doughs, this one will feel different. It's quite dense, sticky, and somewhat slack, so work the dough vigorously against the sides of the bowl with your wooden spoon as you add the flour, rather than turning it out to knead it right away.

4 Turn the dough out onto a floured surface and knead very gently for 3 to 4 minutes, dusting with more flour as necessary. Smear about 2 teaspoons of cooking oil in a large bowl. Transfer the dough to the bowl and rotate it to coat the surface with oil. Cover the bowl with plastic wrap and set aside to rise in a warm spot until doubled in bulk, 1½ to 2 hours.

5 While the dough rises, butter a 13- by 9-inch cake pan with 2 tablespoons soft butter. When the dough has risen, punch it down and transfer it to the pan. Lightly oil a sheet of plastic wrap and place it over the dough, oiled side facing the dough. Set aside for 15 minutes, then press on the plastic to spread the dough out evenly in the pan. Loosen the plastic, but leave it in place. Set the pan aside for 30 to 40 minutes, until the dough is puffy.

MAKES 15 SERVINGS

Oil for the bowl and softened butter for the cake pan

1 large russet potato

¼ cup lukewarm water (105° to 110°F [41–43°C])

1 packet (¼ ounce) active dry yeast

½ cup granulated sugar

¼ cup lukewarm milk (105° to 110°F [41–43°C])

1 large egg, at room temperature

6 tablespoons unsalted butter, melted and partially cooled

1½ teaspoons salt

2½–3 cups all-purpose flour

TOPPING

½ cup light brown sugar

½ cup granulated sugar

½ teaspoon ground cinnamon

6 tablespoons unsalted butter, melted

6 Preheat the oven to 375°F (190°C). Remove the plastic from the dough. Mix the brown sugar, granulated sugar, and cinnamon for the topping in a medium bowl. Spread it evenly over the dough. Using two fingertips, poke the dough repeatedly, making numerous deep impressions. Drizzle the melted butter over the surface, letting it run into the holes.

7 Bake the cake for about 30 minutes, until it is well risen and the surface is crusty brown. (The cake will settle a bit as it cools.) Transfer to a rack and cool in the pan. Serve warm. Reheat slices, wrapped in foil, in a 300°F (150°C) oven for about 10 minutes. This freezes well.

FRESH MINT OREO CHEESECAKE

I grew up in New Jersey, near a stretch of highway many considered the diner capital of the state, so I have cheesecake in my blood. Understand that the diners I frequented didn't cater to dietary trends or serve precious little pieces of cheesecake made with low-fat this or that. These were unabashed slabs roughly the size of those portable concrete highway dividers you see at construction sites. With age has come (slightly) more discipline and an appreciation for the kind of subtlety found in this cheesecake recipe, made with fresh mint from my garden. It's minty, though not powerfully so, and has a natural-looking, soft green hue. (You can add a drop of mint oil for more mint flavor and green food dye for color; see step 4.) The Oreos on top give the cake a fun, festive touch. But depending on your crowd, you can leave them off and apply the chocolate glaze directly to the top of the cake, as pictured here, instead of over the cookies.

1 Crumble the cookies into a food processor. Pulse the machine repeatedly to make fairly fine crumbs. Transfer the crumbs to a bowl and add the melted butter and salt. Mix well. Lightly butter only the sides of a 9-inch springform pan. Add the crumbs, pressing them firmly against the bottom of the pan and about ¼ inch up the sides. (If you press with a meat pounder or another heavy object with a flat surface, it will help you make a nice even crust.) Refrigerate.

2 Have ready a roasting pan or other not-too-deep pan that's large enough to hold the springform pan. Put a kettle of water on to boil. Preheat the oven to 350°F (180°C).

3 Combine the sugar and mint in a food processor. Pulse the machine repeatedly until the mint is finely ground into the sugar, which will turn quite green in the process. Transfer to a bowl.

4 Using an electric mixer — preferably a stand mixer fitted with a flat beater — beat the cream cheese on medium-high speed for about 2 minutes, until smooth and creamy, scraping down the sides several times. Gradually add the minty sugar and beat for another minute. Add the eggs, one at a time, beating until smooth after each addition. Beat in the sour cream on medium speed. With the mixer on low speed, beat in the flour a tablespoon at a time. Beat in the vanilla, lemon juice, and lemon zest. The cheesecake will be mint green, but if you want it greener, blend in a couple of drops of the dye.

5 Tear off two sheets of aluminum foil (see the box on the next page) 16 to 1/ inches long. Put one on top of the other to make a cross, and place the springform pan right in the center. Bunch the foil up around the sides of the pan, sealing off the bottom of the pan from the water that's about to go in the roasting pan. Pour the cheesecake batter into the springform pan, then place it inside the larger pan. Carefully, so you don't spill or splash it onto the cheesecake, add enough hot water to come no more than about ¾ inch up the sides of the cheesecake pan.

MAKES 12 TO 16 SERVINGS

CRUST

Butter for the pan

25 Oreo cookies

4 tablespoons unsalted butter, melted

Pinch of salt

FILLING

1½ cups sugar

1 cup coarsely chopped and loosely packed fresh mint leaves

2 pounds (four 8-ounce packages) cream cheese, at room temperature

4 large eggs, at room temperature

¾ cup sour cream, at room temperature

3 tablespoons all-purpose flour

1½ teaspoons vanilla extract

2 teaspoons lemon juice

1 teaspoon finely grated lemon zest

Drops of green food dye (optional)

Chocolate Glaze (page 288)

8–12 Oreo cookies, for topping

RECIPE CONTINUED ON NEXT PAGE

6 Bake the cake for 30 minutes, then reduce the heat to 325°F (170°C) and bake for another 35 to 45 minutes, until the cake is done. You'll know it's done when the sides are slightly more risen than the middle of the cake. The filling will be wobbly but not at all soupy in the center. If the cake starts puffing up quite a bit, that's an indication that it's overbaking.

7 Remove the roasting pan from the oven and let the cake cool in the roasting pan for 15 minutes. Transfer the cake to a cooling rack, let it cool another 15 minutes, and remove the foil. Cool the cake thoroughly, then refrigerate overnight.

8 To top and glaze the cake before serving, first remove the sides of the pan. Prepare the glaze, and while it is still warm and runny, pour about ⅓ cup of it over the cake, tilting the cake from side to side to spread it out. Crumble the Oreo cookies over the top, and drizzle heavily with more of the warm glaze. Serve right away, or refrigerate until serving.

THE AGE-OLD CHEESECAKE QUANDARY: TO WATER BATH OR NOT?

Baking a cheesecake in a water bath is common practice. A cheesecake is, essentially, a big custard, and custards are partial to steamy spa treatments because they protect them from the direct heat of the oven, keep them moist, and prevent unsightly cracks and wrinkles. Or so the story goes.

Whether you use a water bath or not, it's a good idea to wrap your cheesecake pan in foil. The foil will catch any butter that leaks through the seams of the pan. And it will temper the oven heat so your cheesecake bakes more slowly and evenly.

If you do go the water bath route, a few precautions are in order. If you're using regular aluminum foil, double it up as explained in the recipe. Even a small pinhole will allow water to leak in and saturate your cake. This is much less of an issue with heavy-duty foil; one sheet of it will do.

Also, don't add too much water to the roasting pan. If the level of the water comes above any of the foil, you're in trouble. Keep it low in the pan, about ¾ inch deep.

PUMPKIN CHEESECAKE CRUMB CAKES

What we're calling a crumb cake here starts with a tender, spiced pumpkin cake batter, a bit of which gets spooned into muffin cups. A dollop of "cheesecake" — sweetened cream cheese — is plunked in the middle, followed by more batter and the crumb topping. It makes for an enticing seasonal treat that's especially fun to assemble with kids or grandkids. More cupcake than muffin, these should be served after they've cooled; the cream cheese filling just tastes better at room temperature. It takes a few minutes to whip up the different parts of the recipe, but once you do, the assembly goes quickly.

1 Line a standard-size 12-cup muffin pan with baking cups, or butter the pan with soft butter. Preheat the oven to 400°F (200°C).

2 To make the filling, combine the cream cheese, granulated sugar, egg yolk, and vanilla in a small bowl. Using a handheld electric mixer, beat on medium-high speed for about a minute, until smooth and fluffy. Refrigerate. Keep the mixer nearby; you'll need it. Don't bother to clean the beaters, either.

3 To make the crumb topping, combine the flour, sugar, cinnamon, and salt in a small bowl. Whisk briefly to combine. Add the melted butter and mix it in thoroughly with your fingers; the mixture will be damp and crumbly.

4 To make the batter, sift the flour, baking powder, salt, cinnamon, allspice, ginger, and cloves into a large bowl. Combine the eggs, pumpkin, brown sugar, oil, milk, and vanilla in a separate bowl. Using your mixer, beat the liquid ingredients on medium-high speed for 1 minute. Make a well in the dry ingredients and add the liquid. Stir the batter until smooth, making sure that no dry streaks remain.

5 Spoon enough batter into each cup to fill it by about one-third. Put a big dollop of the cream cheese mixture in the center of each one, pushing it gently into the batter. Cover the dollops with the remaining batter, dividing it evenly among the cups. Sprinkle the top of each with some of the crumbs, and press gently into the batter to embed it slightly.

6 Bake for 10 minutes, then reduce the heat to 375°F (190°C) and continue to bake for another 12 to 13 minutes, until the tops are starting to turn golden brown. Transfer the pan to a cooling rack. Cool for 5 minutes in the pan, remove the cakes, and finish cooling them on the rack.

MAKES 12 CRUMB CAKES

FILLING

- 6 ounces cream cheese, softened
- ⅓ cup granulated sugar
- 1 egg yolk
- ½ teaspoon vanilla extract

CRUMB TOPPING

- ⅓ cup all-purpose flour
- ⅓ cup granulated sugar
- ¼ teaspoon ground cinnamon
- ⅛ teaspoon salt
- 2½ tablespoons unsalted butter, melted

CAKE BATTER

- 1½ cups all-purpose flour
- 2 teaspoons baking powder
- ½ teaspoon salt
- ¾ teaspoon ground cinnamon
- ½ teaspoon ground allspice
- ½ teaspoon ground ginger
- ¼ teaspoon ground cloves
- 2 large eggs
- ¾ cup pumpkin purée, canned or fresh (page 226)
- ¾ cup packed light brown sugar
- ½ cup vegetable oil or other cooking oil
- ¼ cup milk
- ¾ teaspoon vanilla extract

CHOCOLATE-GLAZED PUMPKIN CHEESECAKE WITH GINGERSNAP CRUST

Fall birthdays, Thanksgiving, tailgate parties — I use every excuse in the book to make this cheesecake. For one, I'm a glutton for the predictable reactions — the swooning, the heavenward glances, the toothy smiles. For another, this is on my own short list of best pumpkin recipes of all time, a sinfully rich and creamy cake topped with chocolate glaze. If you're using homemade pumpkin purée (see page 226), take the time to drain the flesh, because you want to remove as much water as possible. Otherwise, it won't taste as creamy, and you'll increase the chances of the cake cracking. (For insurance, this is one recipe where I often do use canned pumpkin.)

1 Preheat the oven to 325°F (170°C). Crumble the gingersnaps into a food processor. Pulse the machine repeatedly to make fairly fine crumbs. Transfer the crumbs to a bowl and add the brown sugar, ginger, and salt. Add the melted butter and mix until evenly combined. Spread the crumbs evenly in a 9-inch springform pan, pressing them into the bottom and ¼ inch up the sides of the pan. Place the pan on a baking sheet and bake the crust for 7 minutes. Transfer to a rack and cool. When the pan has cooled, lightly butter the bare sides. Wrap the bottom in aluminum foil as described in step 5 on page 257. Leave the oven set to 325°F (170°C).

2 Using an electric mixer — preferably a stand mixer fitted with a flat beater — beat the cream cheese on medium speed until soft and creamy. Add the granulated sugar and brown sugar and beat for about 2 minutes, until well mixed, stopping the machine once or twice to scrape down the sides. Beat in the eggs and yolk, one at a time, beating well on medium speed after each one. Add the pumpkin and sour cream and beat on low speed until evenly mixed.

3 Mix the flour, cinnamon, ginger, nutmeg, and salt in a small bowl. Shake the dry mixture over the batter and mix it in on low speed. Add the vanilla and beat slowly until the batter is evenly mixed, scraping down the sides once or twice more.

4 Pour the batter into the springform pan, tapping the pan on the counter several times to settle the batter. Bake for 60 to 75 minutes. When done, the cheesecake will puff very slightly around the edges. Most of the surface will have a dull finish, but the center may still look a little shiny.

5 Turn off the oven and open the door partway to start the cooling process. After 10 minutes, pull out the oven rack about halfway and continue to cool for 20 minutes. Then transfer the cake to a cooling rack and cool thoroughly, for at least 3 or 4 hours. Remove the foil from the bottom of the pan. Cover the pan with a fresh sheet of foil and refrigerate overnight.

MAKES 12 TO 16 SLICES

CRUST

- 1¾ cups finely ground (food-processed) gingersnap cookies (about ½ pound cookies)
- 3 tablespoons packed light brown sugar
- ½ teaspoon ground ginger
- ¼ teaspoon salt
- 4 tablespoons unsalted butter, melted

FILLING

- 1½ pounds cream cheese, softened
- 1 cup granulated sugar
- ½ cup packed light brown sugar
- 4 large eggs plus 1 yolk, at room temperature
- 1½ cups pumpkin purée, canned or fresh (see page 226)
- ½ cup sour cream
- 2 tablespoons all-purpose flour
- 1 teaspoon ground cinnamon
- ½ teaspoon ground ginger
- ¼ teaspoon ground nutmeg
- ½ teaspoon salt
- 2 teaspoons vanilla extract
- Chocolate Glaze (page 288)

6 When you're ready to glaze the cake, prepare the Chocolate Glaze. If you have already and it has begun to set up, rewarm it. Let it cool briefly, so it has a bit more body, and pour it over the cake; you may need all of it. Quickly tilt the cake from side to side, spreading the chocolate right up to the edge. Cool thoroughly. Cover the pan and return the cake to the refrigerator until you're ready to serve it. To serve, run a knife around the edge of the cake to loosen it; then unbuckle the sides of the pan and remove them. Using a sharp knife, cut the cake into slices, rinsing your blade under hot water and drying it before each cut.

8

SWEET PIES AND CROSTATAS

If there's a way to show off the harvest and sum up a season better than a homemade pie or crostata, I'd sure like to know about it. I doubt if anything shrinks worries and brings a smile to someone's face faster than a fresh-fruit filling baked inside a flaky, buttery crust, served up with a scoop of vanilla ice cream.

It's worth mentioning that we're not limited to the usual fruit fillings: green tomato (page 268), carrot (page 266), and sweet potato pies (page 272) can have a similar effect on folks. Just remember to start with good fresh ingredients, add plenty of heart and soul, and you can never go wrong.

CROSTATA DOUGH

There are so many different variations of crostata dough — the dough we use to make open-face fruit tarts (pages 273–277) — that it's difficult to figure out which way to turn. Some versions contain eggs or yolks; some are fairly sweet, while others are only mildly so. A few use cake flour instead of all-purpose flour; others incorporate finely ground nuts. It's more than we can sort out here, but I've tried a lot of them, and I can tell you that this version works as well as any. It has a slightly higher ratio of fat to flour than most American pie dough recipes, and the ingredients are incorporated more thoroughly, yielding a fine-textured crust that's very delicate and tart-like. The buttermilk adds additional tenderness, as does the confectioners' sugar.

1 Combine the flour, confectioners' sugar, and salt in a food processor. Pulse several times to mix.

2 Remove the lid and scatter the butter over the dry ingredients. Give the machine 8 to 10 one-second pulses, until the butter is broken into fine bits. Pulsing the machine again, add ¼ cup buttermilk through the feed tube in a single 5-second stream. Stop pulsing when the mixture starts to form clumps and before the dough balls up around the blade. If the dough seems to need the additional tablespoon of buttermilk, go ahead and add it.

3 Turn the dough out onto a lightly floured surface and shape it into a circular mound. Place the mound on a sheet of plastic wrap and flatten it into a disk about ¾ inch thick. Wrap the dough up in the plastic and refrigerate for at least 1½ hours before rolling.

MAKES ENOUGH FOR 1 LARGE CROSTATA OR A HANDFUL OF SMALLER ONES

1½ cups all-purpose flour

3 tablespoons confectioners' sugar

½ teaspoon salt

¾ cup (1½ sticks) cold unsalted butter, cut into ½-inch cubes

¼ cup cold buttermilk, plus another tablespoon if needed

DEAN'S BLUEBERRY CRUMB PIE

We get virtually all of our fresh blueberries from my brother-in-law, Dean McKitrick. Not only is Dean very generous, he's also a good foot shorter than I am, so he pretty much gives me the run of his high-bush blueberries. Dean loves blueberry crumb pies, and so do I, but if you've baked many yourself, you've probably noticed how, as the fruit juices heat up, they can drown a crumb topping. Not cool. Here's my solution: precooking (and thus prethickening) the berries so the crumbs and juices don't commingle until they reach their destination — your mouth. Good fresh blueberries in season don't need much in the way of embellishment, so we keep it simple with sugar and lemon. If I had to choose one blueberry pie for the summer, this would be it.

1 If you haven't already, prepare the pie dough, and refrigerate it for at least 1½ to 2 hours before rolling, or a little less if you're using the oat and cornmeal dough.

2 On a sheet of lightly floured waxed paper, roll the dough into a 13-inch circle. Invert the pastry over a 9- or 9½-inch deep-dish pie pan, center it, and peel off the paper. Gently tuck the pastry into the pan without stretching it. Sculpt the overhanging dough into an upstanding ridge; flute the edges, if desired. Refrigerate for at least 1 hour, or place in the freezer for 30 minutes.

3 To make the filling, combine the sugar and cornstarch in a large pot. Whisk to combine, then whisk in the juice. Add the blueberries and begin to heat them slowly, so they start to juice. Gradually increase the heat and bring the fruit to a boil, stirring pretty much nonstop. After the fruit begins to boil, continue to cook gently, stirring, for about 1½ minutes, until thickish. Remove from the heat and transfer the fruit to a shallow baking dish so it can cool more quickly. Stir in the lemon juice and lemon zest. Cool.

4 Preheat the oven to 375°F (190°C). Turn the blueberry filling into the pie shell, spreading it evenly. Cover the fruit with a generous layer of the streusel; you probably won't need quite all of it. Bake for 30 minutes, then reduce the heat to 350°F (180°C) and bake for another 25 to 30 minutes, until the topping is golden brown and the filling bubbles up near the edge. Transfer the pie to a rack to cool. Serve the pie warm or at room temperature.

MAKES 8 SERVINGS

Good Basic Pie Dough (page 145) or Oat and Cornmeal Pie Dough (page 147)

1 cup sugar

3 tablespoons cornstarch

¼ cup cranberry juice, grape juice, apple juice, or water

6 cups fresh blueberries

1 tablespoon lemon juice

Finely grated zest of 1 lemon

Brown Sugar Streusel (page 287)

SWEET CARROT PIE

Carrot pie isn't likely to put sweet potato or pumpkin out of business anytime soon, but its resemblance to those traditional pies is unmistakable. Carrots aren't as starchy as potatoes or pumpkin, but adding a little flour to the filling gives it a creamier, more full-bodied texture than you'd have otherwise. (The heavy cream helps in this regard, too.) This one is always fun to serve: They'll think you're passing out slices of pumpkin pie, but the look on their faces will soon tell you they're not so sure. Make them guess, and don't give up the surprise too quickly.

1 Prepare the pie dough, and refrigerate it for at least 1½ to 2 hours before rolling.

2 On a sheet of lightly floured waxed paper, roll the dough into a 13-inch circle. Invert the pastry over a 9- or 9½-inch deep-dish pie pan, center it, and peel off the paper. Gently tuck the pastry into the pan without stretching it. Sculpt the overhanging dough into an upstanding ridge; flute the edges, if desired. Prick the bottom of the shell six or seven times with a fork. Refrigerate for at least 1 hour, or place in the freezer for 30 minutes.

3 Preheat the oven to 375°F (190°C). Tear off a sheet of aluminum foil about 16 inches long. Gently line the pie shell with the foil, pressing it into the creases so it fits like a glove. Add a thick layer of dried beans, banking them up the sides.

4 Bake the pie shell on the center oven rack for 25 minutes. Slide it out and carefully remove the foil and beans. Repoke the holes if they've filled in. Slide the shell back in and bake for another 6 to 8 minutes. Transfer the pie shell to a cooling rack. Once it is cooled, dab a little cream cheese or sour cream into the fork holes to plug them.

5 Preheat the oven to 400°F (200°C). Tear off two long pieces of aluminum foil; butter the middle part of each sheet with the soft butter. Cut the carrots in half, or into thirds, and place them in the middle of each sheet, dividing them up equally. Seal tightly in the foil and bake for about 50 minutes, until soft. Set the packets aside and open the foil so the carrots can cool.

6 Preheat the oven (or turn it down) to 350°F (180°C). When the carrots have cooled, cut them into slices and measure out 2 cups (save any leftovers for use in soups, stews, and other dishes). Put the measured carrots into a food processor with the brown sugar and flour. Process to a smooth purée, scraping down the sides once or twice. Add the eggs, lemon zest, and salt, and process until smooth. Transfer to a bowl and whisk in the heavy cream, half-and-half, vanilla, allspice, and cinnamon.

MAKES 8 TO 10 SERVINGS

Good Basic Pie Dough (page 145)

1 tablespoon butter, softened

1 pound medium-size carrots, trimmed and peeled

1 cup packed light brown sugar

1 tablespoon all-purpose flour

3 large eggs

1 teaspoon finely grated lemon zest

¼ teaspoon salt

¾ cup heavy cream

½ cup half-and-half or light cream

¾ teaspoon vanilla extract

½ teaspoon ground allspice

¼ teaspoon ground cinnamon

Whipped cream, for serving

7 Pour the filling into the pie shell. Bake for approximately 45 to 55 minutes, until the filling is set. When done, the sides of the pie will have puffed up, more so than in the middle, and the filling will jiggle as a whole when you nudge the pie. There should be no evidence of uncooked filling in the center.

8 Transfer the pie to a cooling rack and cool thoroughly. This pie is best served cool or cold, so try to refrigerate it for at least a few hours before serving. Serve with whipped cream.

SPICED GREEN TOMATO PIE

Green tomatoes can be confusing, in part because they're so at odds with their more mature red selves. Red ones are soft and sweetly acidic, and there's almost no limit to how we use them in the kitchen. Green tomatoes are firm and tart and seem to have few aspirations beyond fried tomatoes and pies. That suits me fine, because a good green tomato pie is a thing of beauty, a microseasonal dessert whose season is wedged perfectly between the last of summer's fruit pies and the first apple pies of the year. Another thing about green tomatoes: they're something of a blank canvas, flavorwise, which explains the liberal use of sugar and spice in green tomato pie recipes. This one is no exception, but the mix of cinnamon, crystallized ginger, and orange zest gives this version a unique sparkle that I think you'll love.

1 Prepare the pie dough, and refrigerate it for at least 1½ to 2 hours before rolling.

2 Mix the sugar, cornstarch, cinnamon, cloves, and salt in a large bowl. Add the tomato slices; using your hands, mix well. Add the vinegar, ginger, orange juice, and orange zest; mix again. Set aside for 1 hour.

3 While the tomatoes macerate, roll the pie dough. On a sheet of lightly floured waxed paper, roll the dough into a 13-inch circle. Invert the pastry over a 9- or 9½-inch deep-dish pie pan, center it, and peel off the paper. Gently tuck the pastry into the pan without stretching it. Sculpt the overhanging dough into an upstanding ridge; flute the edges, if desired. Poke the bottom of the shell six or seven times with a fork. Refrigerate for at least 1 hour, or place in the freezer for 30 minutes.

4 Preheat the oven to 375°F (190°C). Using a colander set over a bowl, drain the tomato slices. Pour the juices into a medium-size skillet. Put the tomatoes in a bowl. Gradually bring the juice to a simmer. Simmer for about 30 seconds, just until it begins to thicken. Remove from the heat and stir the juice into the tomatoes, along with the raisins. Transfer the filling to the pie shell and smooth it out.

5 Bake the pie on the middle oven rack for 30 minutes. Then slide out the pie and cover the filling with a thick coating of the streusel topping; you may not need all of it. Reduce the heat to 350°F (180°C) and bake for another 25 to 30 minutes, until the filling bubbles — at least around the edges — and the streusel is golden brown. Don't underbake the pie or the tomatoes won't be fully tender. Transfer to a rack and cool for at least 45 minutes before serving. Refrigerate leftovers.

MAKES 8 SERVINGS

Good Basic Pie Dough (page 145)

¾ cup sugar

1½ tablespoons cornstarch

½ teaspoon ground cinnamon

⅛ teaspoon ground cloves

¼ teaspoon salt

4½ cups cored, quartered, and very thinly sliced green tomatoes

2 tablespoons apple cider vinegar

1½ tablespoons finely chopped crystallized ginger

1 tablespoon orange juice

1 teaspoon grated orange zest

½ cup chopped golden raisins

Brown Sugar Streusel (page 287)

MAPLE-GLAZED ALL-PEAR PIE

This is a shocking admission from someone who has written an entire book about apple pie: given the choice, I'm fairly certain I'd pick a piece of all-pear pie over a piece of all-apple pie any day of the week. What can I say? I just love pears. When we were young and my mom would break out a jumbo can of syrupy pears for dessert (there were nine of us at the dinner table), I thought they were the pinnacle of gourmet dessertdom. Fresh ginger and five-spice powder — an exotic blend of star anise, cloves, cinnamon, Sichuan pepper, and fennel — give the pears in this pie a nice, warm, spicy glow, and the maple glaze, which sets up firm on the top crust, reminds me of those glazed fruit pies that we felt lucky to get in our school lunches.

1 Prepare the pie dough as for a double-crust pie. Refrigerate the dough for at least 1½ to 2 hours before rolling.

2 On a sheet of lightly floured waxed paper, roll the larger half of dough into a 13-inch circle. Invert the pastry over a 9- or 9½-inch deep-dish pie pan, center it, and peel off the paper. Gently tuck the pastry into the pan without stretching it, letting the edge of the pastry drape over the sides of the pan. Loosely cover the pie shell with plastic wrap. Refrigerate.

3 Preheat the oven to 375°F (190°C). Put the pears in a large bowl. Mix the sugar, cornstarch, five-spice powder, and salt in a small bowl. Add to the pears and mix well. Stir in the lemon juice and fresh ginger.

4 Turn the filling into the pie shell and smooth it out evenly. Moisten the edge of the pie shell with a wet fingertip or pastry brush.

5 Roll the other half of the dough into an 11-inch circle, and drape it over the filling. Press the edge of the pastry to seal. Using a paring knife, trim the excess dough flush with the edge of the pan. Crimp the edge with a fork. (Alternatively, you can press the pastry edges together with your fingers and trim the crust with scissors, leaving a ½-inch overhang. Pinch the overhang into an upstanding ridge, and flute or scallop the dough by hand.) Using a paring knife, poke the top pastry several times to make steam vents. Twist the knife slightly to enlarge the holes; this will help you see the juices later in the baking and determine if the pie is done. Lightly brush the top pastry with the egg glaze.

6 Bake the pie for 50 to 55 minutes, until the top is golden brown and you can see thick juice bubbling up through the steam vents. It's important that the juices boil so the cornstarch thickens the pie properly. (If you're in doubt, give it a little more time.) Transfer the pie to a rack. Cool thoroughly, then spoon on the Maple Syrup Glaze, drizzling it liberally over the crust. You may not need all of it. (Refrigerate leftover glaze; rewarm it to use on biscuits, muffins, mini pies, and so on, as desired.)

MAKES 8 SERVINGS

Slab Pie Dough (page 148), as prepared for a double-crust pie

6 cups peeled, cored, and sliced ripe pears

½ cup sugar

2½ tablespoons cornstarch

¾ teaspoon five-spice powder

Pinch of salt

1 tablespoon lemon juice

1 tablespoon minced fresh ginger

1 egg beaten with 1 teaspoon water, for glaze

Maple Syrup Glaze (page 289)

CARAMEL APPLE SLAB PIE

This is not one of those caramel apple pies where you make the caramel sauce separately and drizzle it over the pie after you bake it; there are plenty of recipes out there for that. This one has the caramel built right in, the brown sugar and cream melting together in the filling and coating each tender slice of apple with velvety caramel sauce. This is also a slab pie, something I've become infatuated with lately, at least in part because I love that for essentially the same amount of work and ingredients as your average round pie, you end up with twelve decent-size servings instead of eight, making slab pies a no-brainer for a gathering of any size. This is a great project pie for a fall weekend; you can start out with a trip to a local orchard for fresh-picked apples, team up with family or friends for the assembly and baking, then flag down the neighbors and have them come share your creation.

1 Prepare the slab pie shell. Place in the freezer for at least 30 minutes.

2 Preheat the oven to 400°F (200°C). Combine the apples, brown sugar, flour, cinnamon, and salt in a large bowl. Mix well; hands work best here. Add the cream and lemon juice and mix again.

3 Spread the apples evenly in the pie shell, patting them down lightly so none of the tips stick up and scorch in the oven. Bake for 15 minutes, then reduce the temperature to 375°F (190°C) and bake for 15 minutes more.

4 Slide out the pie and carefully cover it with all of the streusel; it may be easier to place the pie on your work counter while you're doing this, rather than leaving it on the oven rack. Carefully, so you don't burn yourself, press the streusel down gently with the back of a spatula or wooden spoon, to compress. Bake the pie for 25 to 30 minutes more, until the juices are bubbling and the streusel has turned a shade or two more golden. Total baking time will be 50 to 60 minutes.

5 Transfer the pie to a cooling rack and cool for at least 20 to 30 minutes before serving.

MAKES 12 SERVINGS

Slab Pie Dough (and Shell) (page 148)

8 cups peeled, cored, and sliced baking apples (6 to 7 large ones)

½ cup packed light brown sugar

2½ tablespoons all-purpose flour

¾ teaspoon ground cinnamon

¼ teaspoon salt

¼ cup heavy cream

2 teaspoons lemon juice

Brown Sugar Streusel (page 287)

MAPLE SWEET POTATO PIE

My approach to sweet potato pie is much the same as my approach to pumpkin: it needs enough nudging to taste like a credible dessert rather than a trumped-up vegetable side dish. Maple syrup and heavy cream do it here. Keep in mind that sweet potato and pumpkin are custard pies and should therefore be baked in a moderate (not too hot) oven or the eggs might "break" and cause the pie to weep. Lower and slower wins the race. Like all custard pies, I think this is best served cold. But I know there are plenty of you out there in the lukewarm and room temperature camps. Whatever works. Serve with lightly sweetened whipped cream. You're in for a treat.

1 Prepare the pie dough, and refrigerate it for at least 1½ to 2 hours before rolling.

2 On a sheet of lightly floured waxed paper, roll the dough into a 13-inch circle. Invert the pastry over a 9- or 9½-inch deep-dish pie pan, center it, and peel off the paper. Gently tuck the pastry into the pan without stretching it. Sculpt the overhanging dough into an upstanding ridge; flute the edges, if desired. Prick the bottom of the pie shell six or seven times with a fork. Refrigerate for at least 1 hour, or place in the freezer for 30 minutes.

3 Preheat the oven to 375°F (190°C). Tear off a sheet of aluminum foil about 16 inches long. Gently line the pie shell with the foil, pressing it into the creases so it fits like a glove. Add a thick layer of dried beans, banking them up the sides.

4 Bake the pie shell on the center oven rack for 25 minutes. Slide it out and carefully remove the foil and beans. Repoke the holes if they've filled in. Slide the shell back in and bake for another 6 to 8 minutes. Transfer the pie shell to a cooling rack. Once it is cooled, dab a little cream cheese or sour cream into the fork holes to plug them.

5 Set the oven to 375°F (190°C). Whisk the eggs and yolk in a large bowl just until frothy. Add the sweet potato purée, brown sugar, maple syrup, melted butter, cream, half-and-half, and vanilla. Using an electric mixer, beat on low speed until evenly blended. Mix the flour, cinnamon, nutmeg, cloves, and salt in a small bowl. Sprinkle over the filling and blend it in on low speed. Pour the filling into the pie shell.

6 Bake for 20 minutes, then reduce the heat to 350°F (180°C) and bake for another 30 to 40 minutes. When done, the pie will be wobbly, with no sign of liquid in the center; give it a little nudge to be sure. Also, the perimeter will be slightly puffy and have a duller finish than the very center, which will have a bit of a sheen. Transfer to a rack and cool. Refrigerate leftovers.

MAKES 8 TO 10 SERVINGS

Good Basic Pie Dough (page 145)

3	large eggs plus 1 egg yolk, at room temperature
1½	cups sweet potato purée (page 246)
⅔	cup packed light brown sugar
⅓	cup pure maple syrup
4	tablespoons unsalted butter, melted
½	cup heavy cream
½	cup half-and-half
½	teaspoon vanilla extract
1	tablespoon all-purpose flour
½	teaspoon ground cinnamon
½	teaspoon ground nutmeg
¼	teaspoon ground cloves
½	teaspoon salt

FRESH STRAWBERRY CROSTATA

A spoonful of balsamic vinegar and a bit of fresh mint transform ordinary fresh strawberries into a crostata filling with real sparkle. Strawberries can be a bit of a challenge for a crostata because they're so juicy. But by taking a few precautions, like par-freezing the berries (see step 2) and dusting the dough with some sugar and cornstarch, you minimize the chance of a juicy breach. (It's only a very small tragedy if it does happen, and nothing to have a meltdown over. It will still be quite servable.) Garnish slices with soft clouds of whipped cream and sprigs of fresh mint. It's a photo op waiting to happen.

1 Prepare the dough, and refrigerate it for at least 1½ to 2 hours before rolling.

2 Put the strawberries in a shallow baking dish, such as a ceramic or glass pie pan, and place them in the freezer until they're semihard but not frozen solid. (This will delay their juicing, giving the crust more time to set and making it more leak resistant.) When the berries are chilled, preheat the oven to 400°F (200°C). Have ready a large baking sheet, preferably a rimmed one in case the crostata springs a leak. (Leave the berries in the freezer for now.)

3 On a large sheet of parchment paper, roll the dough into a 13-inch circle. Lift the paper and dough onto your baking sheet, trimming the paper to fit the pan. (If you don't have parchment, you can roll the dough on a sheet of waxed paper and invert it onto your baking sheet. Peel off the paper, and you're ready to proceed.)

4 Mix the sugar and cornstarch in a small bowl. Sprinkle a tablespoon of this mixture over the center of the dough in an area roughly equivalent to a 9-inch circle. Put the chilled berries in a large bowl. Sprinkle the lemon juice over the berries, and add the remaining sugar mixture and the mint; mix gently. Spread the berries over the dough, covering the same 9-inch circle as the sugar mixture.

5 Using a spatula or the paper itself to help you lift, fold the uncovered dough border over the filling, working your way around the crostata. The border will sort of self-pleat, enclosing the fruit.

6 Lightly brush the exposed dough with cream, and sprinkle it with sugar. Bake for 20 minutes, then reduce the heat to 375° (190°C) and bake for about 20 minutes more. Stir the balsamic vinegar and strawberry jelly together in a small bowl until smooth. Slide out the crostata and drizzle the mixture over the fruit. Bake the crostata for 10 minutes more. When done, the edge of the crostata will be golden brown and the filling will be bubbling. Transfer the baking sheet to a cooling rack and cool the crostata, directly on the sheet, for at least 30 minutes before serving.

MAKES 6 TO 8 SERVINGS

Crostata Dough (page 263)

3 cups hulled and quartered fresh strawberries

⅓ cup sugar, plus a little for sprinkling

1½ tablespoons cornstarch

1½ teaspoons lemon juice

1–2 tablespoons chopped fresh mint

   Heavy cream, for glaze

2 teaspoons balsamic vinegar

2 tablespoons strawberry jelly or preserves

NOTE: A fruit crostata (an Italian take on the French galette) is an open-face, free-form tart with less filling than your average American pie but a slightly larger footprint. Among many other endearing qualities, it's a real friend to those who suffer from a generalized sense of pie phobia: while there is still a dough to prepare, you don't have to worry about it sticking (if you use parchment), cracking along the edge, or self-destructing when you try to get it into the pan. You simply lift the parchment and dough onto your baking sheet.

THREE-BERRY CROSTATA

Just about every kind of fruit under the sun can go into a crostata, but this berry version has to be the best tasting for the least amount of work. Vanilla ice cream, whipped cream, Vanilla Custard Sauce (page 290), or one of the other usual creamy suspects is a highly recommended accompaniment.

1 If you haven't already, prepare the dough, and refrigerate it for at least 1½ hours before rolling.

2 Preheat the oven to 400°F (200°C). Have ready a large baking sheet, preferably a rimmed one. Combine all of the berries in a large bowl. Mix ⅓ cup sugar and the cornstarch in a small bowl.

3 On a large sheet of parchment paper, roll the dough into a 13-inch circle. Lift the paper and dough onto your baking sheet, trimming the paper to fit the pan. (If you don't have parchment, you can roll the dough on a sheet of waxed paper and invert it onto your baking sheet. Peel off the paper, and you're ready to proceed.)

4 Add the sugar and cornstarch mixture to the fruit; mix well. Mix in the lemon juice, orange zest, and nutmeg. Scrape the fruit out of the bowl and into a mound in the center of the dough. Spread it out evenly to create a 9-inch circle of fruit, with a 2-inch border of dough all around. Using the parchment itself or a spatula to help you lift, fold the edge of the pastry over the filling a few inches at a time. As you make your way around the dough, the border will sort of self-pleat as you go, enclosing a lovely circle of fruit in the middle.

5 Lightly brush the dough border with cream, and sprinkle it with sugar. Bake for 20 minutes, then reduce the heat to 375° (190°C) and bake for about 30 minutes more. When done, the edge of the crostata will be golden brown and the filling will be bubbling. Transfer the baking sheet to a cooling rack and cool the crostata, directly on the sheet, for at least 30 minutes before serving.

MAKES 6 TO 8 SERVINGS

Crostata Dough (page 263)

1½ cups fresh blueberries

1½ cups fresh blackberries (some raspberries are good, too)

1½ cups sliced fresh strawberries

⅓ cup sugar, plus a little for sprinkling

1 tablespoon plus 1 teaspoon cornstarch

1 tablespoon lemon juice

1 teaspoon finely grated orange zest or lemon zest

Pinch of ground nutmeg

Heavy cream, for glaze

INDIVIDUAL CHERRY AND BLACKBERRY CROSTATAS

There's been so much talk about mini pies over the past few years, you'd think that individual crostatas would get carried along in the wake. But crostatas still fly below the radar of many cooks, so maybe this recipe will help. This mini crostata is made with two lovely dark summer fruits that taste wonderful together, cherries and blackberries, lightly sweetened and seasoned with a bit of lemon thyme; some chopped fresh mint would be a fine substitute. Don't be concerned if a breach develops in the pastry and some of the juice leaks onto the baking sheet. Rather, concern yourself with trying to decide whether to serve these with whipped cream, vanilla ice cream, or Vanilla Custard Sauce (page 290).

1 Prepare the crostata dough, dividing it into five or six equal pieces. Shape them into balls, and flatten the balls into disks almost ½ inch thick. Put them on a plate, cover with plastic, and refrigerate for 1 to 1½ hours before rolling.

2 Working with one chilled disk at a time, roll the dough into a 6½-inch-diameter circle. Stack the circles on top of one another, with a piece of plastic wrap or waxed paper in between each one. Refrigerate for 30 minutes.

3 The crostatas will need to be baked on two or more baking sheets because they take up a bit of room, so line a couple of large rimmed baking sheets with parchment, if you have it. Otherwise, you'll have to bake them directly on the sheet. Position one oven rack in the middle of the oven and the second one (if you have a second one) near the bottom of the oven. Preheat the oven to 375°F (190°C).

4 Combine the cherries and blackberries in a mixing bowl. Mix the sugar, cornstarch, and cinnamon in another bowl. Add the mixture to the fruit, along with the lemon juice and lemon thyme. Mix gently, so you don't smash the berries too much.

5 Put two of the dough circles on one of your baking sheets, leaving plenty of room between them. Pile about ½ cup of the fruit mixture in the center of each one, leaving a border of at least 1½ inches of dough all around. Lift and fold the dough up over the edges of the filling; it will self-pleat as you go and nearly enclose the fruit completely. Press the dough gently against the fruit to keep it in place. If there's room on the sheet for a third crostata, assemble it on the side and place it on the sheet. Put the first sheet in the fridge. Repeat for the rest of the crostatas, placing them on the second sheet.

6 When both sheets are ready, place them on separate oven racks and bake for 20 minutes. Then switch the positions of the sheets and bake for another 25 minutes. When the crostatas are done, the juice will bubble and the pastry will be golden brown. Transfer the sheets to cooling racks and cool for 10 minutes. Transfer the crostatas to the cooling racks and continue to cool. If you have any remaining crostatas to bake, start with a fresh baking sheet. Or cool and wash up one of the first ones.

MAKES 5 OR 6 INDIVIDUAL CROSTATAS

Crostata Dough (page 263)

1½ cups halved and pitted sweet cherries

1½ cups fresh blackberries

⅔ cup sugar

4 teaspoons cornstarch

¼ teaspoon ground cinnamon

2 teaspoons lemon juice

1 teaspoon fresh lemon thyme

NOTE: If I don't need six crostatas, I prefer to make five because there's a little more dough to work with and the pastry will be slightly thicker and less likely to spring a leak. If you do make six, make the circles just a tad smaller — about 6 inches in diameter instead of 6½.

PEACH APRICOT CRUMB CROSTATA

Adding a layer of jelly or fruit preserves to a crostata is a simple way to amplify the fruitiness of these open-face tarts without adding a lot of extra fruit. The spread you choose can be made from the same fruit, but more often than not I like to use a complementary one, as we do here with apricot preserves. The preserves are smeared over the dough, followed by a single layer of fresh peaches and some Brown Sugar Streusel. This tart has a ton of seasonal flavor but an elegant, slim profile. It's just right when you want to end your meal with a lovely little slice of summer.

1 Prepare the dough, and refrigerate it for at least 1½ hours before rolling.

2 Preheat the oven to 400°F (200°C). Have ready a large baking sheet, preferably a rimmed one.

3 On a large sheet of parchment paper, roll the dough into a 12½- to 13-inch circle. Lift the paper and dough onto your baking sheet, trimming the paper to fit the pan. (If you don't have parchment, you can roll the dough on a sheet of waxed paper and invert it onto your baking sheet. Peel off the paper, and you're ready to proceed.)

4 Spoon about ⅔ cup of the apricot preserves into a small bowl; stir well to smooth it out. Smear the preserves over the center of the dough in an area equivalent to a 9-inch circle. Starting from the center of the circle and working out, make a single, tight layer of peach slices, placing them in a circular arrangement as you go.

5 When you've covered all of the preserves with peach slices, use the parchment itself or a spatula to fold the uncovered border of the pastry up over the fruit. The dough will form pleats as you work your way around. Brush the exposed dough with a little cream, and sprinkle it with sugar. Stir the remaining preserves until smooth, and dollop it here and there over the fruit.

6 Sprinkle the streusel evenly over the peaches. Bake for 20 minutes, then reduce the heat to 375° (190°C) and bake for about 30 minutes more. When done, the edge of the crostata and the streusel will be golden brown and the filling will be bubbling. Transfer the baking sheet to a cooling rack and cool the crostata, directly on the sheet, for at least 30 minutes before serving.

MAKES 6 TO 8 SERVINGS

Crostata Dough (page 263)

1–1¼ cups apricot or peach preserves (a 12-ounce jar is plenty)

2–3 large ripe peaches, peeled and thickly sliced

Heavy cream, for glaze

Sugar, for sprinkling

1–1½ cups Brown Sugar Streusel (page 287)

PART 4
Top It Off

9

THE HARVEST BAKER'S PANTRY
Sauce, Glaze, Streusel, and More

Here's a little chapter — I like to think of it as a pantry — where we keep the sundry items that complete many of the baked goods found in these pages. Don't think less of them just because they're tucked here at the end. Rather, try to imagine the many uses you'll find for these recipes beyond those mentioned here; I've suggested some that come to mind, and you will, no doubt, come up with many more.

QUICK SUMMER TOMATO SAUCE

My definition of "quick" when it comes to fresh tomato sauce means not having to peel tomatoes, chop a dozen vegetables, or simmer the sauce all day long. This delicious sauce checks all those boxes. In addition to pasta, I'll use this for summer bruschetta or to dress up a meat loaf or frittata slices. And it's really in its element on Grilled Harvest Pizza (page 118). I think the sauce improves when it sits overnight in the fridge, so prepare this a day ahead if you have time. Prefer your sauce without skins? See page 156 for an easy way to peel tomatoes.

1 Heat the olive oil in a large pot. Add the onion and sauté over medium heat for 8 to 10 minutes, until soft and light golden. Stir in the garlic and cook for 30 seconds. Stir in the tomatoes, carrots, sugar, salt, and pepper. Cook for 5 minutes over medium heat, breaking up the tomatoes with your wooden spoon as the sauce simmers.

2 Cover the sauce and simmer gently for about 15 minutes, until good and saucy, stirring occasionally. Stir in the basil and parsley. Stir in the tomato paste, a teaspoon at a time, to give the sauce a little more body. Simmer for a few more minutes, adjusting the seasoning as necessary. Remove from the heat.

3 Cool the sauce thoroughly, then transfer it to a food processor. Pulse the sauce several times to smooth it out, but leave it with some texture.

NOTE: Even though I specify meaty plum tomatoes for this sauce, I'm not dogmatic about it. I often have odd pieces and halves of beefsteak tomatoes sitting in my fridge during the summer, and I don't hesitate to include them. I'll even throw in a handful of halved cherry tomatoes if they need to be used up.

MAKES ABOUT 3½ CUPS

- ¼ cup olive oil
- 1 large onion, finely chopped
- 2 garlic cloves, minced
- 6 cups cored and coarsely chopped plum tomatoes (2 to 2½ pounds; see note)
- 1 cup grated carrots
- 1 teaspoon sugar
- ¾ teaspoon salt
- ¼ teaspoon freshly ground black pepper
- 2–3 tablespoons chopped fresh basil or 1 tablespoon pesto
- 2–3 tablespoons chopped fresh parsley
- 1–3 teaspoons tomato paste

ROASTED PLUM TOMATOES

Roasting plum tomatoes brings out their sweetness and flavor. Think of it as a kind of accelerated ripening, whereby less than perfect tomatoes are changed into valuable currency for the harvest baker. If you've never tried it, start with the Roasted Tomato, Corn, and Cheddar Cheese Quiche (page 186), but don't be surprised if you find yourself tossing roasted tomatoes into all sorts of savory summer pies, savory quick breads, and more.

1 Preheat the oven to 350°F (180°C). Line a large rimmed baking sheet with parchment paper. If you don't have parchment, just rub the sheet with olive oil.

2 Arrange the tomatoes on the baking sheet, cut side up. Salt and pepper them, and dust each one with a tiny pinch of sugar. Drizzle them liberally with olive oil and much less liberally with sprinkles of balsamic vinegar. Sprinkle the minced garlic and the fresh herbs over them.

3 Bake the tomatoes for 1¼ to 1½ hours, until they're soft and wilted. Transfer the baking sheet to a rack. Cool the tomatoes on the sheet, but loosen them while they're still warm so they don't stick. Use right away, or layer the tomatoes in a glass container with olive oil to cover and refrigerate.

MAKES 14 OR MORE ROASTED TOMATO HALVES

2–3 pounds large plum tomatoes, cored, halved lengthwise, and seeded

Salt and freshly ground black pepper

Sugar

Olive oil

Balsamic vinegar

4–5 garlic cloves, minced

1 tablespoon chopped fresh herbs (some combination of rosemary, thyme, and oregano) or 2 to 3 tablespoons chopped fresh basil

FOOD PROCESSOR TOMATO JAM

Tomato jam is a sweet-tart reduction with a relish- or jam-like consistency that a cook can find all manner of creative uses for. You can spread it on sandwiches or burgers in place of ketchup; use it to spice up a grilled cheese sandwich or panino; whisk it into vinaigrette dressing; or spread it on crackers with cream cheese for a shorthand version of our Savory Shortbread Thumbprints with Tomato Jam appetizer (page 71). It's also the spread that gives the Tomato Jam Pizza with Caramelized Onions (page 116) its unique sparkle. Fresh ripe tomatoes are key, so this is a summer endeavor. Once you see how easy this is to make and discover how versatile it is, you'll be hooked. Incidentally, this is a fairly straightforward version of tomato jam. It's not unusual to see recipes with chopped jalapeño peppers, finely chopped red onion, and even more spice than this one. If this is your first time, I'd suggest starting with this recipe as a point of reference before exercising your creative license.

1 Combine the tomatoes in a food processor with the brown sugar, granulated sugar, salt, pepper, lemon juice, apple cider vinegar, ginger, cinnamon, and cloves. Pulse the machine repeatedly until the tomatoes are reduced to a textured purée.

2 Transfer the mixture to a large skillet and bring to a boil. Cook the mixture at a steady boil until it is reduced by slightly less than half and most of the thin liquid has evaporated. As it boils, use a soup spoon to skim some of the foamy matter that rises to the surface. There will be other indications that the jam is ready: it will have a fairly thickish consistency, and there will be a subtle change in the boiling, which will sound more rapid and high-pitched. If in doubt, err slightly on the side of undercooking to keep it from getting too firm as it cools, especially if you're making the Tomato Jam Pizza with Caramelized Onions (page 116), where the extra moisture is welcome. Total cooking time will be 18 to 25 minutes. Remove from the heat and let cool. Transfer to a jar; seal and refrigerate until using.

MAKES 1¼ TO 1½ CUPS

- 2 pounds (about 5 medium) ripe tomatoes, cored and coarsely chopped
- ⅓ cup packed light brown sugar
- ⅓ cup sugar
- ½ teaspoon salt
- ⅛ teaspoon freshly ground black pepper
- 1½ tablespoons lemon juice
- 1½ tablespoons apple cider vinegar
- ½ teaspoon finely grated fresh ginger
- ¼ teaspoon ground cinnamon
- ⅛ teaspoon ground cloves

HOMEMADE CRÈME FRAÎCHE

Crème fraîche is a thick, cultured cream used in French cooking. It adds a pleasant tang and richness to all sorts of dishes, especially in a harvest quiche (see pages 179 and 182). Store brands can be quite expensive, so I always make my own. It's very simple, and if you've ever made yogurt, then you already have the hang of it.

Stir together the cream and buttermilk in a small jar. Place it in a warmish spot, such as near the stovetop or on top of the fridge, and let it sit at room temperature for 12 to 24 hours, until it has thickened. (It seems to make little difference whether you leave it uncovered, cover it with cheesecloth, or use a lid while it sits.) After it thickens, stir, cover, and refrigerate for 24 hours before using. Use within a week.

MAKES ABOUT 1½ CUPS

1½ cups heavy cream

3 tablespoons buttermilk

CURRIED YOGURT DIPPING SAUCE

Here's a simple curry sauce that I serve with a variety of Indian dishes, including the Potato-Stuffed Indian Flatbread on page 72. It's also good with shrimp or grilled salmon. It takes just a minute to prepare, and because it's only mildly spicy, it has widespread appeal. Some curry powders are hotter than others, however, so proceed accordingly. If you happen to want more heat, add some cayenne or chili pepper paste.

Stir together the yogurt, cilantro, onion, jalapeños, honey, curry powder, lime juice, and a pinch of salt and pepper in a small bowl until smooth. Taste, and adjust the balance of ingredients and seasoning as needed. Some Greek yogurts are pretty thick, so if the sauce needs to be thinned, just stir in a little water. If you're using pickled jalapeños, you can add a few teaspoons of the pickling liquid, too, for flavor. Cover and refrigerate until serving.

MAKES ABOUT 1¼ CUPS

- 1 cup plain yogurt
- ¼ cup finely chopped cilantro or flat-leaf parsley, or a combination of the two
- 2 tablespoons minced red onion
- 1–2 tablespoons minced pickled jalapeños or minced fresh jalapeños
- 1 tablespoon honey
- 2–3 teaspoons curry powder
- 2–3 teaspoons lime juice

  Salt and freshly ground black pepper

MINT SUGAR

Mint sugar is just that — fresh mint leaves and granulated sugar ground together in the food processor. As a harvest baker, you'll find lots of creative uses for it: sprinkled on glazed breakfast breads (see the blueberry scones on page 46), dusted over whipped cream on your summer shortcakes, and so much more. Watermelon and cantaloupe aren't the same without it. You'll want to keep a jar handy all summer long. Packed in a pretty jar, it makes a great little summer gift for your favorite baker.

1 Rinse your mint briefly under cold running water, and pat dry between paper towels. Change the paper towels, and pat the mint again to get it good and dry. Examine your mint leaves carefully, removing anything that's the least bit tired, wilted, or otherwise imperfect. Pinch off the small stems right below the leaves, so all that's left are the leaves.

2 Combine the mint leaves and sugar in a food processor. Pulse the mixture repeatedly until the mint leaves are finely chopped, virtually as fine as the sugar. Transfer the mixture to a lidded jar, seal, and refrigerate until using. Because of the moisture in the mint, the sugar may become clumpy, but it's a simple matter to mix or shake the clumps away.

MAKES 1 CUP

1 small bunch fresh mint leaves

1 cup sugar

BROWN SUGAR STREUSEL

Call it streusel topping, crumb topping, or crumble topping — this is my favorite way to finish off a pie, fruit bars, muffins, you name it. I'm never without a bag of this in my freezer, and I'll often make a double batch in the food processor so I have extra on hand. This recipe will make more topping than you need for many of the recipes in this collection. Just put the leftovers in a plastic freezer bag, and pull it out of the freezer when you need it.

1 Cut the butter into ½-inch cubes and put them on a small plate. Place in the freezer for 15 minutes.

2 Combine the flour, brown sugar, cinnamon, and salt in a food processor. Pulse the machine several times to mix. Remove the lid and scatter the butter over the dry ingredients. Pulse the machine repeatedly, perhaps 8 to 12 times, breaking the butter into fine bits; the mixture will be dry and crumbly.

3 Transfer the streusel to a mixing bowl and begin rubbing it between your fingers until it starts sticking together. Aim for small, buttery clumps, which are easier to spread evenly over your baked goods than large clumps. For short-term storage, leave the streusel right in the bowl and refrigerate until needed. For longer storage, refrigerate the streusel until it is cold, then transfer it to a plastic bag and freeze it. (If you put room-temperature streusel in the freezer directly after you mix it, it will freeze into one big lump.)

MAKES ABOUT 2½ CUPS

- ½ cup (1 stick) unsalted butter
- 1¼ cups all-purpose flour
- ¾ cup packed light brown sugar
- ¾ teaspoon ground cinnamon
- ¼ teaspoon salt

CHOCOLATE GLAZE

When you have a chocolate glaze recipe that's as versatile and simple as this one is, it's easy to rely on it time and again. That pretty much sums up the story with this glaze: I use it for quite a few of the cakes in this collection, and once you try it, you'll understand why. It's so quick to prepare that you can wait until the last minute to mix it up. Or you can make it ahead and reheat it to a pourable consistency when you need it. This makes a hefty amount, so if you don't use all of it, just store the leftovers in a sealed container and refrigerate until needed.

1 Bring the cream to a near boil in a small saucepan. Remove the pan from the heat and stir in the vanilla or espresso powder. Immediately add the chocolate chips. Tilt the pan this way and that so the hot cream runs over them. Set the pan aside for 5 minutes, then stir the mixture briefly to start smoothing it out.

2 Let the mixture rest for another 2 to 3 minutes, then whisk briefly, until smooth. The glaze will be a little runny at first, perfect for drizzling on pound cakes and Bundt-type cakes. If you want slightly thicker coverage, such as on a cheesecake or sheet cake, you can let the glaze cool slightly before spreading it. If the sauce cools and starts to thicken and you need to rewarm it to thin it out, heat it very gently in a saucepan. You can also reheat it in a microwavable container, but proceed carefully so you don't burn the chocolate — microwave for no more than 15 seconds at a time, stirring between each round.

MAKES ABOUT 1¼ CUPS

¾ cup heavy cream

½ teaspoon vanilla extract or 1 teaspoon powdered instant espresso or coffee

1¼ cups semisweet chocolate chips

THREE SWEET GLAZES

A sweet glaze can mean the difference between a baked good that looks (and tastes) all put together and one that's missing a little something. So I use glazes all the time to dress up cakes, scones, muffins, and more. Even if the baked item in question already has a crumb topping, a little drizzle of glaze is all it takes to apply the final flourish. Here are a few multipurpose ones that we use with some of the recipes in this collection.

MAPLE SYRUP GLAZE

Combine the butter and maple syrup in a small saucepan. Gently heat the mixture until the butter melts, then whisk in the confectioners' sugar until smooth. Use right away.

MAKES ABOUT ⅔ CUP OF EACH

- 3 tablespoons unsalted butter
- ⅓ cup pure maple syrup
- 1½ cups confectioners' sugar, sifted

CONFECTIONERS' SUGAR GLAZE

Combine the confectioners' sugar, 3 tablespoons milk, and vanilla in a small bowl. Whisk well. The glaze will be stiff at first, but it will smooth right out, along with any lumps. Add the remaining milk, if needed, a teaspoon at a time. You're trying to arrive at a medium-thick, drizzleable consistency.

- 2 cups confectioners' sugar, sifted
- 3–4 tablespoons milk
- ½ teaspoon vanilla extract

CITRUS GLAZE

Prepare the Confectioners' Sugar Glaze, above, adding ½ teaspoon lemon extract and 1 to 2 teaspoons finely grated lemon zest or orange zest.

VANILLA CUSTARD SAUCE

It's easy to get stuck in the same whipped cream or ice cream rut when it comes to garnishing your harvest pies, shortcakes, and other desserts. If you're in the market for an excellent rut unsticker, try this vanilla custard sauce. It's cool, it's smooth and creamy, and it pretty much works anywhere you'd use whipped cream or ice cream. I love it with Blueberry Gingerbread (page 234) and almost any of the fruit crostatas, among other things. Be patient with this custard, and don't try to rush it along by raising the heat, or you'll end up with sweet scrambled eggs.

1 Whisk the egg yolks and sugar together in a medium bowl.

2 Bring the light cream to a near simmer in a medium saucepan over moderate heat. Remove from the heat and gradually whisk it into the yolks, adding about ⅓ cup at a time. Return the mixture to the saucepan. Using a wooden spoon, stir the custard over medium-low heat for about 5 minutes, nonstop, until it thickens enough to coat the back of the spoon. If you draw a finger across the spoon, it should leave a path in the sauce. Be careful not to boil the sauce.

3 Remove from the heat and pour the sauce into a bowl. Stir in the vanilla. Let the sauce cool to room temperature, cover with plastic wrap, and refrigerate until cold. This will keep in the fridge for up to 3 days. Whisk briefly before serving.

MAKES ABOUT 2½ CUPS

- 6 large egg yolks
- ½ cup sugar
- 2 cups light cream or half-and-half
- 1 teaspoon vanilla extract

CONVERTING RECIPE MEASUREMENTS TO METRIC

Unless you have finely calibrated measuring equipment, conversions between US and metric measurements will be somewhat inexact. It's important to convert the measurements for all of the ingredients in a recipe to maintain the same proportions as the original.

WHEN THE MEASUREMENT GIVEN IS	MULTIPLY IT BY	TO CONVERT TO
teaspoons	4.93	milliliters
tablespoons	14.79	milliliters
cups	236.59	milliliters
cups	0.24	liters
pints	473.18	milliliters
pints	0.473	liters

US	=	METRIC
1 teaspoon		5 milliliters
1 tablespoon		15 milliliters
¼ cup		60 milliliters
½ cup		120 milliliters
1 cup		230 milliliters

ACKNOWLEDGMENTS

I wish to thank a number of individuals, in both my professional life and my private life, who have had a hand in the creation of this lovely book or who have otherwise touched my life as a cook and author.

At Storey Publishing, publisher Deborah Balmuth shared my conviction that *The Harvest Baker* would find a sizable audience of likeminded practitioners; my editor Hannah Fries kept me on track and gently nudged my manuscript in the right direction when it veered off course; the talented hand of designer and art director Jeff Stiefel is apparent on every page; the gifted team of Johnny and Charlotte Autry, photographer and stylist, created a visual feast herein; Alee Moncy and Sarah Armour have worked diligently to make sure the world takes notice; and Jennifer Travis did a memorable job of getting the ball rolling.

On the home front, love and gratitude to my children — Ben, Tess, Ali, and Sam — some of my earliest food critics, who taught me that it's fine if it looks pretty, but it really better taste good; my siblings — Joe, Barb, Tom, Bill, Joanne, and Mary — have been an ongoing source of love and support; my brother-in-law Dean could not be more generous with the blueberries and other produce from his garden; Bryan, my main pumpkin pie collaborator, deserves a word of thanks; and love to my wife, Bev, who supports me in all of my endeavors, but who would not hesitate to tell you that I'm a much better cook than I am a kitchen cleaner.

Finally, let me offer sincere words of gratitude to all of you who have followed my career as a food writer, enjoyed my books, and emailed me your thanks and appreciation, including, of course, all of you who follow my latest offerings at my website, ThePieAcademy.com.

INDEX

Q

quiches

SAVOR THE FLAVORS
WITH MORE BOOKS FROM STOREY

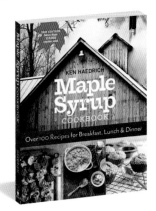

by Ken Haedrich

Maple syrup isn't just for breakfast! From pancakes and scones to fondue, salad dressing, grilled salmon, shrimp and sausage kabobs, cheesecake, and much more, discover how the taste of pure maple syrup enhances any meal.

by Olwen Woodier

Apple pie is just the beginning. Discover the versatility of this iconic fruit with 125 delicious recipes for any meal, including apple frittata, pork chops with apple cream sauce, apple pizza, apple butter, and more.

by Laurey Masterton

Celebrate the flavors and many varieties of honey with more than 80 seasonal recipes. Soups, salads, main dishes, and desserts all radiate with the pleasures of nature's sweetner. With different varieties of honey, such as sage or avocado, try recipes like Pork Tenderloin with Orange Blossom Honey-Mustard or Baked Acorn Squash.

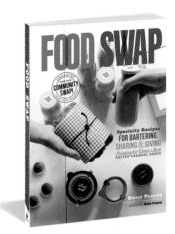

by Emily Paster

Join the growing worldwide food bartering movement with help from this combination cookbook and how-to handbook. More than 80 specialty recipes for the most coveted gourmet items complement full instructions for planning and hosting a successful food swap.
